Mammoth Grab A Pencil®

BOOK OF
Brain Boosters

Mammoth
Grab A Pencil®

BOOK OF  Brain Boosters

Richard Manchester

BRISTOL PARK BOOKS/NEW YORK

Visit www.pennydellpuzzles.com for more great puzzles

First Bristol Park Books edition published in 2017

Bristol Park Books
252 W. 38th Street
NYC, NY 10018

Bristol Park Books is a registered trademark of Bristol Park
Books, Inc.

Published by arrangement with Penny Publications LLC

ISBN: 978-0-88486-655-8

Printed in the United States of America

Contents

PUZZLES

MAGNIFIND

VISUAL ◆ SPATIAL

Figure out which two areas of the drawing have been enlarged.

EASY PICKINGS

LANGUAGE

To solve, simply cross out one letter in each pair below. When the puzzle is completed correctly, the remaining letters will spell out a little truism.

IM FO   TR AH YE   SE HN DO DE

FH NI BT GS,   TY FO US ' WR EH

NU KO TX   AB ML TL ON IW OI NE HG

FC HO RY   GT YR OU WI TF HP.

8

To solve this puzzle, write down the three letters that describe each triangle (a figure with three sides) in this figure. We found nine triangles; how many can you locate?

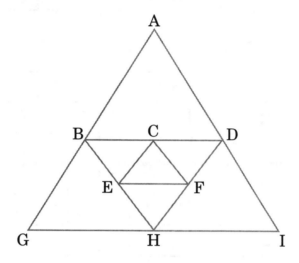

LANGUAGE

ANTONYMS QUIZ

An antonym is a word that is opposite in meaning to another word; for example, "cold" is the antonym of "hot." One of the words following each capitalized word is the antonym of that word.

1. LEADEN	a. light	b. clumsy	c. inclement
2. APPEASE	a. meddle	b. compress	c. enrage
3. DYNAMIC	a. nervous	b. fractious	c. listless
4. PREVALENT	a. grateful	b. rare	c. solemn
5. EXTOL	a. chide	b. increase	c. require
6. SATED	a. decisive	b. reputable	c. hungry
7. INEPT	a. lengthy	b. shocking	c. agile
8. POTENT	a. feeble	b. lofty	c. scrupulous

SUDOKU

Place a number into each box so each row across, column down, and small 9-box square within the larger square (there are 9 of these) contains 1 through 9.

			8	4				5
	6	4		7	9			
			2			4	9	1
		5	4		8		3	
3		1				9		8
	9		3			7	2	
9	7	6			2			
			7	5		6	2	
4				6	3			

TRI, TRI AGAIN

Fit the nine triangles into the big one so six everyday words are spelled out reading across the arrows. Do not rotate the triangles.

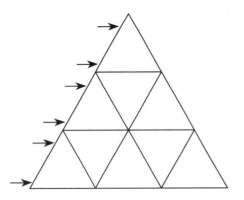

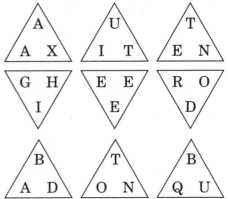

TIPS OF THE ICEBERG

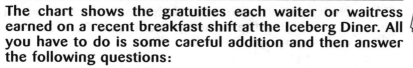

WEEK 1

The chart shows the gratuities each waiter or waitress earned on a recent breakfast shift at the Iceberg Diner. All you have to do is some careful addition and then answer the following questions:

1. Who made the most in total tips?
2. Who made the least?
3. Which two waitpersons made exactly the same amount?

EMPLOYEE	TIP 1	TIP 2	TIP 3	TIP 4	TIP 5
Al	$1.00	$1.10	$1.65	$0.95	$1.05
Brenda	$0.75	$3.00	$0.10	$0.90	$1.55
Charlie	$1.65	$1.10	$1.40	$1.00	$1.00
Dena	$1.00	$0.10	$0.65	$2.50	$1.00
Ed	$1.05	$0.10	$0.90	$0.90	$0.90
Flora	$1.00	$1.70	$0.90	$0.65	$1.00
Greta	$0.90	$0.05	$0.95	$0.90	$0.90

IN THE ABSTRACT

VISUAL ♦ SPATIAL

Fill in each section with one of the four symbols so no sections containing the same symbol touch. Four sections are already complete.

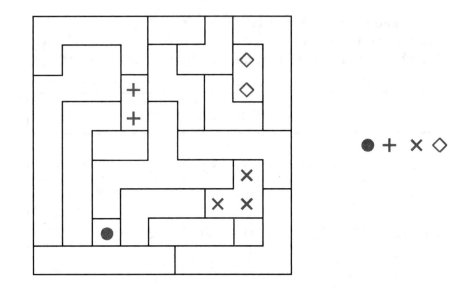

CODE WORD

DECODING

Decipher a truism and the Code Word's eleven letters, represented by the numbers 1 through 11. So, if the Code Word were "FORMULATING," 1 in the truism would be F, 2 would be O, etc.

$$\overline{1} \ \overline{2} \ \overline{3} \ \overline{4} \ \overline{5} \ \overline{6} \ \overline{7} \ \overline{8} \ \overline{9} \ \overline{10} \ \overline{11}$$

3 4 5   3 5 11 3   2 F   F 6 5 5 10 2 1   I 11   7 5 11 11   I 9

W 4 8 3   W 5   8 6 5   F 6 5 5   3 2   10 2   3 4 8 9   I 9

W 4 8 3   W 5   8 6 5   F 6 5 5   9 2 3   3 2   10 2 .

MATH ◆ LOGIC

Can you figure out what missing number goes into the space with the question mark?

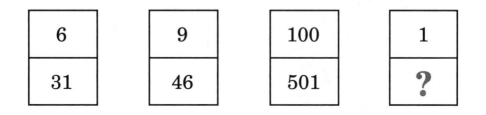

RELATIONSHIPS QUIZ

LANGUAGE

KENNEL is to DOG as STY is to PIG because a DOG lives in a kennel and a PIG lives in a STY. Each of the statements below is a relationship of some kind. Can you select the right word from the four following each?

1. TOMATO is to CAN as EGG is to _____.
   (a) hen   (b) carton   (c) farm   (d) yolk

2. DID is to DAD as GIG is to _____.
   (a) gal   (b) dud   (c) gag   (d) rag

3. APRIL is to JUNE as JANUARY is to _____.
   (a) February   (b) March   (c) May   (d) December

4. MINOR is to MAJOR as SMALL is to _____.
   (a) wee   (b) opposite   (c) medium   (d) large

5. BARACK is to MICHELLE as RONALD is to _____.
   (a) Laura   (b) Nancy   (c) Martha   (d) Barbara

COUNTDOWN

VISUAL

Following the connecting lines, find the only route in this grid that passes through the numbers backward from 9 to 1 consecutively.

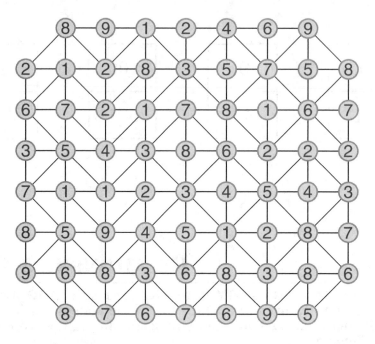

SYMBOL-ISM

DECODING

This is simply a Cryptogram that uses symbols instead of letters to spell out a truism. Each symbol stands for the same letter throughout. For this puzzle, we've already indicated that ❀ = L and 🚲 = U.

14

ROUND TRIP

WEEK
2

When this puzzle has been completed correctly, you will have made a round trip through its set of dots. You must visit every dot exactly once, make no diagonal moves, and return to your starting point. Parts of the right path are shown; can you find the rest?

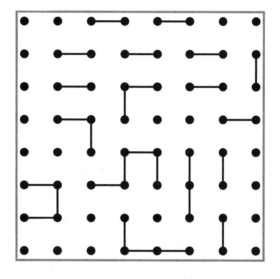

MATH

FUN WITH FACTS AND FIGURES

This puzzle tests you on several little facts and figures. Solve the quiz in the order given since each answer is used in the next statement. There are no fractions used here.

1. Take the number of the date that Saint Patrick's Day falls on in March and add it to the number of sides on a stop sign. _____

2. Next, multiply by the number of seconds in a half of a minute. _____

3. Now subtract the value of the Roman numeral D. _____

4. Divide by the number of cents in a quarter. _____

5. Add the age when citizens can first vote in the U.S. _____

The letters in our answer can be rearranged to form the phrase WEIGHTY TENT. *Can yours?*

ANAGRAM MAZE

VISUAL ◆ LANGUAGE

The diagram contains 36 words, 21 of which are anagrams of other everyday words. Start at the top arrow and anagram SMUG. While solving, move up, down, right, or left to the only adjacent word that can be anagrammed. Continue until you arrive at the bottom arrow. There is only one path through the maze.

1 BALL	2 SMUG	3 PEAS	4 CASK	5 SILO	6 IDLE
7 LARD	8 ZOOS	9 PACK	10 DISC	11 MILL	12 SALT
13 TILL	14 SEWN	15 CORK	16 LACY	17 FILM	18 COLA
19 GEAR	20 WISH	21 PILL	22 BORE	23 CHUM	24 VETO
25 GRAB	26 HARE	27 RACE	28 FOUR	29 MARK	30 WAIT
31 FANG	32 BODY	33 STOP	34 TEND	35 GRIN	36 BAND

ALL IN A ROW

MATH

Which row contains the most groups of consecutive numbers adding up to 11? Look carefully, because some groups may overlap. We've underlined an example of a group in each row to start you off.

A. <u>5 5 1</u> 2 6 9 1 6 4 3 3 3 3 2 9 9 8 1 5 8 1 2 4

B. 7 4 9 4 9 4 8 2 1 5 6 4 <u>1 7 3</u> 2 5 9 4 3 3 3 8 4

C. 8 7 2 3 6 1 1 6 6 9 6 2 1 2 3 4 5 8 <u>9 2</u> 1 5 2 2

ONLINE NETWORK

In each two-column group, take the letters in the left-hand column along the paths (indicated by the lines) and place them in their proper boxes in the right-hand column. When done, you'll find a thought in the two groups by reading the letters in the right-hand columns from top to bottom.

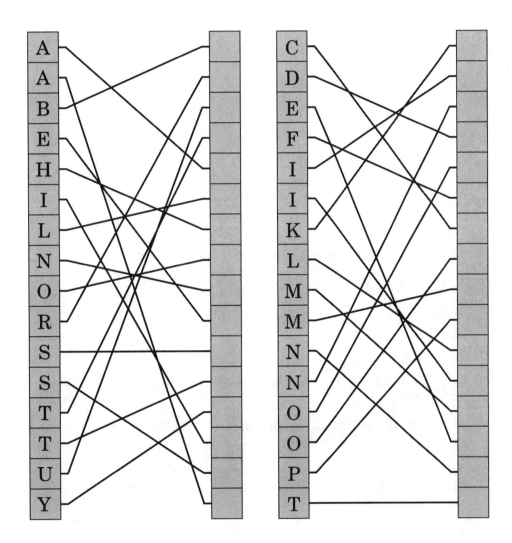

MAGIC NUMBER SQUARES   MATH

Fill in the empty boxes so these groups add up to the number below each diagram: 1. each row; 2. each column; 3. both diagonals. A number will be used only once per diagram.

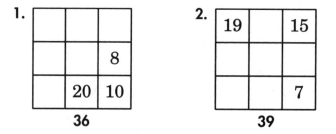

1.

		8
	20	10

36

2.

19		15
		7

39

THE LINEUP   LANGUAGE

While scrutinizing the lineup of letters below, can you answer the five given questions correctly in five minutes or less?

SJIYUDWESTXPRIFLESZOMENKSTRAIGHTVEINQGWC

1. Which letter of the alphabet does not appear in the lineup? _____

2. What 8-letter word — with its letters in correct order and appearing together — can you find in the lineup? _____

3. Which letter of the alphabet appears exactly three times in the lineup? _____

4. What 6-letter word — with its letters in correct order and appearing together — can you find in the lineup? _____

5. Other than the answers to Questions 2 and 4, how many everyday words — with their letters in correct order and appearing together — of four or more letters can you find in the lineup? _____

18

COUNT TO TEN

Examine the sneakers and sandals below and then answer these questions: 1. Which row contains the most SNEAKERS? 2. Which row contains the most SANDALS? 3. Which row contains an equal number of SNEAKERS and SANDALS?

WAYWORDS

An 8-word thought can be found beginning with the word ANY. Then, move to any adjacent box up, down, or diagonally for each following word.

RECENT	FIND	FEELS	TEEMING
PERSON	CHANGE	LIKE	MENTION
ANY	IMPRESSION	LOVELY	IT'S
FIRST	AT	WRONG	CONFIRM

GRAND TOUR

LANGUAGE ◆ VISUAL

Form a continuous chain of 5-letter words moving through the maze from START to FINISH. The second part of one word becomes the first part of the next word. This puzzle starts with UNI-TY-POS (unity, typos).

START

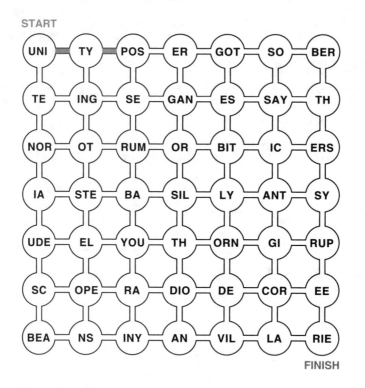

FINISH

BLOCK PARTY

VISUAL ◆ SPATIAL

Study the different views of the block, and draw what should appear on the face that has a question mark.

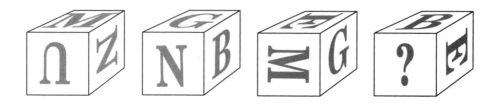

20

LOOSE TILE

The tray on the right seemed the ideal place to store the set of loose dominoes. Unfortunately, when the tray was full, one domino was left over. Determine the arrangement of the dominoes in the tray and which is the Loose Tile.

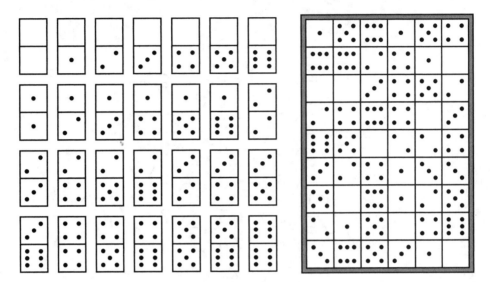

ASSOCIATIONS

Below, you'll find seven groups of three words that can be associated in some way with each other (example: mantel, fireplace, logs). Cross out each group as you find it. The initial letters of the remaining words will spell out the answer to the riddle:

WHAT DOES A KING WEAR ON AN INCLEMENT DAY?

ANCHOR   SPEAK   DISTRIBUTE   REGIONAL

CANBERRA CATEGORIZE EXTRA SAY GROUP ITALY

END   HEAP   GRACIOUS   TERMINATE   ALLOCATE

NERVOUS   PILE   GINGER   SYDNEY   COBRA

VERBALIZE   APPORTION   ORCHARD   CINNAMON

ADELAIDE ACTUAL RANK FINISH STACK NUTMEG

TOMAHAWK

HEXAGON HUNT

VISUAL

In this diagram of six-sided figures, there are 10 "special" hexagons. These 10 are special because the six numbers around each one are all different from each other and the center. We've circled one of the 10. Can you find the other 9?

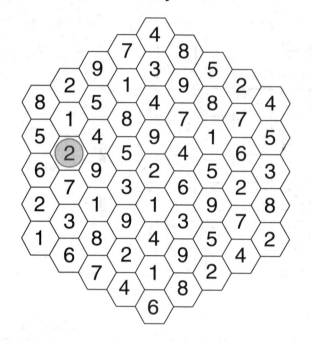

SLIDE RULE

LANGUAGE

Slide each column of letters up or down in the box and form as many everyday 3-letter words as you can in the windows where RUT is now. We formed 36 words, including RUT.

Your list of words:

SEVEN WORD ZINGER

Using each letter once, form seven everyday 3-letter words with the first letter coming from the center, the second from the middle, and the third from the outer circle. Your words may differ from ours.

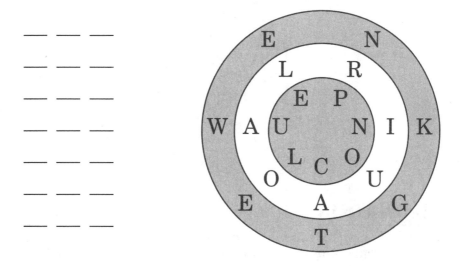

— — —

— — —

— — —

— — —

— — —

— — —

— — —

VISUAL ◆ SPATIAL

STACKED UP

The box on the left can be formed by three of the numbered boxes superimposed on top of each other; do not turn them in any way. Can you figure out which three work?

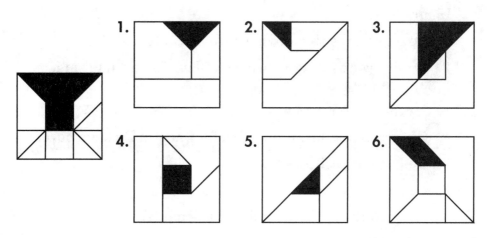

23

CIRCLE SEARCH

LANGUAGE

Move from circle to adjoining circle, horizontally and vertically only, to form 16 common, everyday words of at least three letters. Don't change the order of the letters in the circles that contain more than one letter. Proper names are not allowed.

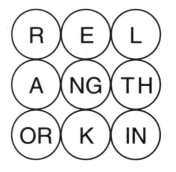

ELIMINATION

LANGUAGE

Cross off the capitalized words below according to the instructions given. The remaining words, in order, will form a thought.

GUARD AGHAST SOME AND ALLITERATION BLAST PEOPLE GOSH GREAT HAIKU CENTER TIDE HAVE CASTE WAIT EGAD DELUSIONS TWELFTH FOR PROTAGONIST OF TACKLE PAST BLIMEY ADEQUACY NO EXPECTATIONS

Eliminate...

1. the four words that rhyme with each other.

2. the five words that go between "Time" and "man" in a famous saying.

3. the three interjections.

4. the words that form the title of a Charles Dickens novel.

5. the football positions.

6. the literary terms.

7. the word that ends with four consonants.

TARGET SHOOT

WEEK 3

Find the two letters which, when entered into the center circle of each target, will form three 6-letter words reading across.

1.

2.

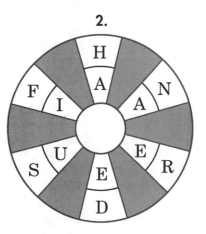

DOVETAILED WORDS

Two related words, with their letters in the correct order, are combined in each row of letters. Can you find both words? In a line like POBOOXDELER, or POboOxDeLEr, you can see the two words **POODLE** and **BOXER**.

1. F R A A R N M C H   _____ _____

2. A U N B O D V E E R   _____ _____

3. G G A I R N G L E I R C   _____ _____

4. M O R D E E T R R O N   _____ _____

5. P R U L B A B S E T I R C _____ _____

25

RING LOGIC

LOGIC

Complete the diagram below by drawing in the links between the rings using the statements below. Assume that all the rings in the picture are locked rigidly into position and cannot be moved in any direction. Consider yourself a true ringmaster if you can find the solution in under six minutes!

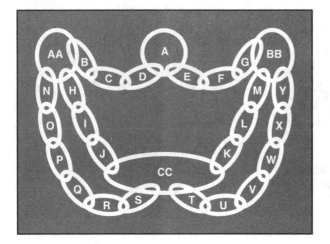

1. The right sides of rings B, K, and Q are to the front.

2. The pattern is symmetrical from left to right.

3. Every ring is linked at least twice.

NEXT TO NOTHING

VISUAL

In the first row below, the A is next to the number zero, and the Y is next to the letter O. First, circle all of the letters next to zeroes. Next, scramble the circled letters to spell out the name of a country.

A0	YO	VO	DO
LO	WO	HO	E0
UO	BO	IO	SO
GO	PO	R0	MO
KO	QO	F0	ZO
N0	C0	XO	JO

ARROW MAZE

Starting at the S and following the arrow to the right, see if you can find your way to F. When you reach an arrow, you MUST follow its direction and continue in that direction until you come to the next arrow. When you reach a two-headed arrow, you can choose either direction. It's okay to cross your own path.

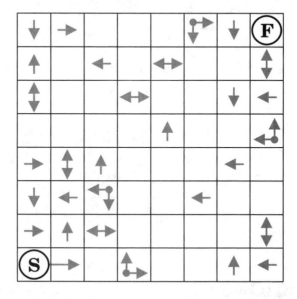

WORD VISIBILITY

There are six 5-letter words below. The first letter of the answer is found in the first pair of letters, and it is either the top or the bottom letter. Continue across each pair.

For example, the word GIRL would be found thus:
<u>G</u> A <u>R</u> <u>L</u>
L <u>I</u> T X

1. H A R C H
   W O S T N

2. P H I Y E
   C L U V D

3. M U D I M
   V E R O A

4. F I B L E
   A M Y E L

5. S E W A T
   G O L U R

6. J Y A R C
   L E R I P

LICENSE PLATES

WEEK 4

Each box contains six letters of the first name and the last name of an Australian actress. The top three are a part of the first name and the bottom three are a part of the last name, in order.

1.
```
A T E
L A N
```

2.
```
C H E
I F F
```

3.
```
U D Y
A V I
```

4.
```
A O M
A T T
```

5.
```
I C O
I D M
```

6.
```
O N I
L L E
```

ASSOCIATIONS

Directions for solving are on page 21. This time around, you'll be looking for eight groups of three words.

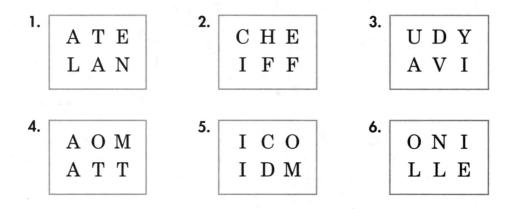

HOW WAS THE FIRST FLEA MARKET STARTED?

MODE AUNT FREEDOM UNIFORM BERLIN REMOVE

MANNER IMITATE GRANDMOTHER OMELET

QUANTITY LOFTY MAJOR STANDARDIZED WAY

SCURRY FRANKFURT BUILDING CARNIVAL

AMOUNT SISTER RIVET MAJESTIC MIMIC ACHE

REGULAR EDIFICE TINSEL MUNICH CHESS APE

PORTION NOBLE HARBOR SKYSCRAPER

SUDOKU

Directions for solving are on page 10.

4		1			6	9		7
	2		7		8	4		
	8	7		1				
	5		6			8	9	
8			3		9			5
	9	4			7		3	
				6		7	2	
		5	4		2		1	
2		9	8			5		6

DISK MEMORY

Here are six discs with different designs. Study them carefully for exactly 30 seconds, and then cover them up with a sheet of paper and try to draw them in proper order in the empty discs on the right. Getting four correct is average, five is good, and six is excellent. Good luck, and no peeking!

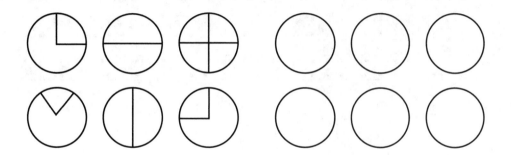

MISSING DOMINOES

VISUAL ◆ LOGIC

In this game you use all 28 dominoes that are in a standard set. Each one has a different combination from 0-0, 0-1, 0-2, to 6-6. Domino halves with the same number of dots lie next to each other. To avoid confusion we have used an open circle to indicate a zero. Can you fill in the missing white dominoes to complete the board?

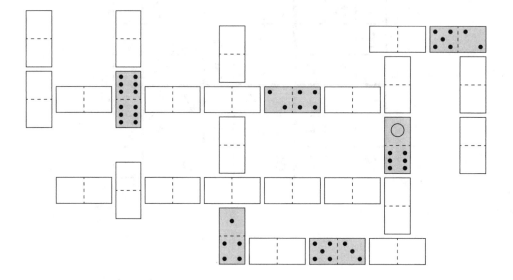

DOMINOES

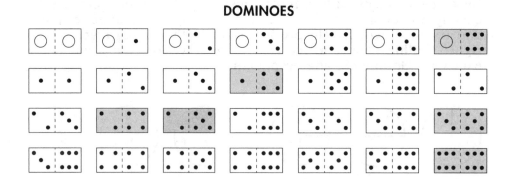

SQUARE LINKS

Write one letter in each empty box so that an everyday 8-letter word is spelled out around each dark box. Each word may read either clockwise or counterclockwise, and may start at any of its letters.

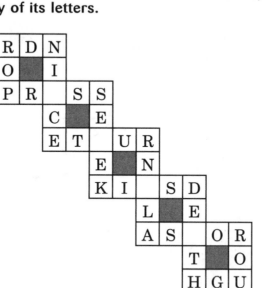

LANGUAGE ◆ SPATIAL

RINGERS

Each Ringer is composed of five rings. Use your imagination to rotate the rings so that you spell out four 5-letter words reading from the outside to the inside when all five rings are aligned correctly.

1.

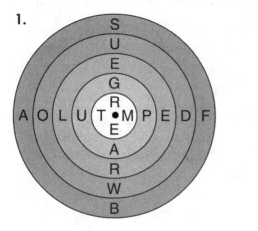

2.

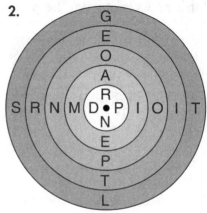

STAR WORDS

Only five of the eight words given will fit together in the diagram. Place them in the directions indicated by the arrows.

BLEW   TALL

LEIS   TEAL

SEAL   WELT

SLAB   WILT

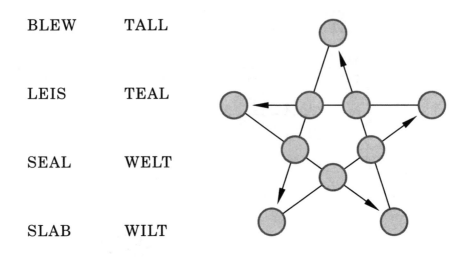

CIRCLE MATH

MATH

Each overlapping circle is identified by a letter having a different number value from 1 to 9. Where some circles overlap, there is a number: It is the SUM of the values of the letters in those overlapping circles. Can you figure out the correct values for the letters? As a starting help, A = 2.

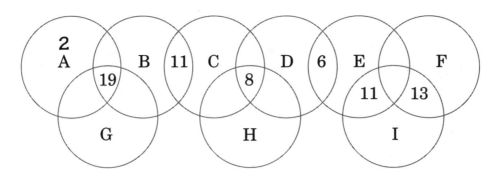

BULL'S-EYE LETTER

Add the SAME single letter to each group of three letters, then rearrange the letters to form six everyday 4-letter words.

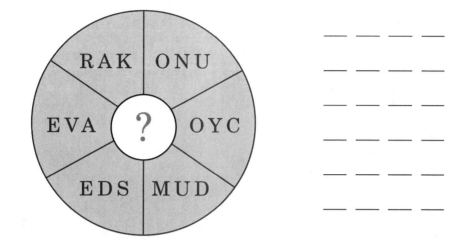

— — — —

— — — —

— — — —

— — — —

— — — —

— — — —

ALPHABET SOUP

Cross off each letter from the alphabet list that appears in the larger group of letters. Then rearrange the letters not crossed out to form the name of the state that entered the Union on July 3, 1890.

```
Q  F  G  F  Q  G  Q  F  Q  E  Z  B  V  B  J  V  Z  B  V  Z

S  K  N  U  S  N  S  K  N  S  P  M  E  P  M  E  M  E  J  M

C  X  C  X  X  C  U  X  R  C  U  J  Q  J  N  K  M  U  J  K

V  B  F  P  F  V  P  L  V  B  K  X  E  K  E  X  K  E  M  N

Z  M  T  M  X  Q  J  V  C  F  K  B  Z  W  G  C  X  Y  M  W
```

A B C D E F G H I J K L M N O P Q R S T U V W X Y Z

State: _____

GOING IN CIRCLES

LANGUAGE

In each circle, insert one letter into each empty space to form an 8-letter word. Words may read either clockwise or counterclockwise and may begin with any letter in the circle.

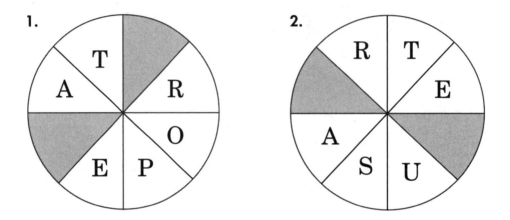

1.

2.

U.S. H'S

LANGUAGE

The list below consists of the names of six U.S. states, but we've removed all of their letters except for the H's. Can you write one letter on each dash to complete the names of the states?

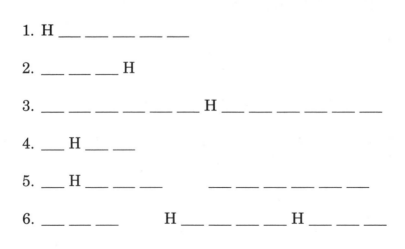

1. H __ __ __ __ __

2. __ __ __ H

3. __ __ __ __ __ __ H __ __ __ __ __ __

4. __ H __ __

5. __ H __ __ __   __ __ __ __ __ __

6. __ __ __   H __ __ __ __ H __ __ __

OVERLAY

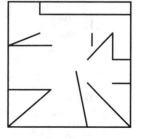

When you overlay the three diagrams in the top row, which of the three lettered diagrams, A, B, or C, will be formed?

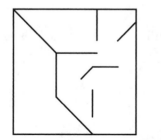

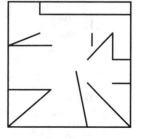

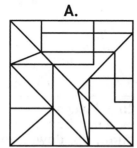
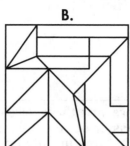
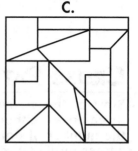

A.   B.   C.

LANGUAGE

COMPOUND IT

Starting at #1, pick a word that will form a compound word with a word chosen in #2. Then with the word you've selected in #2, pick one from #3 to form another compound word. Continue in this manner to #10, so that you've formed nine compound words. In some instances more than one compound word can be formed, but there is only one path to get you to #10.

1. work, sink, oat, spot

2. meal, shop, hole, light

3. house, lift, talk, time

4. table, out, off, hold

5. post, shine, top, up

6. right, standing, script, card

7. sharp, field, board, wing

8. room, tea, grace, walk

9. way, service, clean, taste

10. just, farer, few, build

IN THE MONEY

MATH

How quickly can you convert each bag of money into dollars and cents and determine which one contains the greatest amount?

1. 48 dimes

2. 467 pennies

3. 97 nickels

4. 19 quarters

CROSS PATHS

VISUAL

Start at the arrow. There are three circles in that box, so move three boxes, either across or up. Each time you land in a box, move the number of dots in that box in only one direction, up, down, or across until you reach Finish (F). You may cross your own path, but do not retrace it.

POP!

The balloons in a dart game are arranged so their letters spell out the word "SPEARED." To win, you must pop six different balloons with six different darts, but after each pop the remaining letters must spell out a new word reading across from left to right. Do not rearrange the balloons. Can you determine the order of the balloons to pop and the words formed? Your words may differ from ours.

MATH ◆ SPATIAL

TRIANGULAR SQUARE

Place the nine numbered squares into the diagram so that the four numbers in each of the diagram's four large triangles equal the number outside of it. The patterns have to match and you may not rotate the squares.

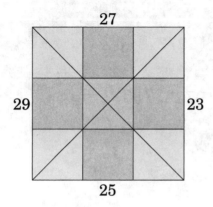

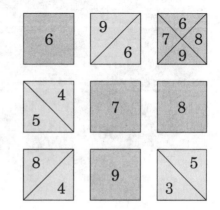

IN THE MONEY

MATH

Directions for solving are on page 36.

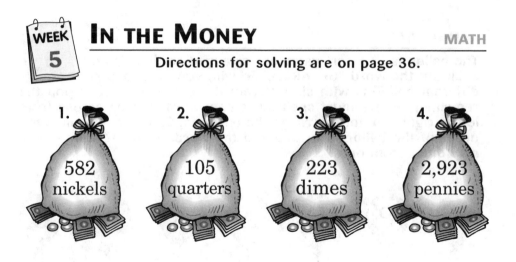

1. 582 nickels
2. 105 quarters
3. 223 dimes
4. 2,923 pennies

HOLE IN ONE

LOGIC

Twenty-four golfers entered a hole-in-one contest. Each golfer was given a ball with a different 4-digit number combination using the numbers 3, 5, 7, and 9 on it. Looking at the 23 balls still on the green, can you figure out what combination is on the ball that won the contest?

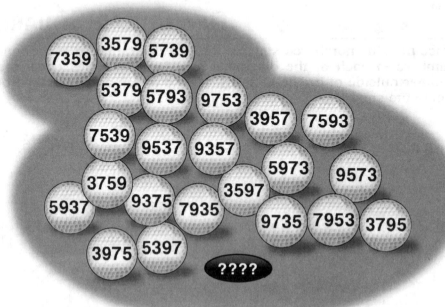

7359 3579 5739
5379 5793 9753
3957 7593
7539 9537 9357
5973 9573
3759 3597
5937 9375 7935
9735 7953 3795
3975 5397
????

POP!

Directions for solving are on page 37. This time, you'll be using the letters in the word "BRIDGES."

VISUAL

CROSS PATHS

Directions for solving are on page 36.

VISION QUEST

Find the row or column that contains five DIFFERENT loaves.

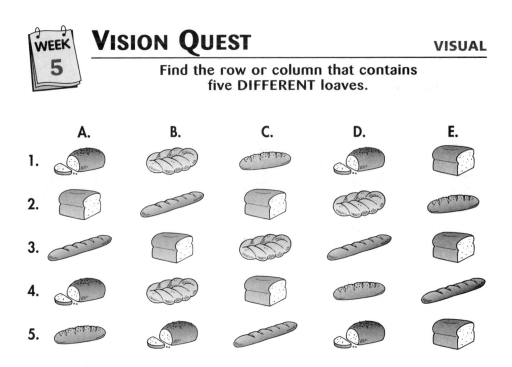

ALTERNATING PRESIDENTS

The list below consists of the names of 8 U.S. Presidents, but we've removed all of the letters in their first and last names except for the second, fourth, sixth, eighth, tenth, twelfth, fourteenth, and sixteenth ones. Can you write one letter on each dash to complete the names of the Chief Executives?

1. __ E __ R __ E   __ A __ H __ N __ T __ N

2. __ O __ D __ O __   W __ L __ O __

3. __ H __ M __ S   __ E __ F __ R __ O __

4. __ B __ A __ A __   L __ N __ O __ N

5. __ A __ T __ N   __ A __   B __ R __ N

6. __ N __ R __ W   __ A __ K __ O __

7. __ A __ V __ N   __ O __ L __ D __ E

8. __ O __ N   __ U __ N __ Y   __ D __ M __

SLIDE RULE

Directions for solving are on page 22. Here, you're to form 4-letter words. We formed 22 words, including DUST.

Your list of words:

DOUBLE DUTY

Cross off each set of matching boxes, and you will see some boxes don't have mates. The letters in the unmatched boxes will spell out something we all look forward to every year.

wo E	o a T	a t N	a e M	v o A	o e A
o e M	e i T	o e T	a e T	w c E	e t N
o i T	i e A	v c A	a i T	u c A	v e A
v e A	i t N	u e A	u e M	o i T	u i T
u e M	o t N	e t N	o e M	e i T	u i E
w c E	a t N	v o A	w o E	i u E	o e T
o e A	a e M	u c A	o a T	i e M	i t N
a e T	u i E	u i T	u e A	i e A	e u E

WORD CHARADE

VISUAL ◆ LANGUAGE

Find each letter in the diagram according to the instructions, and write each letter on its dash to spell out a 6-letter word.

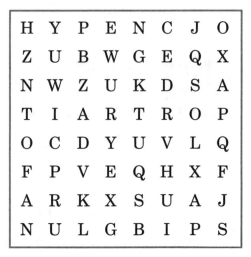

H	Y	P	E	N	C	J	O
Z	U	B	W	G	E	Q	X
N	W	Z	U	K	D	S	A
T	I	A	R	T	R	O	P
O	C	D	Y	U	V	L	Q
F	P	V	E	Q	H	X	F
A	R	K	X	S	U	A	J
N	U	L	G	B	I	P	S

My first letter is directly below a D and directly above a K.

My second letter is the second letter of an 8-letter word reading right to left.

My third letter is in the seventh column, but not in the eighth column.

My fourth letter appears more often than any other letter.

My fifth letter is not in the diagram.

My sixth letter is the only vowel in one of the rows.

— — — — — —

EASY PICKINGS

LANGUAGE

To solve, simply cross out one letter in each pair below. When the puzzle is completed correctly, the remaining letters will spell out a quote by the writer Thomas Carlyle.

HO AI ES CT OE TR GY   IT GS   TR UH NE

BP WI AO GM HR AO PB HI NY   OP SF

GR RM EA EA TB   ME OE TN.

CARD SENSE

Five playing cards were shuffled and put in a pile, one on top of another. Using the clues, can you identify each card's position in the pile?

1. The diamond is somewhere above both hearts.

2. Exactly one heart is somewhere below the nine.

3. The bottom card is not red.

4. The six is somewhere above both black cards.

QUICK FILL

Determine the 10-letter word from the clues. All the letters in the word are listed.

A A C E I N O T V X

1. In the alphabet, letter 6 appears somewhere before letter 1.

2. Letter 5 is from the second half of the alphabet and letter 3 is a consonant.

3. In the alphabet, letter 9 appears immediately after letter 10.

4. Letters 7, 4, 2, and 8 spell out, in order, a metered vehicle.

$$\overline{1} \ \overline{2} \ \overline{3} \ \overline{4} \ \overline{5} \ \overline{6} \ \overline{7} \ \overline{8} \ \overline{9} \ \overline{10}$$

WORD WHEEL

LANGUAGE

Starting with the "M" at the arrow, see how many everyday words of three or more letters you can find going clockwise. Don't skip over any letters. For example, if you saw the letters C, A, R, E, D, you would form five words: CAR, CARE, CARED, ARE, RED. We found 28 words.

KEEP ON MOVING

VISUAL

4	2	1	5	1	2
5	2	3	4	✳	2
2	4	3	3	3	4
4	1	4	1	4	3
3	4	1	3	4	1
2	3	5	1	2	3

The goal is to move from the shaded square to the asterisk. Since the shaded square has the number 1 in it, you must move one square up, down, left, or right, but not diagonally. In the new square will be another number; move that number of squares up, down, left, or right, continuing in this way until you reach the asterisk. It's okay to cross your own path.

WORD EQUATIONS

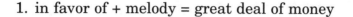

WEEK 6

Determine the three defined words in each equation. The third word is formed when the second is written directly after the first; for example, for "for each + shape = act in a play," you would respond "per + form = perform."

1. in favor of + melody = great deal of money

2. automobile + household animal = wall-to-wall rug

3. armed conflict + cozy room = prison VIP

4. beast of burden + President after Nixon = variety of shoe

5. play on words + polite man = strong-smelling

SQUARE LINKS

Directions for solving are on page 31.

"Change your thoughts and you change your world."
— Norman Vincent Peale

45

ELIMINATION

LANGUAGE

Directions for solving are on page 24. Once again, the remaining words will form a thought.

TWO NETWORK PENNY AGITATE SOLE HEADS
AND HYDROGEN SHAFT GRANOLA PENNY COBALT
ARE GIANT WILL HOUSE BETTER JAWS IODINE
SOON THAN BECOME VERTIGO SPONGE ONE
MANY GUEST

Eliminate…

1. the names of chemical elements.

2. the six words that, when read together, form a saying that means "multiple encephalic structures surpass the productivity of an individual said formation."

3. all one-word movie titles.

4. the two words that, when the letters are scrambled together, form the names of a southern state and its capital.

5. the word whose six letters are in reverse (but not consecutive) alphabetical order.

6. the name of a fish.

7. the two words that, when put together, can form a compound word no matter the order of the words.

BLOCK PARTY

VISUAL ◆ SPATIAL

Directions for solving are on page 20.

WORD HUNT

WEEK
6

Find words by moving from one letter to any adjoining letter. You may start a word with any letter in the diagram. In forming a word you may return to a letter as often as you wish, but do not stand on a letter using it twice in direct succession. In this Word Hunt, you are searching for 4-letter words that contain "TH" (such as MATH). We found 18 words.

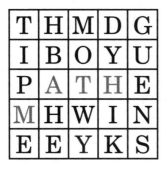

Your list of words:

ROUND TRIP

Directions for solving are on page 15.

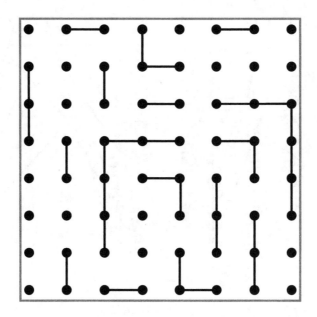

ONLINE NETWORK

VISUAL

Directions for solving are on page 17.

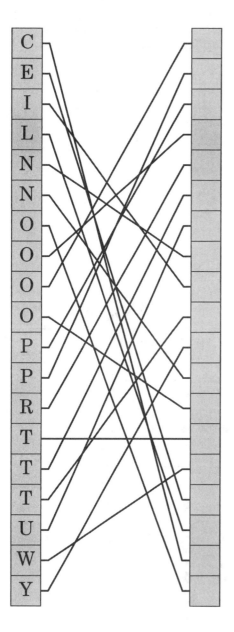

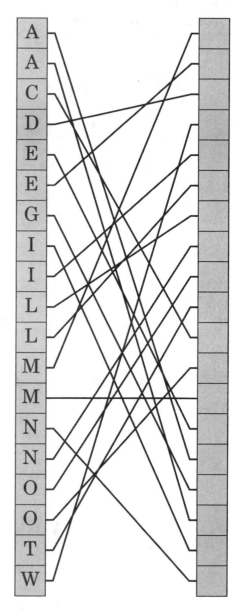

48

ANAGRAM MAZE

WEEK
7

Directions for solving are on page 16. This time, there are 19 words to anagram and the first word you'll be anagramming is FAST.

1 NEON	2 SLAP	3 EDIT	4 FERN	5 HIGH	6 FAST
7 MILE	8 DUMB	9 SOWN	10 MEAT	11 CURL	12 BATS
13 RIOT	14 MOAT	15 JINX	16 EARL	17 HOSE	18 LUGE
19 ROAR	20 NEWT	21 MEAL	22 PERT	23 FARM	24 BOLD
25 VOLT	26 PULL	27 WHAT	28 MAKE	29 MYTH	30 ZINC
31 LANE	32 PIER	33 DAWN	34 SOCK	35 MAZE	36 BUFF

LANGUAGE

SKILLS TEST

There are five everyday, uncapitalized 5-letter words that begin with F and end with N. Can you determine all four?

F — — — N

F — — — N

F — — — N

F — — — N

F — — — N

Directions for solving are on page 10.

1					7	4		6
2	5	3						
	6				1	3		
	3		9				5	8
	4		5	7	3		6	
9	7				6		4	
		8	2				7	
						5	8	2
5		7	4					1

LICENSE PLATES

LANGUAGE

Each box contains three letters of a South American capital's name and three letters of its country's name. The top three are a part of the city's name and the bottom three are a part of the nation's, in order.

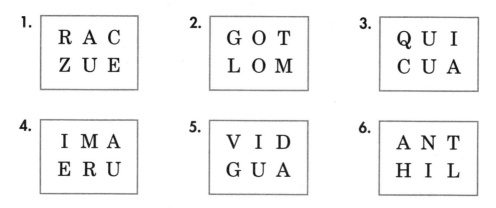

1.

```
R A C
Z U E
```

2.

```
G O T
L O M
```

3.

```
Q U I
C U A
```

4.

```
I M A
E R U
```

5.

```
V I D
G U A
```

6.

```
A N T
H I L
```

MAGIC NUMBER SQUARES

Fill in the empty boxes so these groups add up to the number below each diagram: 1. each row; 2. each column; 3. each long diagonal; 4. the four center squares; 5. the four corner squares; and 6. each quarter of the diagram. A number will be used only once per diagram.

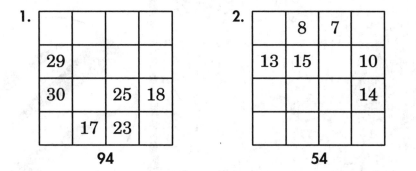

1.

29			
30		25	18
	17	23	

94

2.

	8	7	
13	15		10
			14

54

THE LINEUP

Directions for solving are on page 18.

VQBKEEPHCDAFFODILWMILKVGUZZLEMAREXYTNS

1. Which letter of the alphabet does not appear in the lineup? _____

2. What 8-letter word — with its letters in correct order and appearing together — can you find in the lineup? _____

3. Which letter of the alphabet appears exactly three times in the lineup? _____

4. What 6-letter word — with its letters in correct order and appearing together — can you find in the lineup? _____

5. Other than the answers to Questions 2 and 4, how many everyday words — with their letters in correct order and appearing together — of four or more letters can you find in the lineup? _____

Figure out which area of the drawing has been enlarged.

ANTONYMS QUIZ

LANGUAGE

Directions for solving are on page 9.

1. FORTITUDE a. ideology b. cowardice c. fortune

2. IMPEDE a. free b. publish c. subdue

3. OBLIQUE a. mature b. lewd c. direct

4. AFFABLE a. unfriendly b. needy c. youthful

5. JUDICIOUS a. vast b. imprudent c. perpetual

6. BRAZEN a. shy b. idealistic c. kinetic

7. TRAITOROUS a. encumbered b. elective c. loyal

8. LETHARGIC a. cyclical b. inconsistent c. lively

TIPS OF THE ICEBERG

We're back at the Iceberg Diner. After doing some careful addition, answer the following questions:

1. Who made the most in total tips?
2. Who made the least?
3. Which two waitpersons made exactly the same amount?

EMPLOYEE	TIP 1	TIP 2	TIP 3	TIP 4	TIP 5
Hank	$0.95	$1.65	$1.45	$2.70	$1.25
Inez	$1.30	$3.40	$2.30	$2.20	$2.10
Jack	$2.45	$1.50	$2.10	$2.05	$2.15
Ken	$2.30	$1.80	$1.95	$1.50	$3.15
Laura	$1.45	$2.30	$0.85	$2.60	$1.85
Marty	$0.95	$1.80	$1.80	$1.90	$1.90
Noel	$2.10	$1.90	$0.95	$2.80	$1.30

RINGERS

Directions for solving are on page 31.

1.

2.

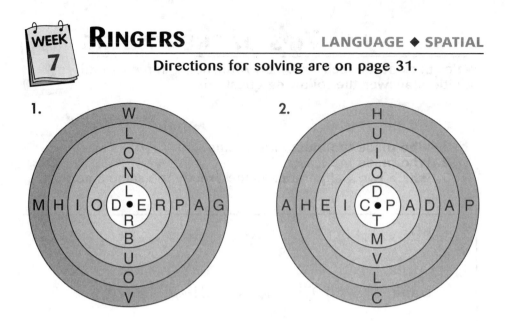

CODE WORD

DECODING

Directions for solving are on page 12. Here, determine a 12-letter Code Word.

$$\overline{1}\ \overline{2}\ \overline{3}\ \overline{4}\ \overline{5}\ \overline{6}\ \overline{7}\ \overline{8}\ \overline{9}\ \overline{10}\ \overline{11}\ \overline{12}$$

6 W A 11 6   3 A V 8   A 11   A 10 9   4 F   B 8 10 11 12

2 9 4 1 D ,   6 7 1 2 10 D ,   A 11 D   M 10 6 C 3 10 8 V 4 16 ;

Q 1 A 5 10 7 10 8 6   7 3 A 7   12 4   W 8 55   7 4 12 8 7 3 8 9 .

---

*"He is indebted to his memory for his jests
and to his imagination for his facts."*
— *Richard Sheridan*

TRI, TRI AGAIN

Directions for solving are on page 10.

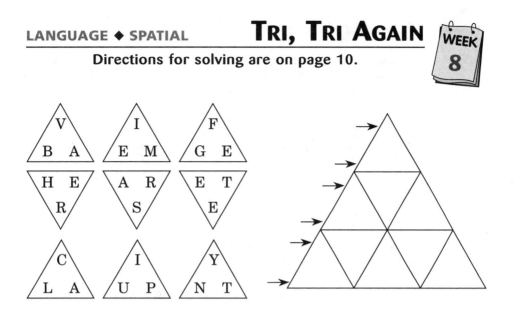

FUN WITH FACTS AND FIGURES

Directions for solving are on page 15.

1. Take the number of vowels in the word FLATTER and multiply it by the number of consonants in the word. _____

2. Next, add the number of keys on a piano. _____

3. Now divide by the number of riders on a tandem bicycle. _____

4. Subtract the number of letters in the name of the state that contains Buffalo and Syracuse. _____

5. Divide by the number of eggs in half a dozen. _____

Our answer is the number most likely to come up when you roll a pair of dice. *Is yours?*

GRAND TOUR

Directions for solving are on page 18. This time, you'll be looking for a chain of 5-letter words, starting with KNA-VE-NOM (knave, venom).

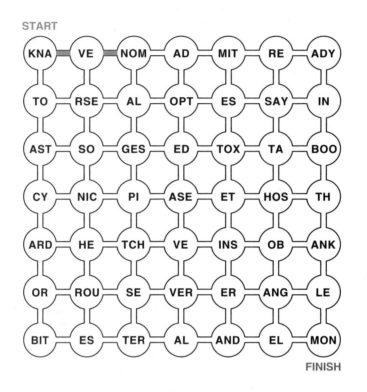

START

KNA	VE	NOM	AD	MIT	RE	ADY
TO	RSE	AL	OPT	ES	SAY	IN
AST	SO	GES	ED	TOX	TA	BOO
CY	NIC	PI	ASE	ET	HOS	TH
ARD	HE	TCH	VE	INS	OB	ANK
OR	ROU	SE	VER	ER	ANG	LE
BIT	ES	TER	AL	AND	EL	MON

FINISH

DOVETAILED WORDS

Directions for solving are on page 25.

1. C W A L T O C C H K   _____ _____

2. F H U R O M I S D T Y   _____ _____

3. S F L U G O A U R R   _____ _____

4. M O L E R S A S O L N   _____ _____

5. L A G I U G G G H L E   _____ _____

56

MARCHING ORDERS

WEEK
8

Using a different two-step sequence of addition, can you make your way from Start to Finish in each puzzle? We've started the first one for you using the sequence +2 and +6; continue this sequence to reach Finish. You will not cross your own path or pass through any square twice.

1.   FINISH ↑

18	20	26	34	40	42
15	23	19	30	32	26
9	12	10	25	29	24
7	8	11	16	18	20
2	5	9	12	14	15
0	3	7	10	11	13

↑ START

2.   FINISH ↑

12	10	17	15	19	27
14	9	12	16	24	26
13	11	16	19	21	23
8	10	11	14	20	19
5	7	9	12	13	16
4	6	8	10	11	14

↑ START

SKILLS TEST

Complete the factual sentence below by writing A, E, I, O, or U on each dash.

TH __ R __ V __ L __ T __ __ N __ F TH __

M __ __ N __ R __ __ ND TH __ __ __ RTH __ S

__ RR __ G __ L __ R B __ C __ __ S __ __ F __ TS

__ LL __ PT __ C __ L __ RB __ T.

COUNTDOWN

VISUAL

Directions for solving are on page 14.

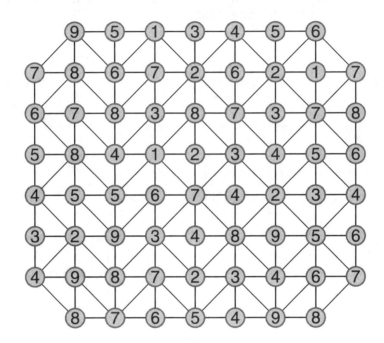

WAYWORDS

LANGUAGE

Directions for solving are on page 19. This time, you'll be looking for a 10-word thought beginning with LIVE.

WOLF	JUSTICE	LIVE	CREATE
NICEST	THE	LIFE	BLUE
FEAR	SHEEP	AND	AS
GRATEFUL	FOREVER	A	PURCHASE

STAR WORDS

Directions for solving are on page 32.

WEEK
8

DEAL   MEAL

DEEM   PLED

LEER   REAL

MALL   REAP

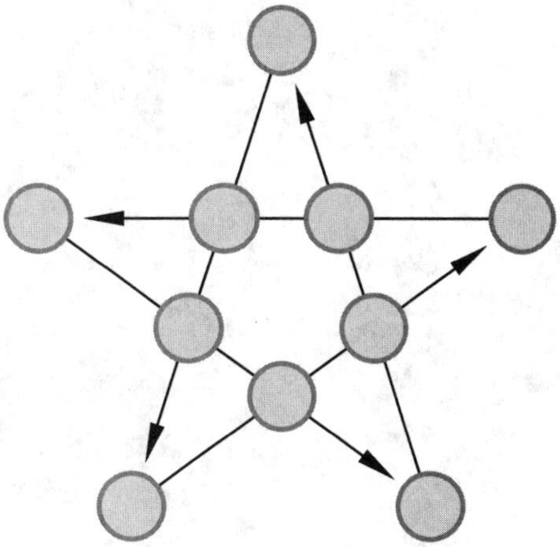

ASSOCIATIONS

Directions for solving are on page 21. This time around, you'll be looking for eight groups of three words.

WHAT KIND OF ENTRYWAYS DO HAUNTED HOUSES HAVE?

SURPASS   SUGAR   REDUCE   MIX   INVOLVED

CRANBERRY PACKERS EXCEED TWINE RODENT

DECREASE BEETHOVEN EMANATE BLEND ECLIPSE

ANCHOVY   LEAGUE   LESSEN   MEDICINE

COMPLICATED GIANTS DRAMATIC STRING MOZART

OCELOT   MINGLE   ASSOCIATION   OPULENT

COMPLEX ROMANTIC EAGLES CORD BRAHMS

SUNSHINE PARTNERSHIP

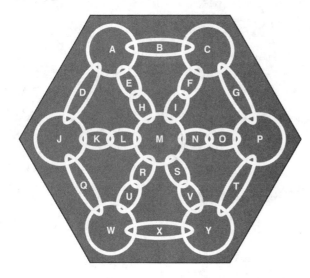

RING LOGIC

LOGIC

Directions for solving are on page 26.

1. Every ring is linked at least twice.

2. The pattern repeats radially.

3. The bottom sides of rings K and X are to the front.

ALL IN A ROW

MATH

Directions for solving are on page 16. This time, look for the most groups of consecutive numbers adding up to 18.

A. 9 7 2 3 8 1 5 6 6 9 6 2 1 2 3 4 5 8 9 7 1 5 2 2

B. 6 4 9 4 9 4 8 2 1 5 5 5 1 7 3 2 5 9 4 3 3 3 8 9

C. 5 5 5 3 6 9 1 6 4 3 3 3 3 3 9 9 8 1 5 8 1 2 4

"The brain is as strong as its weakest think."
— *Eleanor Doan*

LETTER, PLEASE

The numbers below stand for certain letters on the telephone dial. You will see that one number may stand for more than one letter — for example, 3 may be D, E, or F. By finding the correct letter for each number in the puzzle below, you will have spelled out a truism.

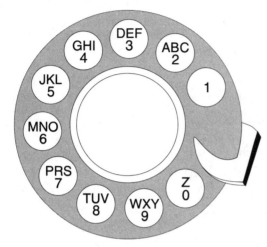

2 3665 6878

669 263 8436

23 74448 29

242623.

F COUNT

Here's an eye exam that's also an F exam! First, read the sentence below. Next, go back and read the sentence again, but this time count all of the F's. How many are there?

IF FIFI FAFFNER'S RIFFRAFF FRIEND

EFFIE OFFENSIVELY OFFERS FIFTY-FIVE

FRANCS FOR FIFI'S FAITHFUL MASTIFF

FLUFFY, I FEAR FOR THE AFTEREFFECTS...

FISTICUFFS OR A FACE-OFF, FEASIBLY.

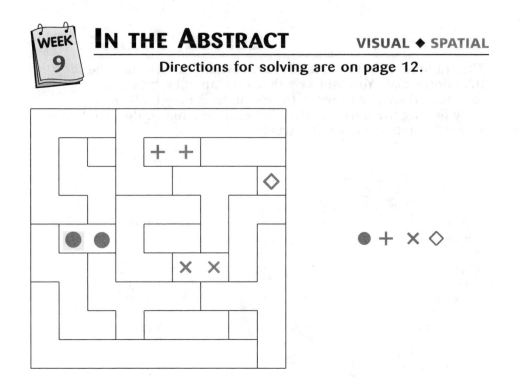

CROSS-UPS

LANGUAGE

Using only the letters given above each diagram, fill in the boxes in such a way that an everyday compound word is formed, one part reading across and the other part reading down. The letter already in the diagram is a letter shared by both parts of the word. Note: Each part of the compound word is an entire word on its own.

1. A B M O O R

2. C D E E H H

3. B I L O S T

4. A C E K N O

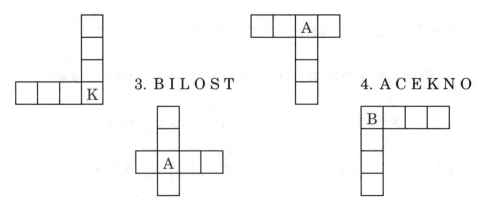

FILLING STATION

Place the given consonants on the dashes to form words. The vowels have already been placed for you, and as an additional help, each entry lists its category beside its given consonants.

1. B G H P R S T T (U.S. city)

    __ I __ __ __ __ U __ __ __

2. F G R R R R T (household sight)

    __ E __ __ I __ E __ A __ O __

3. D R S S S T T W (movie)

    " __ E __ __   __ I __ E   __ __ O __ Y "

4. D D G G H L N T Z (food)

    __ __ A __ E __   __ O U __ __ __ U __

5. B G L R R Z Z (animal)

    __ __ I __ __ __ Y   __ E A __

SKILLS TEST

Bob is a hardware-store clerk who last week sold a different number of nails each day, Monday through Friday. Monday's nail number was 200 lower than Tuesday's, which was 400 higher than Wednesday's, which was 500 lower than Thursday's, which was 600 higher than Friday's.

If Bob sold 800 nails on the day of his lowest sales, how many nails did he sell on each day?

LOOSE TILE

VISUAL ◆ SPATIAL

The tray on the right seemed the ideal place to store the set of loose dominoes. Unfortunately, when the tray was full, one domino was left over. Determine the arrangement of the dominoes in the tray and which is the Loose Tile.

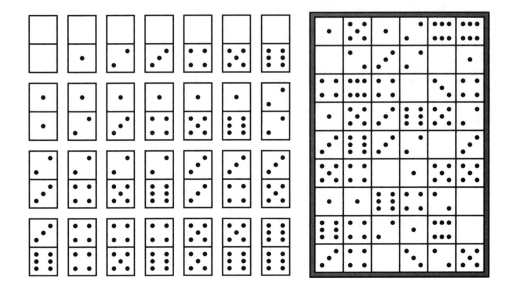

CIRCLE SEARCH

LANGUAGE

Directions for solving are on page 24.
Here you're looking to form 12 words.

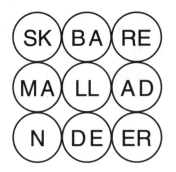

VISION QUEST

WEEK 9

Find the row or column that contains
five DIFFERENT pairs of eyeglasses.

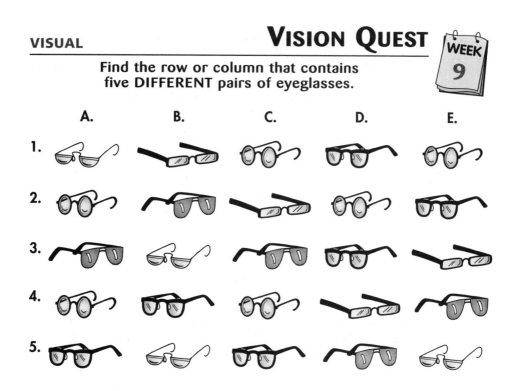

A.   B.   C.   D.   E.

1.

2.

3.

4.

5.

SEVEN WORD ZINGER

Directions for solving are on page 23.

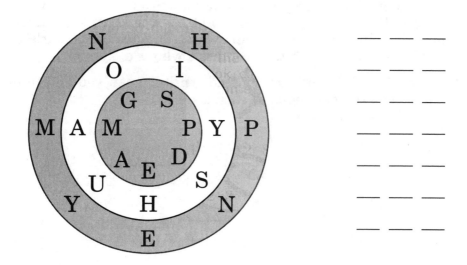

— — —

— — —

— — —

— — —

— — —

— — —

— — —

ALPHABET SOUP

VISUAL ◆ LANGUAGE

Cross off each letter from the alphabet list that appears in the larger group of letters. Then rearrange the letters not crossed out to form the title of a 1970 movie.

```
Z  P  B  B  P  Z  P  Z  P  B  P  L  K  L  P  L  K  P  K  L
B  P  L  K  Z  L  B  P  E  K  R  C  W  C  W  R  C  R  W  C
L  Z  F  O  Z  O  F  L  O  Z  D  W  K  L  B  U  K  W  D  U
X  G  Q  G  X  Q  Z  O  R  P  N  P  T  C  O  I  W  Q  J  B
W  K  V  J  X  T  B  L  E  J  Q  Y  O  I  Z  B  T  L  C  V
```

A B C D E F G H I J K L M N O P Q R S T U V W X Y Z

Movie title: _____

DEDUCTION PROBLEM

LOGIC

Tim, Lou, Mark, and Jack escorted their girlfriends to a dance last week. All of them brought corsages for their dates; Jack's consisted of yellow roses. The young ladies' names are Amy, Bea, Clea, and Donna. Bea is a junior and Clea wore a pink gown with a pink camellia in her dark, curly hair. The two senior girls are Tim's date who wore white and Mark's who is a blonde.

Knowing that Tim and Amy are not an item, can you determine the names of the two teens in each couple?

MISSING DOMINOES

In this game you use all 28 dominoes that are in a standard set. Each one has a different combination from 0-0, 0-1, 0-2, to 6-6. Domino halves with the same number of dots lie next to each other. To avoid confusion we have used an open circle to indicate a zero. Can you fill in the missing white dominoes to complete the board?

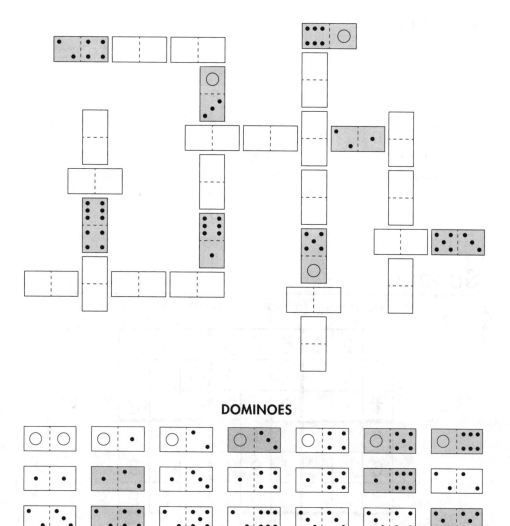

DOMINOES

67

CHANGELINGS

LANGUAGE

Can you change the first word into the second word by changing only one letter at a time? Do not rearrange the order of the letters with each change. Each change must result in an everyday word, and words beginning with a capital letter, slang, or obsolete words aren't allowed.

1. FIND

_____

_____

_____

LOVE
(4 changes)

2. FILE

_____

_____

_____

NAIL
(4 changes)

3. SWAP

_____

_____

_____

DEAL
(4 changes)

SUDOKU

LOGIC

Directions for solving are on page 10.

	2	3	5	4	1			
	5				8	9	4	
1			9					3
8	7			1				
6			7	9	5			8
				6			2	9
4					3			7
	3	7	4				1	
			6	5	7	3	8	

CARD SENSE

Directions for solving are on page 43.

1. Exactly one card is between the two black cards.

2. Neither the two nor the seven is on the bottom.

3. The ace is somewhere above the two.

4. The five is directly above the four.

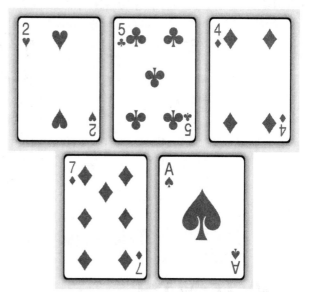

LANGUAGE

U.S. R'S

The list below consists of the names of six U.S. States, but we've removed all of their letters except for the R's. Can you write one letter on each dash to complete the names of the states?

1. __ __ __ __ __ __ R __ __ __

2. __ __ __   __ __ R __

3. __ __ R __ __ __ __

4. __ R __ __ __ __

5. __ __ __ __ R __ __ __

6. __ R __ __ __ __ __

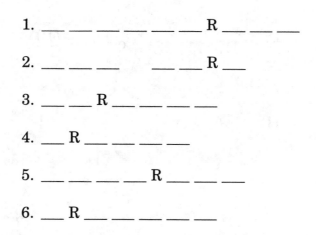

WORD HUNT

LANGUAGE ◆ SPATIAL

Directions for solving are on page 47. This time, you'll be searching for words that begin with S and end with D (such as SLINKED). We found 30 words.

Your list of words:

T	L	A	D	I
E	S	I	N	R
D	E	K	O	C
N	P	W	L	S
U	O	S	I	D

CIRCLE MATH

MATH

Directions for solving are on page 32. We've started you off by telling you that B = 2.

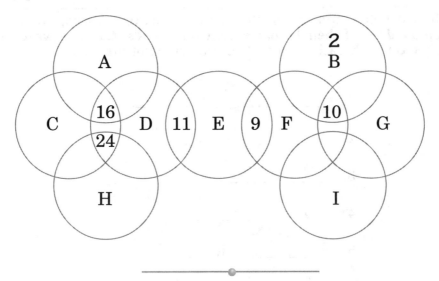

"A prudent question is one-half of wisdom."
— Francis Bacon

GOING IN CIRCLES

Directions for solving are on page 34.

WEEK
10

1.

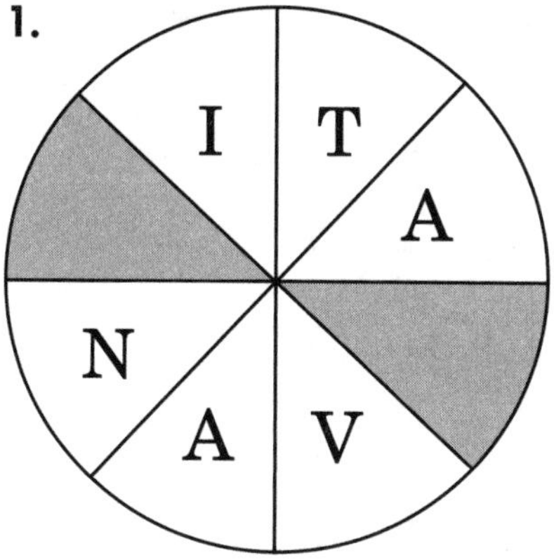

I T
A
N
A V

2.

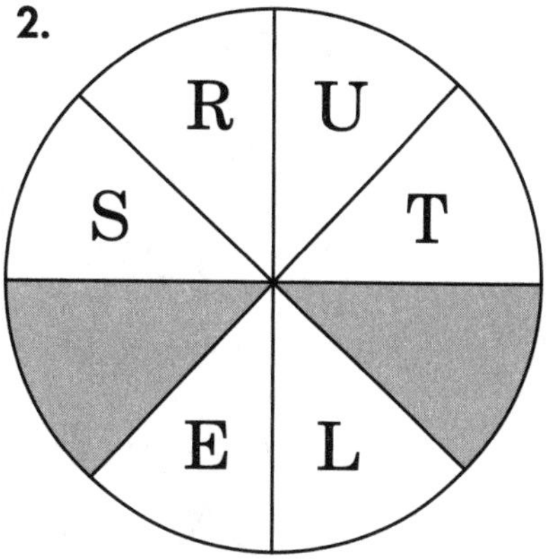

R U
S T
E L

RELATIONSHIPS QUIZ

Directions are on page 13.

1. QUARTER is to NICKEL as HUNDRED is to _____.
   (a) one   (b) five   (c) twenty   (d) fifty

2. AUTUMN is to RAKE as WINTER is to _____.
   (a) shovel   (b) ski   (c) snow   (d) blizzard

3. MUSIC is to HEAR as ODOR is to _____.
   (a) aroma   (b) taste   (c) smell   (d) air

4. BEAR is to BARE as HORSE is to _____.
   (a) pony   (b) saddle   (c) race   (d) hoarse

5. FEAR is to TREMBLE as JOY is to _____.
   (a) sadness   (b) smile   (c) quake   (d) happiness

HEXAGON HUNT

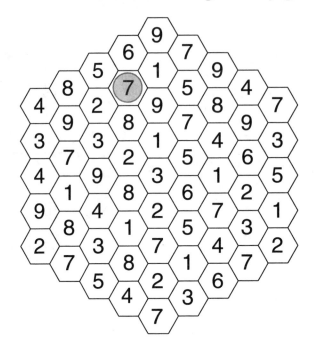

Directions for solving are on page 22.

VISUAL

LETTER, PLEASE

DECODING

Directions for solving are on page 61.

2 626 266846233

2424678 447 9455

47 668 266846233.

COMPOUND IT

WEEK
10

Directions for solving are on page 35.

1. mouse, cat, snow, mast

2. drift, head, fish, nap

3. tail, bowl, wood, strong

4. gate, pipe, and, men

5. dream, lady, power, line

6. up, team, love, house

7. boat, wind, scale, sick

8. bag, mill, fall, room

9. jump, turn, mate, back

10. style, ground, rug, sight

LANGUAGE

WORD WHEEL

Directions for solving are on page 44. Beginning with the "W" at the top of the wheel, we formed 32 words of three or more letters.

BULL'S-EYE LETTER

LANGUAGE

Directions for solving are on page 33.

— — — — —

— — — — —

— — — — —

— — — — —

— — — — —

— — — — —

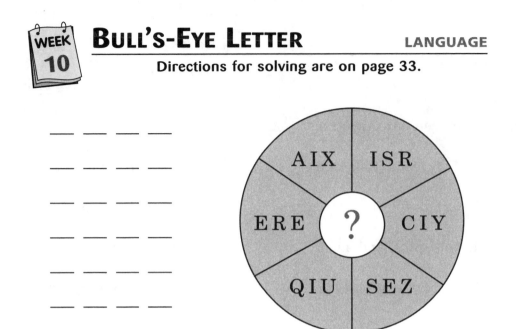

DISK MEMORY

SPATIAL

Directions for solving are on page 29.

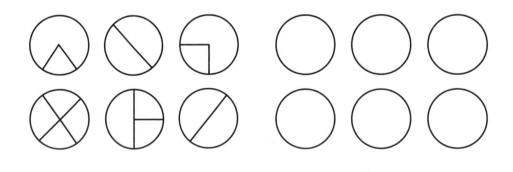

"Many live by their wits but few by their wit."
— Laurence Peter

WHAT'S YOUR NUMBER?

Can you figure out the sequence of numbers in the boxes below and what missing number goes into the space with the question mark?

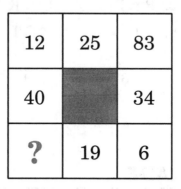

12	25	83
40		34
?	19	6

ANIMAL CHARADES

Each line contains a clue to a letter of the alphabet. These letters, in the given order, will spell out the name of an animal. The animal's identity is also hinted at in the last sentence of the Charade.

My FIRST is in PERCH and in SCRAWL; ____

My SECOND is in CARIBOU and in BRAWL; ____

My THIRD is in MOUSE but not in SMEAR; ____

My FOURTH is in RACCOON but not in ENDEAR; ____

My FIFTH is in PORPOISE and in ESCORT; ____

My SIXTH is in SARDINE and in DEPORT; ____

My SEVENTH is in PENGUIN but not in HEADSTRONG; ____

My EIGHTH is in STARLING but not in SARONG; ____

My NINTH is in LEOPARD and in APPLAUSE. ____

My WHOLE is a critter with massive jaws.

_____

75

COUNT ON IT!

LANGUAGE

Use the given letters to fill in the familiar saying, one letter per dash. All the letters following 1 are the first letters of each word, the letters following 2 are the second letters of each word, etc. It is up to you to determine which letter goes where.

1. M P P   2. R A E   3. R K A   4. C E F

5. T E S   6. C I   7. C T   8. E

$\overline{\quad}\ \overline{\quad}\ \overline{\quad}\ \overline{\quad}\ \overline{\quad}\ \overline{\quad}\ \overline{\quad}\ \overline{\quad}$ $\overline{\quad}\ \overline{\quad}\ \overline{\quad}\ \overline{\quad}\ \overline{\quad}$
  1 2 3 4 5 6 7 8   1 2 3 4 5

$\overline{\quad}\ \overline{\quad}\ \overline{\quad}\ \overline{\quad}\ \overline{\quad}\ \overline{\quad}\ \overline{\quad}$.
  1 2 3 4 5 6 7

WORD CHARADE

LANGUAGE ◆ VISUAL

Directions for solving are on page 42.

My first letter is surrounded by an 8-letter word, reading clockwise, composed of letters from the first half of the alphabet.

My second letter appears more often in one of the columns than any other letter.

K	Q	N	X	P	A	H	J
S	Q	T	H	U	S	X	P
A	O	P	X	I	L	K	T
T	W	G	L	M	E	M	U
P	X	G	A	D	I	A	B
W	U	S	X	P	Q	G	E
L	G	B	K	E	M	R	J
H	L	P	X	D	N	E	T

My third letter is to the immediate left or immediate right of my second letter wherever it appears.

My fourth letter appears only in the top half of the diagram.

My fifth letter is the only letter from the second half of the alphabet in one of the rows.

My sixth letter is the first letter of four 4-letter words that read up, down, left, or right.

— — — — — —

G COUNT

Directions for solving are on page 61. This time, see how many G's you can count in the sentence.

BEGRUDGINGLY ZIGZAGGING ALONG THE GARDEN EDGE IN GOGGLES, GREGG IS JOGGING TO MAGGIE'S GORGEOUS GARAGE TO GORGE ON GALLONS OF THE GIRL'S ENGAGING, GRATIFYING EGGNOG.

LANGUAGE

ELIMINATION

Directions for solving are on page 24. Once again, the remaining words will form a thought.

EMPIRE BALUSTRADE CENT THE ALL COFFEE WOLVERINES STATE FORM LABORATORY PUNISHMENT DEFROST OXIDE MY FOR CHIANTI HURRICANES ALBATROSS VANITY LEMONADE LOVING IS VOLUNTEERS SEVERE BUILDING FLATTERY ALE

Eliminate...

1. the words that begin with the same three letters in any order.

2. the team nicknames of the University of Michigan, University of Miami (Florida), and University of Tennessee.

3. the words that form the title of a Beatles hit that begins: "Close your eyes and I'll kiss you, Tomorrow I'll miss you."

4. the names of beverages.

5. the 7-letter word that begins with three letters from the first half of the alphabet and ends with four letters from the second half.

6. the words that form the name of a New York City attraction.

7. the words that form other words when "per" is put before them.

QUICK FILL

Directions for solving are on page 43.

D E I I N N O P P T

1. In the alphabet, letter 10 appears somewhere before letter 7.

2. Letters 2 and 5 are vowels.

3. Letters 1, 6, and 9 spell out, in order, a crusty bakery treat.

4. Letters 2, 6, 9, and 10 are from the first half of the alphabet.

5. In the alphabet, letter 3 appears somewhere before letter 4, which appears somewhere before letter 8.

$$\overline{1} \quad \overline{2} \quad \overline{3} \quad \overline{4} \quad \overline{5} \quad \overline{6} \quad \overline{7} \quad \overline{8} \quad \overline{9} \quad \overline{10}$$

TARGET SHOOT

Directions for solving are on page 25.

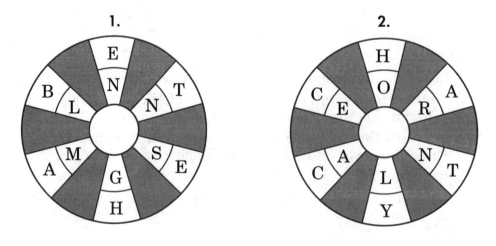

"Ignorance is the primary source of all misery and vice."
— Victor Cousin

TRI, TRI AGAIN

Directions for solving are on page 10.

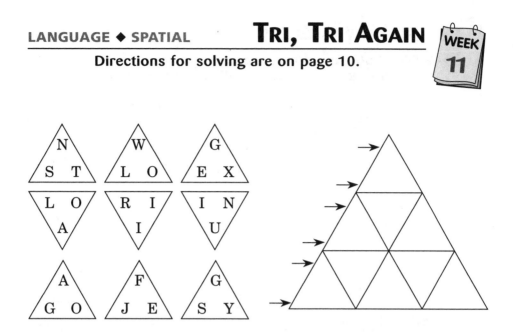

SUDOKU

Directions for solving are on page 10.

	8		6		1			
		2		3			8	6
7		1	8	2				
	4	7			3	6	5	
		5	7		9	3		
	1	8	5			4	7	
				7	8	5		4
8	7			5		2		
			9		4		3	

ALL IN A ROW

MATH

Directions for solving are on page 16. This time, look for the most groups of consecutive numbers adding up to 21.

A. 5 5 5 2 6 9 1 6 4 3 7 1 3 3 2 9 4 8 1 5 8 1 2 4

B. 6 4 9 4 8 4 8 2 1 5 9 5 1 6 3 2 5 9 5 3 3 3 8 4

C. 8 7 2 3 8 1 9 6 5 9 6 1 1 2 3 4 5 8 9 7 1 4 2 2

ANIMAL CHARADES

LANGUAGE

Directions for solving are on page 75.

My FIRST is in WOMBAT and in MOIST; ____

My SECOND is in CONDOR and in REJOICED; ____

My THIRD is in EGRET but not in TEEN; ____

My FOURTH is in NUTHATCH but not in CUISINE; ____

My FIFTH is in POLECAT and in POINT; ____

My SIXTH is in IGUANA and in ANOINT; ____

My SEVENTH is in SALMON but not in LAMP; ____

My EIGHTH is in PANTHER but not in STAMP. ____

My WHOLE is a shell-encased reptile, one not particularly mobile.

KEEP ON MOVING

Directions for solving are on page 44. Here, start in the shaded square with the number 3.

2	2	5	3	2	5
3	4	2	3	4	1
2	1	3	3	1	3
4	3	2	2	2	1
2	4	2	3	2	✳
1	4	1	4	5	3

MATH ◆ VISUAL

COUNT TO TEN

Examine the ears of corn and tomatoes below and then answer these questions: 1. Which row contains the most EARS OF CORN? 2. Which row contains the most TOMATOES? 3. Which row contains an equal number of EARS OF CORN and TOMATOES?

1.

2.

3.

4.

5.

6.

7.

8.

9.

10.

ARROW MAZE

VISUAL

Directions for solving are on page 27. This time, you'll begin by moving to the right from the starting box.

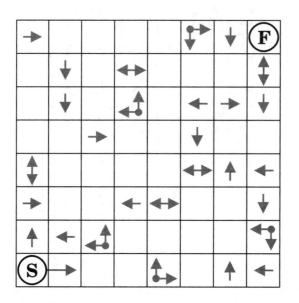

WAYWORDS

LANGUAGE

Directions for solving are on page 19. This time, you'll be looking for a 10-word thought beginning with SEVEN.

GUEST	WEAK	ONE	ANYBODY
BEFORE	DAYS	VALUES	MAKE
ON	PLEAD	SEVEN	CAN
A	CRASH	DIET	PERCENT

FUN WITH FACTS AND FIGURES

WEEK 12

Directions for solving are on page 15.

1. Take the number of kings on a chessboard at the beginning of a game and add the number of players in a traditional checkers game. _____

2. Next, multiply by the number heard before "Skiddoo!" in the catchphrase of the 1920s. _____

3. Now subtract the number of people in 15 quartets. _____

4. Add the number of months in the year that have names of one syllable. _____

5. Divide by the number of continents on the earth. _____

Our answer is the number of rings on the Olympics flag. Is yours?

VISUAL ◆ SPATIAL

STACKED UP

Directions for solving are on page 23.

1.

2.

3.

4.

5.

6.

SKILLS TEST

LANGUAGE

The words of a little 2-line rhyme are printed in alphabetical order. The slash indicates the end of the first line, capitalized words indicate the beginnings of the two lines, and a period indicates the end of the rhyme. Can you recreate the rhyme?

and	nastiest	thing
Diplomacy	nicest	to
do	say/	way.
in	the	
is	The	

Your answer: _____

_____

SLIDE RULE

LANGUAGE

Directions for solving are on page 22. This time, we formed 31 words, including SLAM.

Your list of words:

WORD EQUATIONS

WEEK 12

Directions for solving are on page 45.

1. actor Gibson + opposite of high = full-flavored, as wine

2. poker stake + casual walking gait = African mammal

3. hobo, maybe + wharf = more jolting, as a bus ride

4. opposite of pro + biology or chemistry = feeling of morality

5. map, for one + take advantage of again = yellowish-green color

RHYMING REPLACEMENTS

Each pair of words below will become a familiar phrase when you replace each word in capital letters with a word that rhymes with it. For example, CORK & SCENES would be replaced by the rhyming PORK & BEANS. Can you figure out all 12 pairs?

1. LONG & PANTS

2. BRIDE & NEW

3. FLED & RUN

4. SLANT & WAVE

5. SEEK & CHILD

6. HAT & BLOUSE

7. TAX & PAIN

8. CHILL & BLEW

9. PICK & WIN

10. CARS & PIPES

11. SHOCK & BOWL

12. KITES & ROUNDS

HEXAGON HUNT

VISUAL

Directions for solving are on page 22.

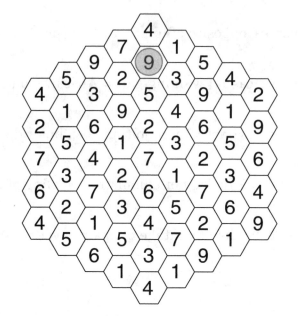

OVERLAY

VISUAL ◆ SPATIAL

Directions for solving are on page 35.

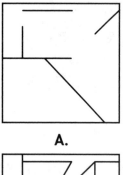

A.

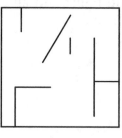

B.

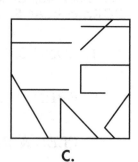

C.

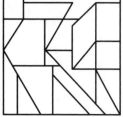

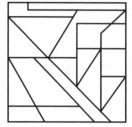

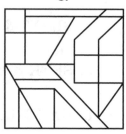

ANAGRAM MAZE

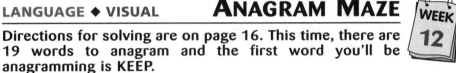

WEEK 12

Directions for solving are on page 16. This time, there are 19 words to anagram and the first word you'll be anagramming is KEEP.

1 KEEP	**2** ANTS	**3** DOES	**4** FEAT	**5** INCH	**6** HUNT
7 OOZE	**8** FIVE	**9** PURR	**10** CUFF	**11** PALE	**12** PLUS
13 WHIM	**14** FOIL	**15** SHAM	**16** RAID	**17** STUD	**18** ALOE
19 DECK	**20** GOAT	**21** KEEN	**22** FALL	**23** INTO	**24** WAIT
25 WINE	**26** BOWL	**27** CREW	**28** REAM	**29** MODE	**30** VEER
31 KNOW	**32** BAKE	**33** REAR	**34** FACE	**35** CULT	**36** NEAR

EASY PICKINGS

To solve, simply cross out one letter in each pair below. When the puzzle is completed correctly, the remaining letters will spell out a quote by the writer Norman Cousins.

HE OD EP CE   AI NS

DI ON OD EH PI GE NM DI EJ NV OT   KO HF

ET HE IE   AN YP PI IA SR AS IT UJ SN

OT FT   LC IO VG IJ LC.

IN THE ABSTRACT

VISUAL ◆ SPATIAL

Directions for solving are on page 12.

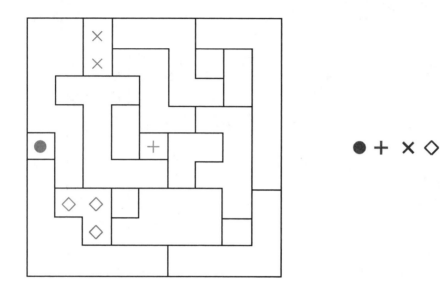

● + × ◇

WHAT'S YOUR NUMBER?

MATH ◆ LOGIC

Can you figure out what number goes into the space with the question mark?

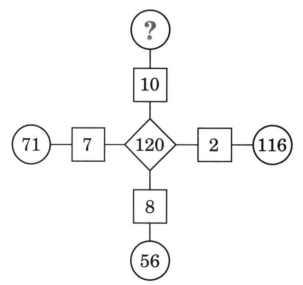

SUDOKU

Directions for solving are on page 10.

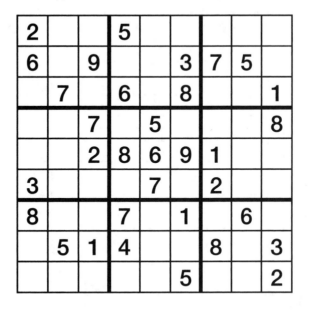

LANGUAGE

FILLING STATION

See page 63 for solving directions.

1. B D F F H L R S (game)

   __ __ U __ __ __ E __ O A __ __

2. B G H H M P R R T (actor)

   __ U __ __ __ __ E Y   __ O __ A __ __

3. D H M R R R S T W (TV show)

   "__ U __ __ E __ ,   __ __ E   __ __ O __ E "

4. C C L N N S S T T (things)

   __ O __ __ A __ __   __ E __ __ E __

5. D G H L L N N R S T (fictional characters)

   __ A __ __ E __   A __ __   __ __ E __ E __

ARROW MAZE

Starting at the **S** and following the arrow up, see if you can find your way to **F**. When you reach an arrow, you MUST follow its direction and continue in that direction until you come to the next arrow. When you reach a two-headed arrow, you can choose either direction. It's okay to cross your own path.

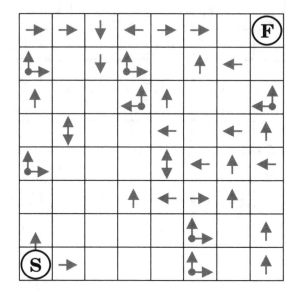

QUICK FILL

Determine the 10-letter word from the clues. All the letters in the word are listed.

A B E I L O P R R V

1. Letter 8 is a vowel.

2. In the alphabet, letter 4 is four letters after letter 2.

3. Letters 10, 9, and 7, in order, spell out a science workroom.

4. Letters 1, 3, 6, and 5, in order, spell out a skin opening.

$$\overline{1}\ \overline{2}\ \overline{3}\ \overline{4}\ \overline{5}\ \overline{6}\ \overline{7}\ \overline{8}\ \overline{9}\ \overline{10}$$

COUNT TO TEN

WEEK
13

Examine the rakes and clippers and then answer these questions: 1. Which row contains the most rakes? 2. Which row contains the most clippers? 3. Which row contains an equal number of rakes and clippers?

1.
2.
3.
4.
5.
6.
7.
8.
9.
10.

EASY PICKINGS

To solve, simply cross out one letter in each pair below. When the puzzle is completed correctly, the remaining letters will spell out a truism.

SE NO TE MN IY WE SF   AW ER EV

MU MA DI ET, IN DO TA

BR FO RE DN.

THE LINEUP

LANGUAGE

While scrutinizing the lineup of letters below, can you answer the five given questions correctly in five minutes or less?

ZYTAXIJSLIMWCORRECTDSPONGEKHFBUMPQM

1. Which letter of the alphabet does not appear in the lineup? _____

2. What 7-letter word — with its letters in correct order and appearing together — can you find in the lineup? _____

3. Which letter of the alphabet appears exactly three times in the lineup? _____

4. What 6-letter word — with its letters in correct order and appearing together — can you find in the lineup? _____

5. Other than the answers to Questions 2 and 4, how many everyday words — with their letters in correct order and appearing together — of four or more letters can you find in the lineup? _____

SUDOKU

LOGIC

3					8	9		
9		7	4				1	
	6	4			9			2
	4		7		2		5	8
	9			4			2	
5	2		3		1		7	
4			2			8	9	
	7				3	5		1
		9	6					7

Place a number into each box so each row across, column down, and small 9-box square within the larger square (there are 9 of these) contains 1 through 9.

IN THE ABSTRACT

Fill in each section with one of the four symbols so no sections containing the same symbol touch. Four sections are already complete.

● + ✕ ◇

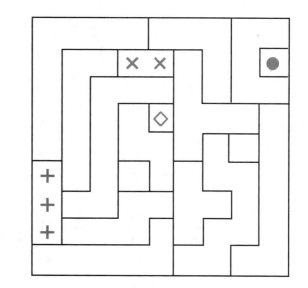

B COUNT

Here's an eye exam that's also a B exam! First, read the sentence below. Next, go back and read the sentence again, but this time count all of the B's. How many are there?

BARBARA AND BOBBY BALBOA'S

CHUBBY BABIES BABBLE, JABBER,

AND BLUBBER WHEN BOBBY

BOBBLES BUBBLES OR BARBARA

BURLESQUES THE BUZZING HUBBUB

OF BUMBLEBEES.

HEXAGON HUNT

VISUAL

In this diagram of six-sided figures, there are 10 "special" hexagons. These 10 are special because the six numbers around each one are all different from each other and the center. We've circled one of the 10. Can you find the other 9?

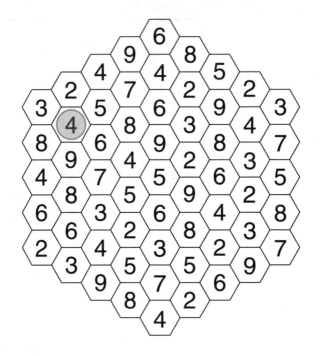

COMPOUND IT

LANGUAGE

Starting at #1, pick a word that will form a compound word with a word chosen in #2. Then with the word you've selected in #2, pick one from #3 to form another compound word. Continue in this manner to #10, so that you've formed nine compound words. In some instances more than one compound word can be formed, but there is only one path to get you to #10.

1. clean, fuss, cat, low

2. shaven, up, nip, budget

3. wind, bringing, town, swing

4. shield, storm, burn, ship

5. watch, sides, shape, out

6. pouring, run, shine, cast

7. down, away, around, beat

8. turn, play, right, about

9. field, wing, over, time

10. keep, blank, moist, come

ONLINE NETWORK

In each two-column group, take the letters in the left-hand column along the paths (indicated by the lines) and place them in their proper boxes in the right-hand column. When done, you'll find three related words reading down each of the two right-hand columns.

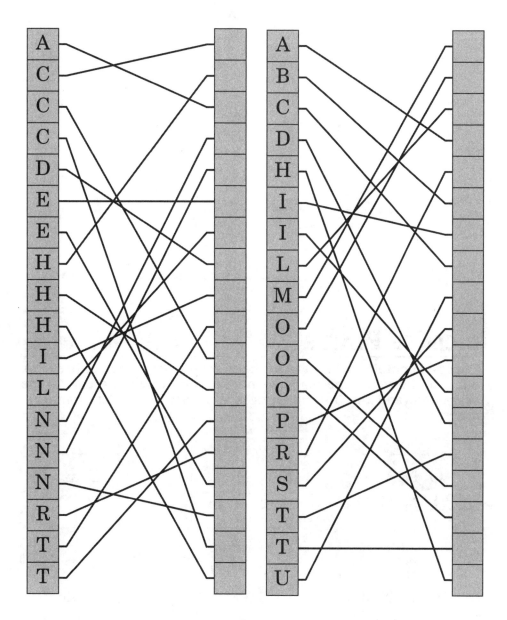

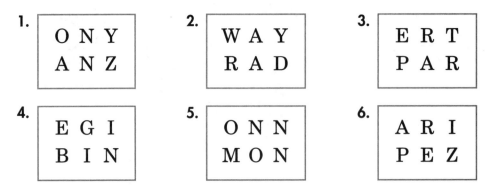

COUNT THE TRIANGLES

VISUAL ◆ SPATIAL

To solve this puzzle, write down the three letters that describe each triangle in this figure. We found 27 triangles; how many can you locate?

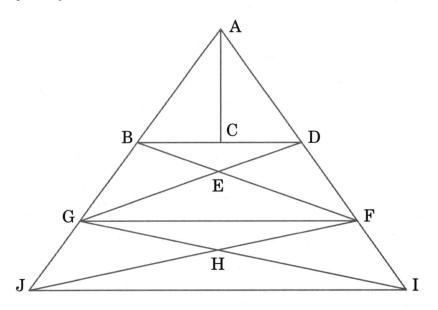

LICENSE PLATES

LANGUAGE

Each box contains six letters of the first and last names of previous hosts of the Miss America pageant. The top three are a part of the first name and the bottom three are a part of the last name, in order.

1.
```
O N Y
A N Z
```

2.
```
W A Y
R A D
```

3.
```
E R T
P A R
```

4.
```
E G I
B I N
```

5.
```
O N N
M O N
```

6.
```
A R I
P E Z
```

LOOSE TILE

The tray on the right seemed the ideal place to store the set of loose dominoes. Unfortunately, when the tray was full, one domino was left over. Determine the arrangement of the dominoes in the tray and which is the Loose Tile.

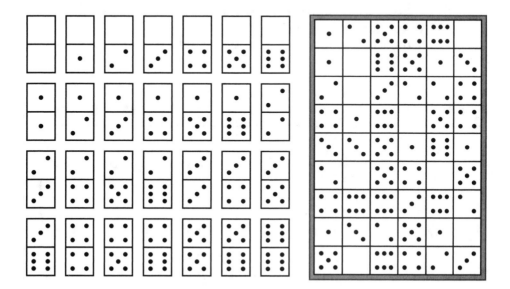

ALL IN A ROW

Which row below contains the most groups of consecutive numbers adding up to 10? Look carefully, because some groups may overlap. We've underlined an example of a group in each row to start you off.

A. 4 1 8 7 2 2 9 3 6 1 <u>5 3 2</u> 8 1 4 7 2 6 1 1 2 4 2

B. 9 <u>4 1 5</u> 6 2 7 4 1 1 2 3 3 8 1 4 7 9 3 2 2 1 6 4

C. 2 1 7 4 3 2 3 6 2 1 4 2 1 8 3 9 2 <u>4 6</u> 3 2 4 5 1

TIPS OF THE ICEBERG

MATH

The chart shows the gratuities each waiter or waitress earned on a recent breakfast shift at the Iceberg Diner. All you have to do is some careful addition and then answer the following questions:

1. Who made the most in total tips?
2. Who made the least?
3. Which two waitpersons made exactly the same amount?

EMPLOYEE	TIP 1	TIP 2	TIP 3	TIP 4	TIP 5
Al	$1.10	$1.80	$1.15	$1.05	$1.00
Brenda	$1.70	$2.10	$2.10	$2.70	$1.05
Charlie	$1.10	$3.10	$1.10	$1.10	$1.90
Dena	$1.90	$1.90	$1.35	$6.60	$1.00
Ed	$3.00	$3.90	$1.00	$1.00	$3.85
Flora	$1.10	$3.40	$5.80	$1.55	$1.70
Greta	$1.00	$1.85	$1.05	$1.00	$1.80

COUNTDOWN

Following the connecting lines, find the only route in this grid that passes through the numbers backward from 9 to 1 consecutively.

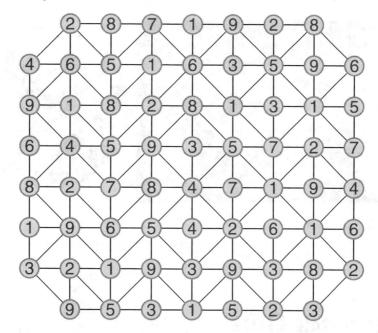

SYMBOL-ISM

This is simply a Cryptogram that uses symbols instead of letters to spell out a truism. Each symbol stands for the same letter throughout. For this puzzle, we've already indicated that ❖ = O and ≈ = D.

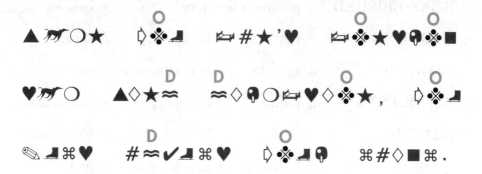

MAGNIFIND

Figure out which area of the drawing has been enlarged.

ANTONYMS QUIZ

An antonym is a word that is opposite in meaning to another word; for example, "cold" is the antonym of "hot." One of the words following each capitalized word is the antonym of that word.

1. ABRIDGE   a. abolish   b. augment   c. delay

2. PRECISE   a. inexact   b. swift   c. amiable

3. IMPOVERISHED   a. prosperous   b. reputable   c. extinct

4. SLAPDASH   a. petty   b. slovenly   c. thorough

5. IMMENSE   a. minute   b. permissive   c. torrid

6. CONQUEST   a. inquiry   b. defeat   c. competition

7. DEARTH   a. union   b. discipline   c. abundance

8. COMELY   a. hideous   b. principal   c. joyful

ANIMAL CHARADES

Each line contains a clue to a letter of the alphabet. These letters, in the given order, will spell out the name of an animal. The animal's identity is also hinted at in the last sentence of the Charade.

My FIRST is in MACAW and in CATCH;   _____

My SECOND is in PARTRIDGE and in SCRATCH;   _____

My THIRD is in PORCUPINE but not in PROVIDE;   _____

My FOURTH is in WILDCAT but not in CRIED;   _____

My FIFTH is in BARRACUDA and in CARRY;   _____

My SIXTH is in DONKEY and in DAIRY.   _____

My WHOLE is a critter who won't steer you wrong,
    If your desire is to have your home filled with song.

_____

CODE WORD

Decipher a quote and the Code Word's eleven letters, represented by the numbers 1 through 11. So, if the Code Word were "THUNDERCLAP," 1 in the quote would be T, 2 would be H, etc.

$$\overline{1}\ \overline{2}\ \overline{3}\ \overline{4}\ \overline{5}\ \overline{6}\ \overline{7}\ \overline{8}\ \overline{9}\ \overline{10}\ \overline{11}$$

10 9 9 10 2 8 11 2 V 2 1 7 9 9 9 5 D 7 9 5 2 6 1 10 ,

W H 8 C H 8 11 W H Y 11 9 M 2 P 2 9 P 5 2 K 2 2 P

P 4 7 7 8 10 3 8 7 9 F F .

ELIMINATION

WEEK 14

LANGUAGE

Cross off the capitalized words below according to the instructions given. The remaining words, in order, will form a thought.

ANGEL THERE BEST REMEDY IS GRAND
REGULATION ALWAYS PORTER VEST SOMEONE
CURE ROYAL READY TEST INTESTINES TO HEAL
TWIN SAY RAPIDS YOU REST CAN'T STOUT
RANGER

Eliminate the…

1. four words that rhyme with each other.
2. four words that are names of American League baseball players.
3. three words that have the same meaning.
4. two words that form a Michigan city.
5. word in which every letter appears exactly twice.
6. word that contains all five vowels (a, e, i, o, and u).
7. two words that are types of beers.

GOING IN CIRCLES

LANGUAGE

In each circle, insert one letter into each empty space to form an 8-letter word. Words may read either clockwise or counterclockwise and may begin with any letter in the circle.

1.

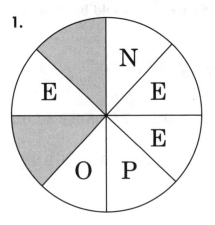

2.

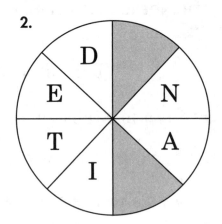

ANAGRAM MAZE

The diagram contains 36 words, 21 of which are anagrams of other everyday words. Start at the top arrow and anagram SACK. While solving, move up, down, right, or left to the only adjacent word that can be anagrammed. Continue until you arrive at the bottom arrow. There is only one path through the maze.

1 SACK	2 WHIP	3 SILO	4 WHEN	5 HEAR	6 HEAT
7 MUSH	8 FADE	9 ADDS	10 CALL	11 ZINC	12 COAL
13 CUED	14 PODS	15 PRAY	16 APSE	17 RING	18 NAIL
19 SUNS	20 PALM	21 WARY	22 WOES	23 TWIN	24 WISE
25 LEND	26 REAL	27 COPY	28 WOOL	29 FANG	30 TOOK
31 POPS	32 STUD	33 PASS	34 BANE	35 RUNT	36 RACE

WHAT'S YOUR NUMBER?

Can you figure out the sequence of numbers in the box and what missing number goes into the space with the question mark?

85	80	75	70	65
90	25	20	15	60
95	30	5	10	55
100	35	40	45	?
105	110	115	120	125

STAR WORDS

VISUAL ◆ LOGIC

Only five of the eight words given will fit together in the diagram. Place them in the directions indicated by the arrows.

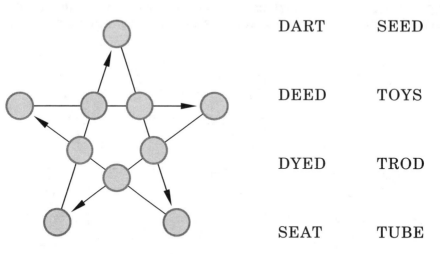

DART   SEED

DEED   TOYS

DYED   TROD

SEAT   TUBE

ASSOCIATIONS

LANGUAGE

You'll find eight groups of three words that can be associated in some way with each other (example: mantel, fireplace, logs). Cross out each group as you find it. The initial letters of the remaining words will spell out the answer to the riddle:

**AFTER THE RAIN FALLS,
WHEN DOES IT GO UP AGAIN?**

PROMISE   AREA   JOIN   ITCH   ORLANDO   GUIDE

NEST   CONNECT   VOW   DRIP   CLINTON   ELEVATE

STRICT   REGION   WITCH   LINK   STEER   BUSH

PROHIBIT   TRADITION   SEVERE   TAMPA   INNING

LOCALE   OBAMA   MATCH   DIRECT   BAN   HARSH

EDGE   MIAMI   OATH   FORBID

BULL'S-EYE LETTER

Add the SAME single letter to each group of three letters, then rearrange the letters to form six everyday 4-letter words.

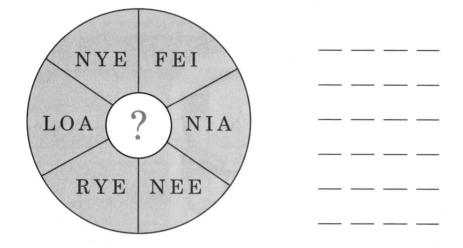

— — — —

— — — —

— — — —

— — — —

— — — —

— — — —

SLIDE RULE

Slide each column of letters up or down in the box and form as many everyday 3-letter words as you can in the windows where CON is now. We formed 41 words, including CON.

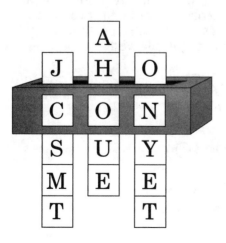

Your list of words:

OVERLAY

VISUAL ◆ SPATIAL

When you overlay the three diagrams in the top row, which of the three lettered diagrams, A, B, or C, will be formed?

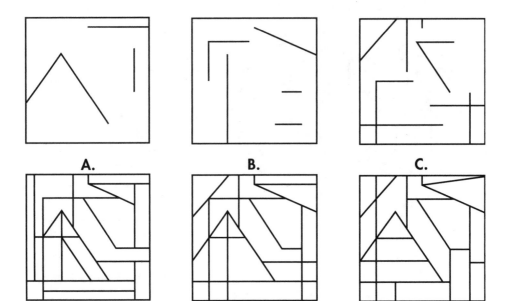

A. B. C.

CIRCLE SEARCH

LANGUAGE

Move from circle to adjoining circle, horizontally and vertically only, to form 14 common, everyday words of at least three letters. Don't change the order of the letters in the circles that contain more than one letter. Proper names are not allowed.

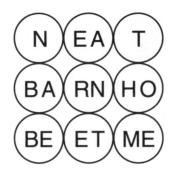

WORD VISIBILITY

WEEK 15

There are six 5-letter words below. The first letter of the answer is found in the first pair of letters, and it is either the top or the bottom letter. Continue across each pair.

For example, the word GIRL would be found thus: G A R L
L I T X

1. M R O P E
   E A W D G

2. H O P L R
   A P N S E

3. M C O D H
   K O E S E

4. P R A M H
   T I U T K

5. O A I I G
   B R B E T

6. S Y M I F
   M I D O C

CARD SENSE

Five playing cards were shuffled and put in a pile, one on top of another. Using the clues, can you identify each card's position in the pile?

1. The jack is somewhere below both spades.

2. The three is somewhere above both the six and the diamond.

3. The heart is not on the bottom.

4. The club is not on the top.

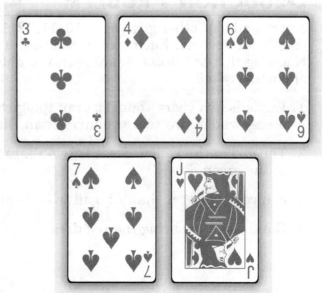

VISION QUEST

VISUAL

Find the row or column that contains five DIFFERENT ducks.

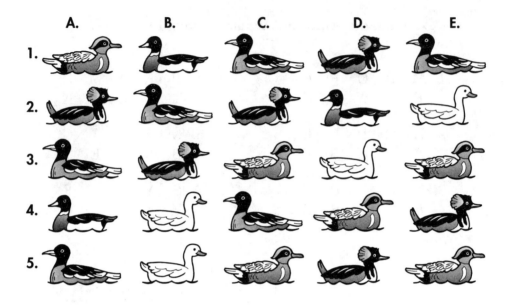

DEDUCTION PROBLEM

LOGIC

Nancy and four other girls, aged 10, 11, 12, 13, and 14, are walking together to school. Each girl is wearing a different color dress. Knowing that one dress is pink, can you determine each girl's age and dress color?

1. Leslie is two years younger than the girl wearing the blue dress (who is two years younger than Diane.)

2. The girl in the yellow dress is two years younger than the girl in the green dress.

3. Janice is younger than Abigail (who is not wearing green.)

4. Diane is not wearing the red dress.

RELATIONSHIPS QUIZ

KENNEL is to DOG as STY is to PIG because a DOG lives in a kennel and a PIG lives in a STY. Each of the statements below is a relationship of some kind. Can you select the right word from the four following each?

1. JOG is to RUN as TROT is to _____.
   (a) fly (b) dance (c) swim (d) gallop

2. DECK is to CARD as PIE is to _____.
   (a) crust (b) cherries (c) slice (d) bake

3. ELEPHANT is to CALF as KANGAROO is to _____.
   (a) joey (b) kid (c) cub (d) whelp

4. MOUNTAIN is to CREST as HOUSE is to _____.
   (a) roof (b) door (c) hill (d) home

5. JURY is to JUDGE as COMMITTEE is to _____.
   (a) member (b) chairman (c) issue (d) council

WAYWORDS

A 9-word thought can be found beginning with the word ONE. Then, move to any adjacent box up, down, or diagonally for each following word.

ONE	THING	CHORE	MIXTURE
WE	WAY	SURPRISE	GRATEFUL
ALWAYS	NEVER	OF	IS
BELIEVE	OUT	RUN	SINGLE

SUDOKU
LOGIC

Directions for solving are on page 92.

7		5	9			6		
			1				9	4
9	4	1			3			
3	9		6					5
4			2	5	8			3
8					9		1	6
			8			5	2	9
	6	9			4			
		8				1	3	4

FUN WITH FACTS AND FIGURES
MATH

This puzzle tests you on several little facts and figures. Solve the quiz in the order given since each answer is used in the next statement. There are no fractions used here.

1. Take the number of the date that Halloween falls on in October and add to that the number of innings in a regulation professional baseball game. _____

2. Next, divide by the number of nickels in one dollar. _____

3. Now, multiply by the value of the Roman numeral V. _____

4. Add the number of musicians in fifteen quartets. _____

5. Divide by the number of digits on both hands. _____

Our answer is a number that many consider to be lucky.
Is yours?

LETTER, PLEASE

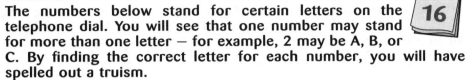

The numbers below stand for certain letters on the telephone dial. You will see that one number may stand for more than one letter — for example, 2 may be A, B, or C. By finding the correct letter for each number, you will have spelled out a truism.

843   7623   86

7822377   47

368833   9484

6269   83678464

7275464   772237.

SEVEN WORD ZINGER

Using each letter once, form seven everyday 3-letter words with the first letter coming from the center, the second from the middle, and the third from the outer circle. Your words may differ from ours.

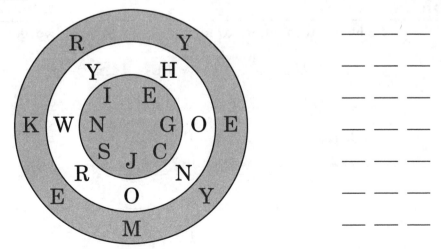

__ __ __'

__ __ __

__ __ __

__ __ __

__ __ __

__ __ __

__ __ __

111

GRAND TOUR

LANGUAGE ◆ VISUAL

Form a continuous chain of 5-letter words moving through the maze from START to FINISH. The second part of one word becomes the first part of the next word. This puzzle starts with CO-VER-SE (cover, verse).

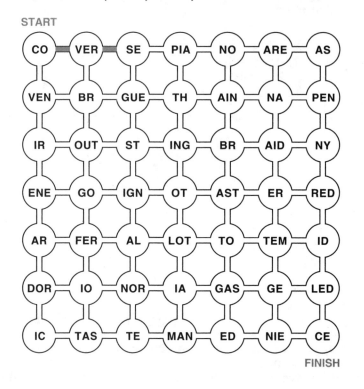

SKILLS TEST

LANGUAGE

Fill in the blanks with letters to form pairs of rhyming words.

1. R O U __ __ & G R U __ __

2. C O U __ __ & G O __ __

3. L __ __ __ & H __ __ N

4. C H O __ __ & T I __ __

5. B R O __ __ & F R A __ __

6. H A __ __ & L A __ __ H

COUNT ON IT!

Use the given letters to fill in the familiar saying, one letter per dash. All the letters following 1 are the first letters of each word, the letters following 2 are the second letters of each word, etc. It is up to you to determine which letter goes where.

1. L B C A M B   2. A Y I R A L   3. N V E O N

4. A E N T   5. E D

$$\overline{\underset{1}{}\ \overline{\underset{2}{}}\ \overline{\underset{3}{}}\qquad \overline{\underset{1}{}}\ \overline{\underset{2}{}}\ \overline{\underset{3}{}}\ \overline{\underset{4}{}}\ {}^{,}\qquad \overline{\underset{1}{}}\ \overline{\underset{2}{}}\ \overline{\underset{3}{}}\ \overline{\underset{4}{}}$$

$$\overline{\underset{1}{}}\ \overline{\underset{2}{}}\qquad \overline{\underset{1}{}}\ \overline{\underset{2}{}}\ \overline{\underset{3}{}}\ \overline{\underset{4}{}}\ \overline{\underset{5}{}}\qquad \overline{\underset{1}{}}\ \overline{\underset{2}{}}\ \overline{\underset{3}{}}\ \overline{\underset{4}{}}\ \overline{\underset{5}{}}.$$

FILLING STATION

Place the given consonants on the dashes to form words. The vowels have already been placed for you, and as an additional help, each entry lists its category beside its given consonants.

1. D F H K L R R R S S T T (movie)
   " _ A I _ E _ _   O _   _ _ E
   _ O _ _   A _ _ "

2. G N N P (bird)
   _ E _ _ U I _

3. L N V Z (country)
   _ E _ E _ U E _ A

4. H P R R R T T Y (fictional character)
   _ A _ _ _   _ O _ _ E _

5. C D G N N N R Y (natural wonder)
   _ _ A _ _   _ A _ _ O _

TARGET SHOOT

Find the two letters which, when entered into the center circle of each target, will form three 6-letter words reading across.

1.   **2.**

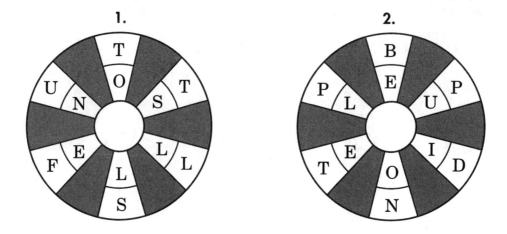

U.S. O'S

The list below consists of the names of six U.S. states, but we've removed all of their letters except for the O's. Can you write one letter on each dash to complete the names of the states?

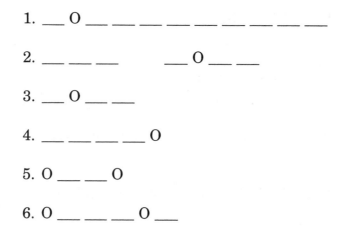

1. __ O __ __ __ __ __ __ __ __ __

2. __ __ __   __ O __ __

3. __ O __ __

4. __ __ __ __ O

5. O __ __ O

6. O __ __ __ O __

114

KEEP ON MOVING

The goal is to move from the shaded square to the asterisk. Since the shaded square has the number 3 in it, you must move three squares up, down, left, or right, but not diagonally. In the new square will be another number; move that number of squares up, down, left, or right, continuing in this way until you reach the asterisk. It's okay to cross your own path.

2	1	2	3	3	2
4	3	4	2	3	5
5	1	4	3	✳	5
2	2	1	3	1	1
4	3	1	2	3	1
4	1	2	2	3	5

DOVETAILED WORDS

Two related words, with their letters in the correct order, are combined in each row of letters. Can you find both words? In a line like POBOOXDELER, or POboOxDeLEr, you can see the two words POODLE and BOXER.

1. VNEORUNB _____ _____

2. HOSUNGEARY _____ _____

3. SMOKULNEK _____ _____

4. SVENNAOMKE _____ _____

5. CSHONECLHL _____ _____

"Our greatest glory is not in never failing, but in rising up every time we fail."
— *Ralph Waldo Emerson*

WORD HUNT

LANGUAGE ◆ SPATIAL

Find words by moving from one letter to any adjoining letter. You may start a word with any letter in the diagram. In forming a word you may return to a letter as often as you wish, but do not stand on a letter using it twice in direct succession. In this Word Hunt, you are searching for 4-letter words that end with NT (such as BUNT). We found 21 words, including BUNT.

Your list of words:

H	P	B	D	H
A	U	E	I	L
T	R	N	T	M
N	F	A	P	S
O	W	L	C	J

MARCHING ORDERS

LOGIC ◆ MATH

Using a different two-step sequence of addition and/or subtraction, can you make your way from Start to Finish in each puzzle by moving up, down, or diagonally? We've started the first one for you using the sequence +2 and +3; continue this sequence to reach Finish. You will not cross your own path or pass through any square twice.

1. FINISH ⬆

17	21	19	39	41	44
16	22	15	36	34	31
12	11	14	16	19	29
9	10	8	19	17	26
6	5	12	14	21	24
4	7	9	10	15	19

⬆ START

2. FINISH ⬆

27	30	32	27	37	38
22	28	35	33	22	21
14	19	27	23	16	18
11	9	10	15	13	17
6	4	8	12	25	21
3	7	9	13	15	19

⬆ START

MISSING DOMINOES

In this game you use all 28 dominoes that are in a standard set. Each one has a different combination from 0-0, 0-1, 0-2, to 6-6. Domino halves with the same number of dots lie next to each other. To avoid confusion we have used an open circle to indicate a zero. Can you fill in the missing white dominoes to complete the board?

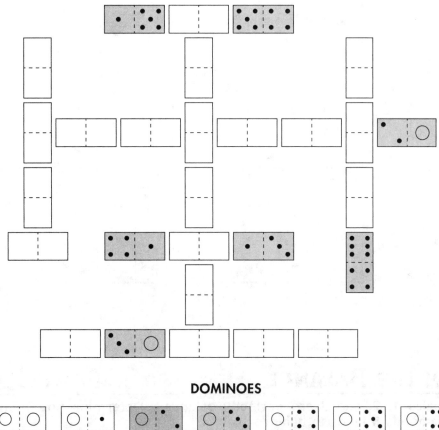

DOMINOES

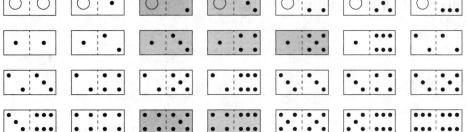

CROSS PATHS

VISUAL

Start at the arrow. There are six circles in that box, so move six boxes, either across or up. Each time you land in a box, move the number of dots in that box in only one direction, up, down, or across. You may cross your own path, but do not retrace it.

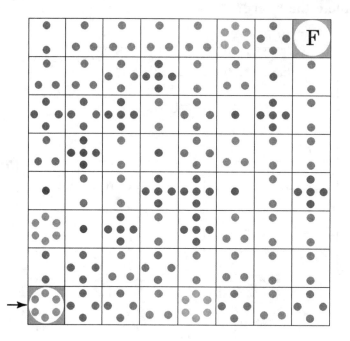

IN THE BALANCE

MATH ◆ LOGIC

Scales 1, 2, and 3 are perfectly balanced. Determine how many diamonds it takes to balance scale 4.

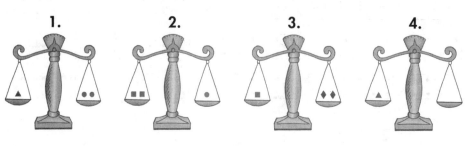

HOLE IN ONE

Twenty-four golfers entered a hole-in-one contest. Each golfer was given a ball with a different 4-digit number combination using the numbers 2, 3, 6, and 8 on it. Looking at the 23 balls still on the green, can you figure out what combination is on the ball that won the contest?

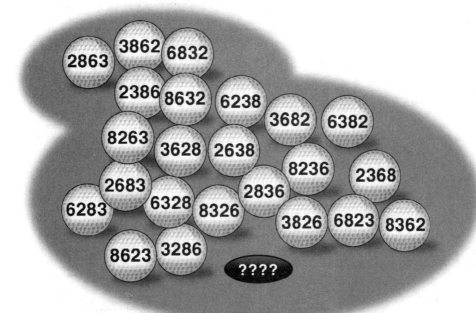

POP!

The balloons in a dart game are arranged so their letters spell out the word "STOWING." To win, you must pop six different balloons with six different darts, but after each pop the remaining letters must spell out a new word reading across from left to right. Do not rearrange the balloons. Can you determine the order of the balloons to pop and the words formed? Your words may differ from ours.

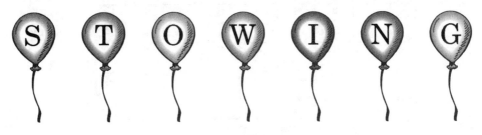

TRIANGULAR SQUARE

MATH ◆ SPATIAL

Place the nine numbered squares into the diagram so that the four numbers in each of the diagram's four large triangles equal the number outside of it. The patterns have to match and you may not rotate the squares.

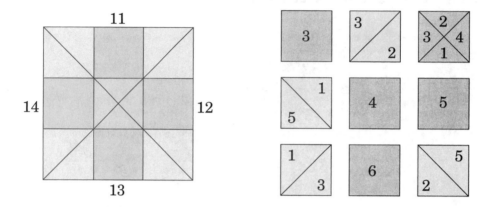

CROSS PATHS

VISUAL

Directions for solving are on page 118.

HOLE IN ONE

Directions for solving are on page 119. This time, the 4-digit number combination uses 4, 5, 7, and 9.

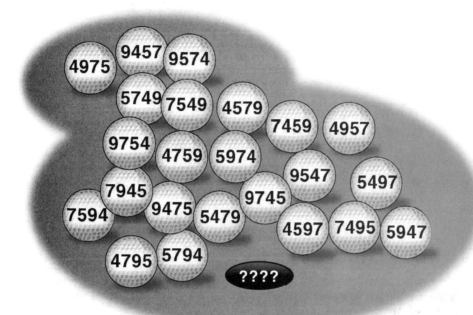

LOGIC ◆ MATH

IN THE BALANCE

Directions for solving are on page 118. This time, determine how many triangles it takes to balance scale 4.

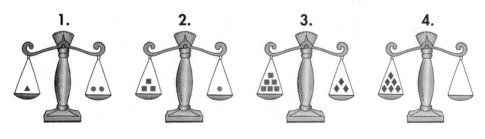

NEXT TO NOTHING

VISUAL

In the first row below, the A is next to the number zero, and the Y is next to the letter O. First, circle all of the letters next to zeroes. Next, scramble the circled letters to spell out a man's name.

A0	YO	JO	WO
IO	DO	HO	EO
U0	BO	LO	S0
GO	QO	R0	M0
NO	PO	FO	ZO
KO	C0	XO	VO

WORD WHEEL

LANGUAGE

Starting with the "S" at the arrow, see how many everyday words of three or more letters you can find going clockwise. Don't skip over any letters. For example, if you saw the letters C, A, R, E, D, you would form five words: CAR, CARE, CARED, ARE, RED. We found 31 words.

ONLINE NETWORK

WEEK 17

Directions for solving are on page 95.

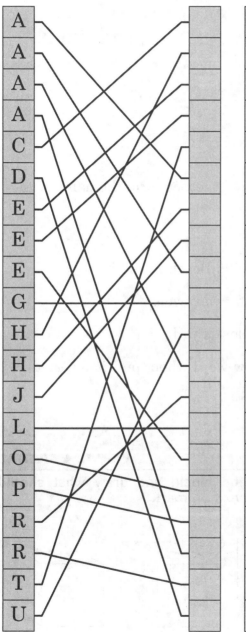

ELIMINATION

LANGUAGE

Directions for solving are on page 102. Once again, the remaining words will form a thought.

OPERATION CANOE BETTER EVER BASE TO
REED DARE RAVEN GOOD GREAT ACCUMULATE
TRIVIA THINGS CARDINAL FATIGUE THAN
DIMENSION PERMISSIBLE VIBRATIONS DARE
GLADES ENNUI NOTHING WORLD VULTURE

Eliminate the...

1. birds.

2. two words that, when put together, form the name of a Florida marshland.

3. three four-syllable words.

4. two words that form a 1966 Beach Boys hit.

5. four words that end with two vowels.

6. three words that can follow "third."

7. word that becomes a new word when "put" is inserted somewhere in the middle of it.

BLOCK PARTY

VISUAL ◆ SPATIAL

Study the different views of the block, and draw what should appear on the face that has a question mark.

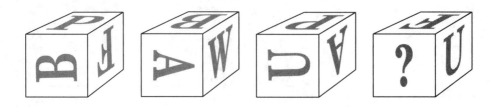

IN THE ABSTRACT

WEEK
18

Directions for solving are on page 93.

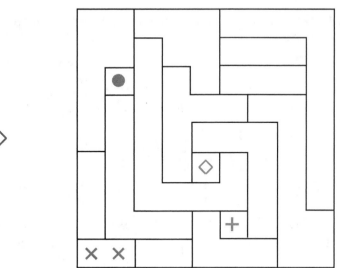

● + × ◇

TRI, TRI AGAIN

Fit the nine triangles into the big one so six everyday words are spelled out reading across the arrows. Do not rotate the triangles.

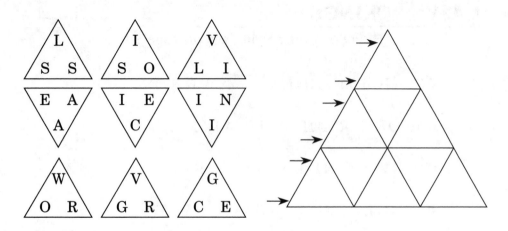

WORD CHARADE
LANGUAGE ◆ VISUAL

Find each letter in the diagram according to the instructions, and write each letter on its dash to spell out a 6-letter word.

My first letter appears only once in every other column, starting with the first column.

P	N	E	R	T	X	A	U
G	A	I	D	W	E	Z	H
W	D	B	H	F	A	S	A
R	K	T	A	N	G	U	B
F	D	W	E	X	P	Q	K
N	O	I	T	A	L	E	R
I	U	G	H	P	X	W	D
A	T	Z	R	I	N	Z	H

My second letter appears more often than any other letter.

My third letter appears only in the outer rows and columns.

My fourth letter appears only to the immediate left or right of my first letter.

My fifth letter appears in the top two rows, but not in the bottom two rows.

My sixth letter is the eighth letter of a word reading backwards in one of the rows.

— — — — — —

EASY PICKINGS
LANGUAGE

Directions for solving are on page 91.

TO AH EM CR NE   AT GR EX

AM OF NR EH   IR AD ML EL

EB RV EA RI EN SN   KT MH AW NZ

TI VD LI EN   GH AH NW DV WS.

ALPHABET SOUP

WEEK 18

Cross off each letter from the alphabet list that appears in the larger group of letters. Then rearrange the letters not crossed out to form the name of the state that entered the Union on December 29, 1845.

```
I  P  K  D  G  P  I  Y  M  L  W  H  G  P  I  Y

P  R  H  Z  C  H  R  H  V  P  I  N  F  R  P  F

J  Q  L  B  W  Q  C  D  H  C  V  I  W  V  N  M

H  D  Z  H  D  U  O  Y  D  H  N  Q  V  P  I  R
```

```
A B C D E F G H I J K L M N O P Q R S T U V W X Y Z
```

State: _____

SKILLS TEST

Which figure does not belong in the group below?

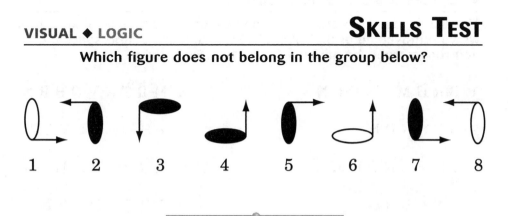

1   2   3   4   5   6   7   8

"It's surprising how much memory is built around things unnoticed at the time."
— *Barbara Kingsolver*

127

ARROW MAZE

VISUAL

Directions for solving are on page 90. This time, you'll begin by moving to the right from the starting box.

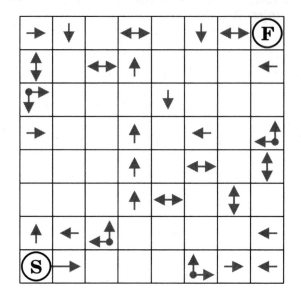

CONDENSED PRESIDENTS

LANGUAGE

The list below consists of the names of 10 U.S. Presidents, but we've removed all of their A's, E's, I's, O's, U's, Y's, and spaces. Can you reconstruct the names of the Chief Executives?

1. B R H M L N C L N

2. B R C K B M

3. J H N Q N C D M S

4. R N L D R G N

5. L S S S G R N T

6. M R T N V N B R N

7. T H D R R S V L T

8. H R R T R M N

9. R C H R D N X N

10. L N D N J H N S N

CHANGELINGS

WEEK 18

Can you change the first word into the second word by changing only one letter at a time? Do not rearrange the order of the letters with each change. Each change must result in an everyday word, and words beginning with a capital letter, slang, or obsolete words aren't allowed.

1. NAME

————————

————————

————————

SONG
(4 changes)

2. PEEP

————————

————————

————————

NEST
(4 changes)

3. DEER

————————

————————

————————

PARK
(4 changes)

RING LOGIC

Complete the diagram by drawing in the links between the rings using the statements below. Assume that all the rings in the picture are locked rigidly into position and cannot be moved in any direction. Consider yourself a true ringmaster if you can find the solution in under six minutes!

1. The right side of ring I is to the front.

2. Ring C is linked to four rings.

3. Rings E and G are each linked to two rings.

4. The pattern is symmetrical from left to right.

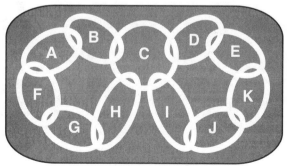

HEXAGON HUNT

Directions for solving are on page 94.

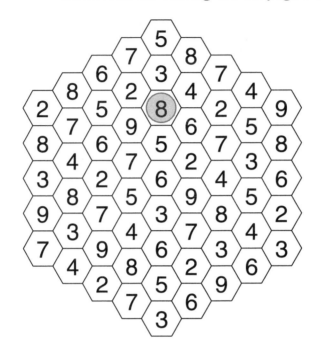

RINGERS

Each Ringer is composed of five rings. Use your imagination to rotate the rings so that you spell out four 5-letter words reading from the outside to the inside when all five rings are aligned correctly.

1.   2.

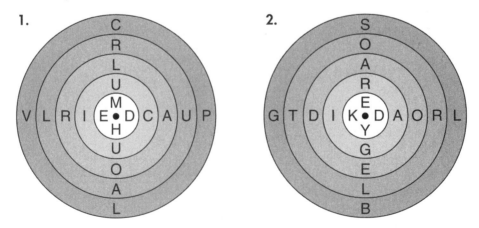

CARD SENSE

Directions for solving are on page 107.

1. A queen is somewhere below both clubs.

2. The heart is somewhere above both queens.

3. The red cards are not adjacent.

4. The diamond is somewhere above the five.

WAYWORDS

Directions for solving are on page 109. This time, you'll be looking for a 9-word thought beginning with THE.

THINK	CONVEY	CONSTANT	BLESSED
THAT	GUILTY	THE	THEM
BREEZE	ALL	OF	IS
CHOICE	NEVER	TALK	WANT

ROUND TRIP

VISUAL ◆ LOGIC

When this puzzle has been completed correctly, you will have made a round trip through its set of dots. You must visit every dot exactly once, make no diagonal moves, and return to your starting point. Parts of the right path are shown; can you find the rest?

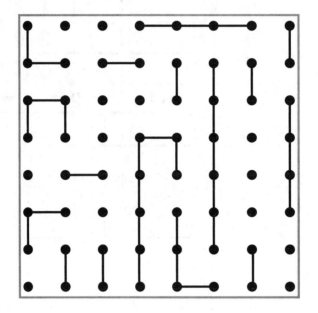

C COUNT

VISUAL

Directions for solving are on page 93. This time, how many C's are there?

CYNICAL CECIL CEDRIC CACKLED,

"CAN CHUCK CHURCH CORRECTLY

CHECK THE ACCURACY OF CACTUS

CHOICES IN COCOA BEACH?"

SUDOKU

WEEK 19

Directions for solving are on page 92.

	6	2		5		9		
	3				6		4	1
4					7			2
		3		1			5	6
	4			6			2	
7	1		5		2			
9			6					7
3	2		4				6	
		8		1		3	9	

FILLING STATION

Directions for solving are on page 113.

1. L M N N P S (city)

   __ I __ __ E A __ O __ I __

2. L P P R R T Z Z (thing)

   __ U __ I __ __ E __   __ __ I __ E

3. B C D K L L N R S (actress)

   __ A __ __ __ A   __ U __ __ O __ __

4. C F F H T (television show)

   " __ __ E   O __ __ I __ E "

5. C H M R S S T (holiday)

   __ __ __ I __ __ __ A __

ON THE LINE

VISUAL ◆ LOGIC

Can you trace this figure without lifting your pencil from the paper, crossing, or retracing your own path?

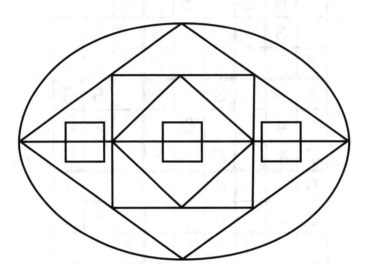

SLIDE RULE

LANGUAGE

Directions for solving are on page 105. This time, you'll be looking for 36 4-letter words, including PRAY.

Your list of words:

RELATIONSHIPS QUIZ

Directions for solving are on page 109.

1. WHEEL is to SPOKE as LADDER is to _____.
   (a) tree   (b) climb   (c) height   (d) rung

2. HEAD is to HAT as FOOT is to _____.
   (a) toe   (b) shoe   (c) ankle   (d) inch

3. NURSERY is to SHRUB as SCHOOL is to _____.
   (a) whale   (b) principal   (c) pupil   (d) parent

4. EGYPT is to PYRAMID as ENGLAND is to _____.
   (a) Stonehenge   (b) London   (c) Parthenon   (d) Colossus

5. XI is to ELEVEN as XL is to _____.
   (a) ninety   (b) sixty   (c) nineteen   (d) forty

MATH

MAGIC NUMBER SQUARES

Fill in the empty boxes so these groups add up to the number below each diagram: 1. each row; 2. each column; 3. each long diagonal; 4. the four center squares; 5. the four corner squares; and 6. each quarter of the diagram. A number will be used only once per diagram.

1.

3			9
	15		
	23	11	
			33

72

2.

			16
	20		
	28		
34	14	12	

100

ANAGRAM MAZE

VISUAL ◆ LANGUAGE

Directions for solving are on page 103. This time, there are 21 words to anagram and the first word you'll be anagramming is BLOW.

				↓	
1 CHAR	2 LEAK	3 NODE	4 ONCE	5 BLOW	6 WHIM
7 VEER	8 JIVE	9 WILD	10 CITY	11 EYES	12 FLAP
13 COAT	14 ISLE	15 ROAD	16 VOTE	17 REAM	18 ODES
19 CUFF	20 TILL	21 TUBA	22 LIFE	23 WING	24 LEFT
25 GREW	26 THUG	27 FOUR	28 BOLD	29 LEGS	30 DIRE
31 MELT	32 OVER	33 SALT	34 CLAY	35 DENT	36 MARK

ALL IN A ROW

MATH

Directions for solving are on page 97. This time, look for the most groups of consecutive numbers adding up to 14.

A. 5 5 7 2 6 3 1 6 4 3 3 3 3 3 2 8 5 8 2 5 4 1 2 4

B. 1 4 9 1 9 7 4 2 1 5 7 5 1 3 3 2 5 9 4 3 3 3 2 4

C. 3 7 2 1 1 1 1 6 5 8 4 2 1 2 3 4 3 5 3 1 1 1 2 2

STACKED UP

WEEK 19

The box on the left can be formed by three of the numbered boxes superimposed on top of each other; do not turn them in any way. Can you figure out which three work?

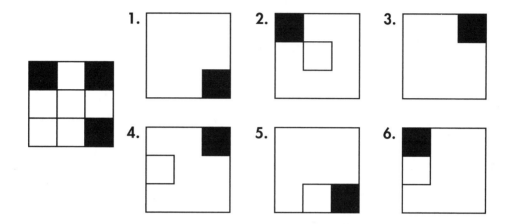

SQUARE LINKS

Write one letter in each empty box so that an everyday 8-letter word is spelled out around each gray box. Each word may read either clockwise or counterclockwise, and may start at any of its letters.

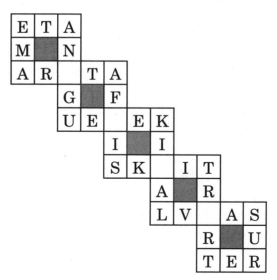

137

LICENSE PLATES

Each box contains three letters of a capital city that begins with "B" and three letters of its country's name. The top three are a part of the city's name and the bottom three are a part of the country's, in order.

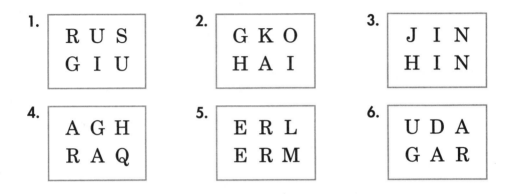

1.

R U S
G I U

2.

G K O
H A I

3.

J I N
H I N

4.

A G H
R A Q

5.

E R L
E R M

6.

U D A
G A R

THE LINEUP

LANGUAGE

Directions for solving are on page 92.

LYBWVOFCJHUSKPSCRATCHZTIMEEXCESSQHAREGN

1. Which letter of the alphabet does not appear in the lineup? _____

2. What 7-letter word — with its letters in correct order and appearing together — can you find in the lineup? _____

3. Which letter of the alphabet appears exactly three times in the lineup? _____

4. What 6-letter word — with its letters in correct order and appearing together — can you find in the lineup? _____

5. Other than the answers to Questions 2 and 4, how many everyday words — with their letters in correct order and appearing together — of four or more letters can you find in the lineup? _____

U.S. E'S

The list below consists of the names of six U.S. states, but we've removed all of their letters except for the E's. Can you write one letter on each dash to complete the names of the states?

1. __ E __ __ __ __

2. __ E __ __ __

3. __ E __ __ E __ __ E E

4. __ __ __ __ E

5. __ E __   __ E __ __ E __

6. __ E __ __ __ __ __ E

SENTENCE TEASER

Read the four statements A–D below, and assume that the statements are all true for the residents of Logic Heights. Next, read statements 1–4, and, using the information received from statements A–D, try to determine whether the four people could be found living in this community.

A. All athletes like milk.

B. All singers who like milk are good drivers.

C. Men who like milk enjoy sailing.

D. The only people who enjoy surfing are women who are good drivers.

•••

1. Mark, a male athlete who enjoys surfing.

2. Maria, the famous Logic Heights singer, who enjoys drinking a glass of milk each day but dislikes surfing.

3. John Jones, Logic Heights' champion sprinter, who also enjoys sailing.

4. A Logic Heights singer who enjoys sailing, dislikes milk, and is a good driver.

MAGNIFIND

VISUAL ◆ SPATIAL

Figure out which areas of the drawing have been enlarged.

STAR WORDS

VISUAL ◆ LOGIC

Directions for solving are on page 104.

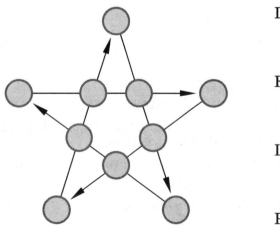

DRIP	PLAY
FILL	SURF
LAUD	TILE
PLAT	TURF

140

ALPHABET CIRCLE MAZE

Start at A at the bottom, continue through the alphabet only once, and finish at the Z in the center. You will pass through other letters when going from one letter to the next, but move in only one direction, either around a circle or along a spoke. Don't enter or cross through the Z until you are finished.

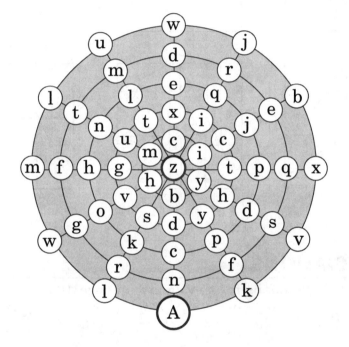

MATH ◆ LOGIC

WHAT'S YOUR NUMBER?

Can you figure out the sequence of numbers in the figures below and what missing number goes into the space with the question mark?

2   6   ?   9   11   10   19   8   5

OVERLAY

VISUAL ◆ SPATIAL

Directions for solving are on page 106.

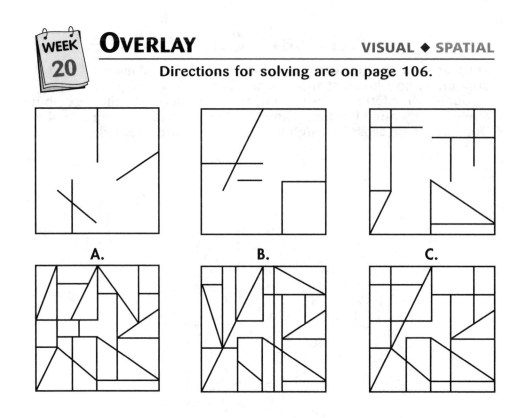

A.   B.   C.

ASSOCIATIONS

LANGUAGE

Directions for solving are on page 104.

WHAT DO YOU CALL A DUCK THAT GETS STRAIGHT A'S IN SCHOOL?

FINISH ASPHALT SLEEP WEIRD ACTIVE WORK
ISLAND ROME LIVELY SEARCH COLLAPSE TOIL
ANIMATED ENERGY DOZE QUIP MILAN VICTORY
COMPLETE UNTIL NAP TRIUMPH ACHE THYME
CRASH LABOR CRAM END BREAKDOWN KILT
MARJORAM EBONY CONQUEST NAPLES REVEAL
OREGANO

VISION QUEST

Find the row or column that contains five DIFFERENT cooking utensils.

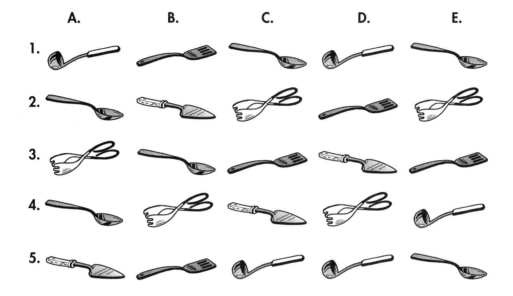

A.   B.   C.   D.   E.

COMPOUND IT

Directions for solving are on page 94.

1. crab, look, barn, file

2. storm, apple, alike, yard

3. stick, bird, work, tree

4. pin, horse, brain, ball

5. room, wheel, park, wave

6. land, mate, well, way

7. farer, lay, side, mine

8. man, out, up, ways

9. handle, power, hole, gun

10. list, house, pride, sun

CIRCLE MATH

MATH

Each overlapping circle is identified by a letter having a different number value from 1 to 9. Where some circles overlap, there is a number: It is the SUM of the values of the letters in those overlapping circles. Can you figure out the correct values for the letters? As a starting help, H = 9.

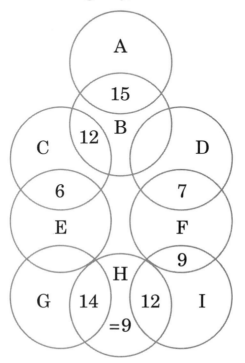

SYMBOL-ISM

DECODING

Directions for solving are on page 99. For this puzzle, we've indicated that 🔔 = D.

MISSING DOMINOES

Directions for solving are on page 117.

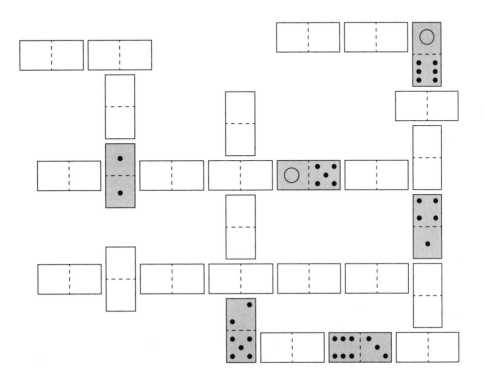

DOMINOES

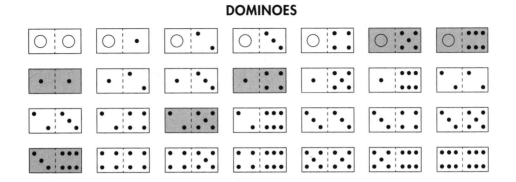

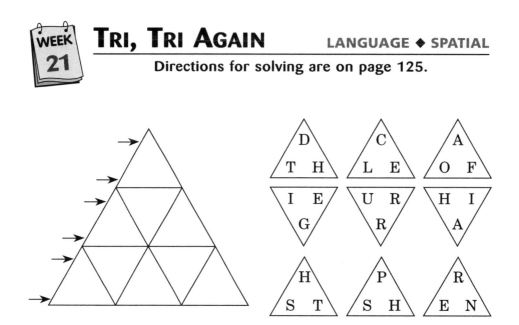

WEEK 21 — TRI, TRI AGAIN

LANGUAGE ◆ SPATIAL

Directions for solving are on page 125.

CODE WORD

DECODING

Directions for solving are on page 101. This time you'll be looking for a 12-letter word.

$$\overline{1}\ \overline{2}\ \overline{3}\ \overline{4}\ \overline{5}\ \overline{6}\ \overline{7}\ \overline{8}\ \overline{9}\ \overline{10}\ \overline{11}\ \overline{12}$$

L 9 V 6   4 12   5 9 7   12 9 F 7   L 4 11 6   8 2 7 6 10 ;   4 7

4 12   H 2 10 D   L 4 11 6   10 9 1 11 ,   9 5   8 H 4 1 H   7 H 6

8 2 V 6 12   9 F   H 2 7 10 6 D   3 6 2 7   4 5   V 2 4 5 .

"Knowledge comes, but wisdom lingers."
— *Alfred Lord Tennyson*

SUDOKU

WEEK 21

Directions for solving are on page 92.

8	4				2			
		5		1	7	3	4	
7		6		5			9	
	7				1		2	4
5			9		2			8
4	6		7				3	
	2			7		4		5
	5	7	4	6		9		
		4					7	3

LANGUAGE

ANTONYMS QUIZ

Directions for solving are on page 100.

1. LAGGARDLY   a. continuous   b. forbidden   c. rapid

2. UNCOUTH   a. habitual   b. cultured   c. amiss

3. SUBSTANTIATE   a. quake   b. deny   c. barter

4. OPTIMISM   a. desperation   b. aptitude   c. dominion

5. BENEFICENCE   a. appeal   b. scrutiny   c. evil

6. LOLL   a. incline   b. interfere   c. labor

7. OBSCURITY   a. abstract   b. renown   c. discernment

8. ANTAGONIST   a. sanction   b. ally   c. pedant

TIPS OF THE ICEBERG

MATH

We're back at the Iceberg Diner. After doing some careful addition, answer the following questions:

1. Who made the most in total tips?
2. Who made the least?
3. Which two waitpersons made exactly the same amount?

EMPLOYEE	TIP 1	TIP 2	TIP 3	TIP 4	TIP 5
Hank	$1.15	$1.15	$1.30	$1.10	$1.85
Inez	$1.10	$1.95	$1.10	$0.60	$1.00
Jack	$1.10	$1.10	$1.05	$0.45	$5.00
Ken	$1.50	$1.35	$1.15	$1.05	$3.00
Laura	$1.00	$1.35	$0.40	$0.85	$3.00
Marty	$1.60	$1.10	$1.00	$1.00	$1.00
Noel	$1.80	$0.85	$1.00	$1.10	$1.00

WORD CHARADE

Directions for solving are on page 126.

My first letter appears more often than any other letter in one of the columns.

My second letter is the fifth letter of six letters in consecutive alphabetical order reading right to left.

My third letter appears in the first four columns, but not in the last four columns.

My fourth letter is surrounded by four 3-letter words (two reading across and two reading down).

My fifth letter appears in the top four rows, but not in the bottom four rows.

My sixth letter is not in the diagram.

Q	N	H	P	F	V	D	Y
U	S	L	I	M	K	W	J
K	B	V	M	D	O	G	X
J	E	R	H	I	T	A	Z
U	L	S	K	M	A	P	K
Z	Y	X	W	V	U	N	B
Q	O	M	T	M	G	R	H
D	T	F	B	Q	J	E	L

___ ___ ___ ___ ___ ___

ALPHABET SOUP

Directions for solving are on page 127. This time, rearrange the letters not crossed out to form the name of a vegetable.

W	F	E	Y	O	C	W	F	E	N	E	L	W	F	E	N	M	V	U	V	M
L	J	Q	Z	U	V	M	V	N	U	V	P	G	B	X	G	P	G	K	J	P
X	P	G	L	X	G	Q	J	Z	J	Q	N	T	Y	Z	J	K	Z	J	V	N	Z

A	B	C	D	E	F	G	H	I	J	K	L	M	N	O	P	Q	R	S	T	U	V	W	X	Y	Z

Vegetable: _____

149

KEEP ON MOVING

VISUAL

Directions for solving are on page 115. Here, start in the shaded square with the number 4.

5	1	3	3	1	5
4	4	3	3	3	3
5	1	4	❊	1	4
4	1	3	3	2	3
1	4	4	3	3	4
2	2	3	3	2	1

COUNT ON IT!

LANGUAGE

Directions for solving are on page 113.

1. F M T D A L   2. A N E U H A   3. E T N C D S

4. C I E S   5. E C

$\overline{1}\ \overline{2}\ \overline{3}\ \overline{4}$, $\overline{1}\ \overline{2}\ \overline{3}\ \overline{4}$ $\overline{1}\ \overline{2}\ \overline{3}$ $\overline{1}\ \overline{2}\ \overline{3}\ \overline{4}\ \overline{5}$

$\overline{1}\ \overline{2}\ \overline{3}$ $\overline{1}\ \overline{2}\ \overline{3}\ \overline{4}\ \overline{5}$!

"If you don't like something, change it; if you can't change it, change the way you think about it." — *Mary Engelbreit*

TARGET SHOOT

Directions for solving are on page 114.

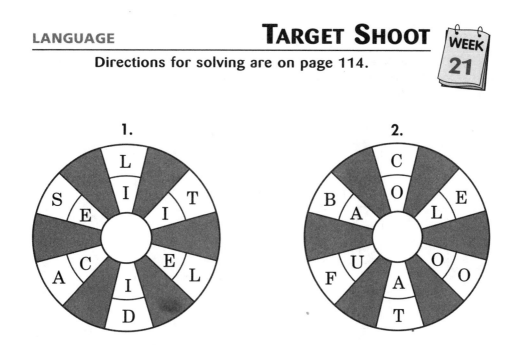

1.

2.

LANGUAGE ◆ SPATIAL

WORD HUNT

Directions for solving are on page 116. This time, you'll be searching for 4- to 7-letter last names of Vice Presidents (such as Gerald FORD). We found 11 Vice Presidents, including FORD.

D	A	M	U	R	T
N	O	L	E	D	O
S	H	J	L	F	G
B	U	X	Y	N	A
D	I	O	A	E	H
E	N	Q	U	W	C

Your list of words:

COUNT TO TEN

VISUAL ◆ MATH

Examine the leaves and acorns and then answer these questions: 1. Which row contains the most leaves? 2. Which row contains the most acorns? 3. Which row contains an equal number of leaves and acorns?

1.
2.
3.
4.
5.
6.
7.
8.
9.
10.

WHAT'S YOUR NUMBER?

LOGIC ◆ MATH

Can you figure out the sequence of numbers in the boxes below and what missing numbers go into the spaces with the question marks?

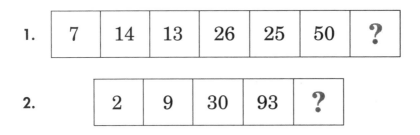

| 1. | 7 | 14 | 13 | 26 | 25 | 50 | ? |

| 2. | 2 | 9 | 30 | 93 | ? |

GOING IN CIRCLES

Directions for solving are on page 102.

1.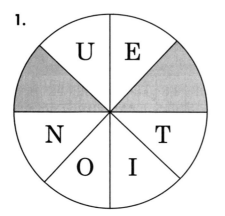

2.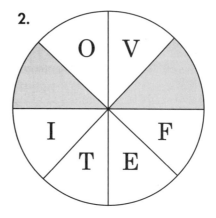

RING LOGIC

Directions for solving are on page 129.

1. The pattern looks the same even when it's rotated like a wheel.

2. Every ring is linked at least twice.

3. The right side of ring E is to the front.

4. The left side of ring N is to the front.

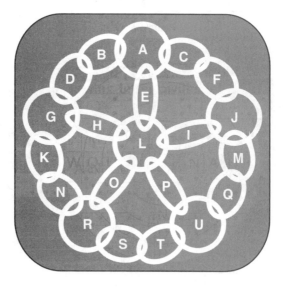

SEVEN WORD ZINGER

LANGUAGE

Directions for solving are on page 111.

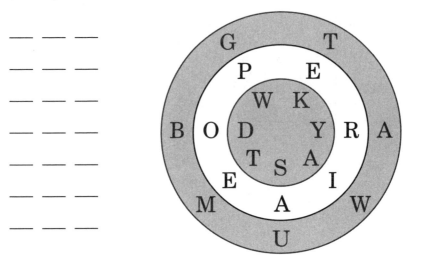

STACKED UP

VISUAL ◆ SPATIAL

Directions for solving are on page 137.

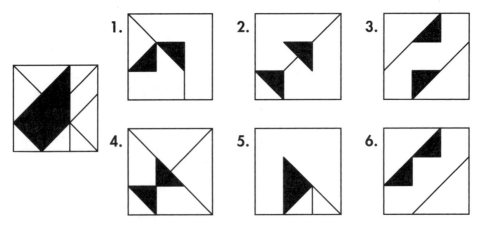

GRAND TOUR

WEEK 22

Directions for solving are on page 112. This time, you'll be looking for a chain of 5-letter words, starting with SAU-NA-CRE (sauna, nacre).

START

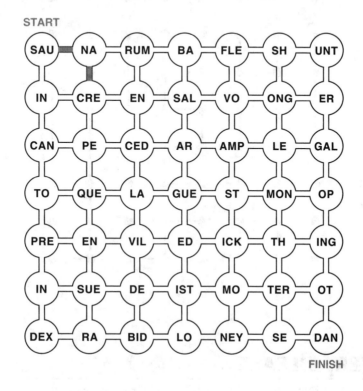

FINISH

EASY PICKINGS

Directions for solving are on page 91. This time, the remaining letters will spell out a quip.

PE OE OS CP AL ET   WN RI ST HD

HA ON DR OS VE   AS EV EN SI EF

KT NO OA RW   CW HM EC HN

TI IO   VS AR GY   "NG BA YX."

ROUND TRIP

VISUAL ◆ LOGIC

Directions for solving are on page 132.

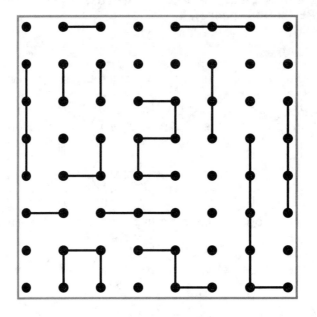

LETTER, PLEASE

DECODING

Directions for solving are on page 111.

5 6 6 5   2 3 3 6 7 3

9 6 8   5 3 2 7 .

SUDOKU

Directions for solving are on page 92.

	3	7	9		2			4
2	8		5				6	
5				4			8	3
				1		9		7
			4		8			
4		1		2				
7	2			6				8
	4				3		7	6
3			8		7	4	2	

ARROW MAZE

Directions for solving are on page 90. This time, you'll begin by moving to the right from the starting box.

ALL IN A ROW

MATH

Directions for solving are on page 97. This time, look for the most groups of consecutive numbers adding up to 25.

A. 9 2 5 3 6 7 1 6 2 9 5 3 4 5 6 2 1 3 5 9 5 4 5 1

B. 7 7 3 5 1 4 2 7 9 8 9 4 5 1 6 2 3 8 2 7 3 6 6 1

C. 2 1 9 3 4 5 7 6 2 2 3 2 9 1 6 8 3 5 1 3 5 9 6 7

HEXAGON HUNT

VISUAL

Directions for solving are on page 94.

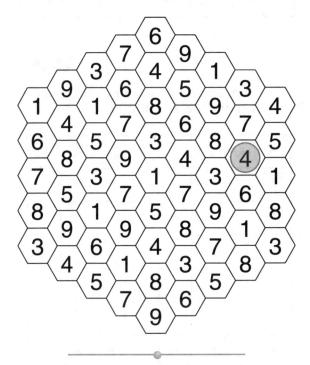

"If you want to be happy, be."

— Leo Tolstoy

CIRCLE SEARCH

Directions for solving are on page 106. Here you're looking to form 14 words, and proper names are not allowed.

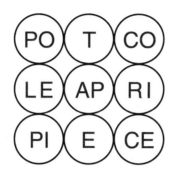

DECODING

SWITCHEROO

In each group, for the first word and its number equivalent given, determine what the number equivalent is for the second word.

1. POLE is to 4612 as LOPE is to:
   (a) 6412 (b) 1624 (c) 1462 (d) 1642

2. SPAT is to 3952 as PAST is to:
   (a) 9532 (b) 9523 (c) 9235 (d) 3259

3. READ is to 6713 as DEAR is to:
   (a) 3167 (b) 3761 (c) 3716 (d) 3617

4. LIFE is to 5492 as FILE is to:
   (a) 9452 (b) 9524 (c) 9245 (d) 9542

5. COAL is to 1364 as COLA is to:
   (a) 1643 (b) 1436 (c) 1346 (d) 1634

6. GEAR is to 2795 as RAGE is to:
   (a) 2579 (b) 5927 (c) 5972 (d) 5297

MARCHING ORDERS

MATH ◆ LOGIC

Directions for solving are on page 116.

1. FINISH ⬆

7	10	6	16	24	29
9	8	13	11	26	21
3	4	9	14	19	23
5	1	7	12	10	18
0	3	6	8	17	20
2	4	5	10	12	15

⬆ START

2. FINISH ⬆

6	11	12	14	11	15
9	10	8	9	10	13
5	8	7	10	8	9
3	7	4	11	12	11
6	2	5	6	10	8
4	1	3	7	5	9

⬆ START

DEDUCTION PROBLEM

LOGIC

Eileen, Jerri, and Melinda are three college students who are on the track team. After completing a practice race, each made a statement to their coach. Two of them told the truth while the one who finished last lied. They were the only ones who raced and there were no ties. From the following statements, can you determine how they finished?

Eileen: "I didn't finish last."

Jerri: "Melinda didn't finish last."

Melinda: "I came in first."

There are four 7-letter, everyday words beginning with the letters COMPA. Can you think of all four?

C O M P A __ __

C O M P A __ __

C O M P A __ __

C O M P A __ __

LANGUAGE

SLIDE RULE

Directions for solving are on page 105. We formed 41 4-letter words, including DOCK.

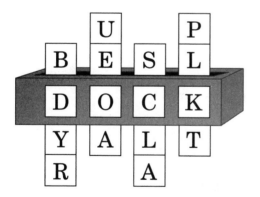

Your list of words:

"The most important thing in communication is to hear what isn't being said."
— *Peter F. Drucker*

LOOSE TILE

WEEK 23

Directions for solving are on page 97.

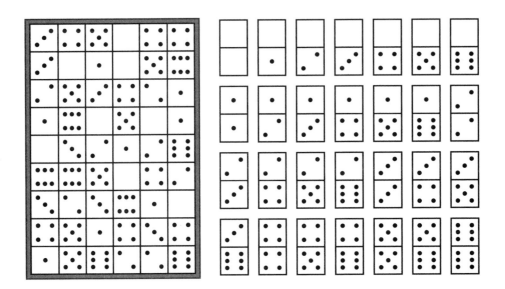

QUICK FILL

LANGUAGE

Directions for solving are on page 90.

A A D E I I L N T V

1. Letter 10 is a vowel.
2. Letter 1 appears elsewhere in the word.
3. In the alphabet, letter 6 is five letters after letter 7.
4. Letters 3, 8, and 9, in order, spell out a large factory container for holding liquid.
5. Letter 2 is from the second half of the alphabet and letter 5 is a consonant.
6. In the alphabet, letter 7 is three letters after letter 4.

$$\overline{1}\ \overline{2}\ \overline{3}\ \overline{4}\ \overline{5}\ \overline{6}\ \overline{7}\ \overline{8}\ \overline{9}\ \overline{10}$$

COUNTDOWN

Directions for solving are on page 99.

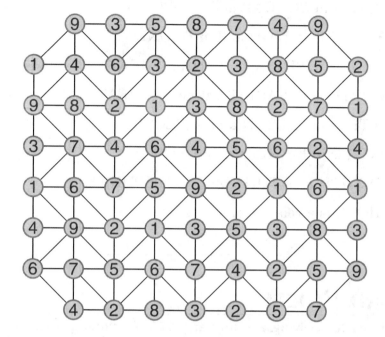

BLOCK PARTY

Directions for solving are on page 124.

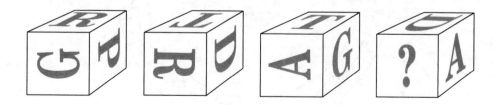

ANIMAL CHARADES

Directions for solving are on page 101.

My FIRST is in COUGAR and in GROWN; ————

My SECOND is in LION and in DRONE; ————

My THIRD is in SHREW but not in WHEAT; ————

My FOURTH is in RABBIT but not in TREAT; ————

My FIFTH is in FALCON and in CLOSE; ————

My SIXTH is in EAGLE and in GLOWS; ————

My SEVENTH is in TUNA but not in SPUNKY. ————

My WHOLE is a relative of a monkey.

————————

WORD WHEEL

Directions for solving are on page 122. Beginning with the "F" at the top of the wheel, we formed 31 words of three or more letters.

ASSOCIATIONS

Directions for solving are on page 104.

WHAT'S GREEN AND MAKES HOLES?

BARON ASTOUND ASPIRIN MUSTARD FLAUNT DIME

BIOLOGY   PETTICOAT   ROMANCE   VISCOUNT

REFUGE ITALY SURPRISE SUPPORT LOLLIPOP

PHYSICS   LIST   KETCHUP   PINAFORE   PERIOD

PARADE IMMEDIATE BACK SANCTUARY CHANGE

EXHIBIT KILOMETER DUKE AMAZE SARONG

UPHOLD LAVISH RELISH ASYLUM ESTIMATE

CHEMISTRY

LANGUAGE

WAYWORDS

Directions for solving are on page 109. This time, you'll be looking for an 11-word thought beginning with WHY.

THOSE	EAGER	WHEN	SECRET
THAT	WON'T	LISTEN	HISTORY
PEOPLE	IT	SURE	REPEATS
WHEREVER	WHY	IS	ITSELF

DOVETAILED WORDS   LANGUAGE

Directions for solving are on page 115.

1. O K I V L E N N   _____ _____

2. O G R R E A E N N G E   _____ _____

3. C R K O N C I H E T T   _____ _____

4. C Y A A N C O H E T   _____ _____

5. S L E P I T N T A U C C E H _____ _____

ELIMINATION   LANGUAGE

Directions for solving are on page 102. Once again, the remaining words will form a thought.

SHOULDN'T FIBER DEMAND BIRDS TAILS SNAKE
EXCELLENCE COSTUME WINE OF AND CHURCH
BE NASTY A THROW WILLING AURA TO HOUR
FEATHER PAY ILL SANITARY FLOCK FOR
STONES TOGETHER IT INDEFINITE

Eliminate the...

1. two words that, when put together, form the last name of a British prime minister.

2. two words that, when scrambled together, form the name of a neighbor of New Zealand.

3. words that complete the proverb: "People who live in glass houses…"

4. two words that contain three consecutive letters of the alphabet, in order.

5. three words that begin with the same three letters, in some order.

6. three words that, when followed by "glass," form three new words.

7. words that form the saying that means "avians bearing analogous plumage rendezvous."

ANAGRAM MAZE

Directions for solving are on page 103. This time, there are 19 words to anagram and the first word you'll be anagramming is LIFT.

1 QUAD	2 DIRT	3 LIFT	4 SHOE	5 CANE	6 MEAT
‒‒‒‒	‒‒‒‒	‒‒‒‒	‒‒‒‒	‒‒‒‒	‒‒‒‒
7 ZONE	8 GONE	9 AFAR	10 TURF	11 LOCK	12 INCH
‒‒‒‒	‒‒‒‒	‒‒‒‒	‒‒‒‒	‒‒‒‒	‒‒‒‒
13 VEIL	14 LISP	15 PALE	16 FAIL	17 LIEU	18 CAPE
‒‒‒‒	‒‒‒‒	‒‒‒‒	‒‒‒‒	‒‒‒‒	‒‒‒‒
19 BUST	20 LOUT	21 SURF	22 MASH	23 RIPE	24 PEST
‒‒‒‒	‒‒‒‒	‒‒‒‒	‒‒‒‒	‒‒‒‒	‒‒‒‒
25 DUNE	26 CUKE	27 ALOE	28 CLEF	29 FINE	30 CLAP
‒‒‒‒	‒‒‒‒	‒‒‒‒	‒‒‒‒	‒‒‒‒	‒‒‒‒
31 NONE	32 WEAK	33 CORK	34 DROP	35 FOIL	36 TINY
‒‒‒‒	‒‒‒‒	‒‒‒‒	‒‒‒‒	‒‒‒‒	‒‒‒‒

LANGUAGE

CROSS-UPS

Using only the letters given above each diagram, fill in the boxes in such a way that an everyday compound word is formed, one part reading across and the other part reading down. The letter already in the diagram is a letter shared by both parts of the word. Note: Each part of the compound word is an entire word on its own.

1. C E E H I N O S T

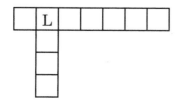

2. C C K K L R W

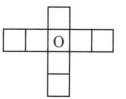

1.   **2.**

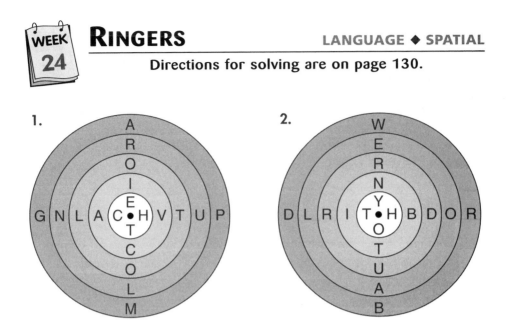

FUN WITH FACTS AND FIGURES

MATH

Directions for solving are on page 110.

1. Take the number of vowels in the word FREEZING and multiply it by the number of consonants in the word. _____

2. Next, add the number of legs on a tripod. _____

3. Now subtract the number of players in a chess game. _____

4. Multiply by the number of letters in the name of the country that contains Cairo and Alexandria. _____

5. Subtract the number halfway between one and seven. _____

Our answer, when spelled out, can be anagrammed to form the phrase ENVY EXISTS. *Can yours?*

IN THE ABSTRACT

Directions for solving are on page 93.

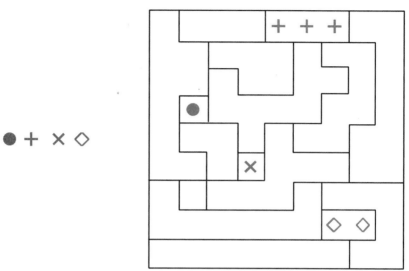

BULL'S-EYE LETTER

Directions for solving are on page 105.

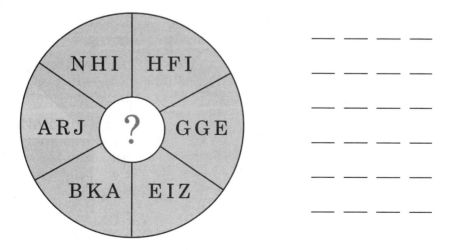

Directions for solving are on page 137.

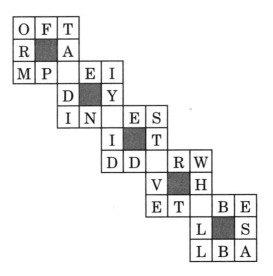

CARD SENSE

LOGIC

Directions for solving are on page 107.

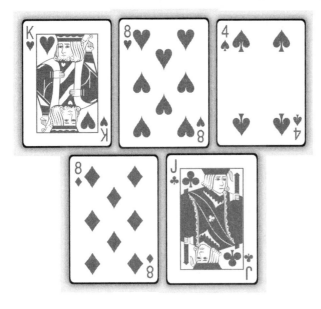

1. One eight is somewhere above the king; the other is somewhere below it.

2. The four is somewhere above both face cards.

3. Exactly two of the red cards are adjacent; they are not of the same suit.

4. The face cards are not adjacent.

ON THE LINE

Can you trace this figure without lifting your pencil from the paper, crossing, or retracing your own path?

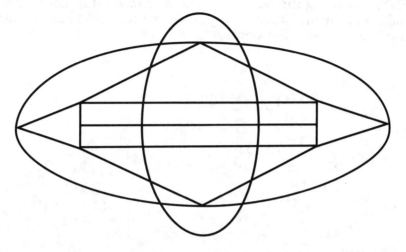

MATH

CIRCLE MATH

Directions for solving are on page 144. We've started you off by telling you that C = 7.

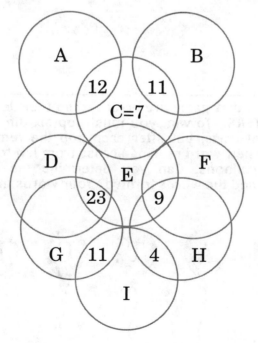

HOLE IN ONE

LOGIC

Twenty-four golfers entered a hole-in-one contest. Each golfer was given a ball with a different 4-digit number combination using the numbers 1, 3, 4, and 6 on it. Looking at the 23 balls still on the green, can you figure out what combination is on the ball that won the contest?

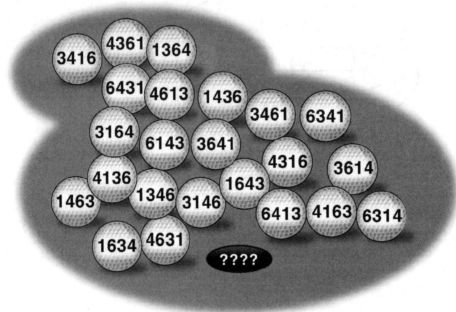

POP!

LANGUAGE

The balloons in a dart game are arranged so their letters spell out the word "CRATERS." To win, you must pop six different balloons with six different darts, but after each pop the remaining letters must spell out a new word reading across from left to right. Do not rearrange the balloons. Can you determine the order of the balloons to pop and the words formed? Your words may differ from ours.

CROSS PATHS

Start at the arrow. There are four circles in that box, so move four boxes, either across or up. Each time you land in a box, move the number of dots in that box in only one direction, up, down, or across. You may cross your own path, but do not retrace it.

IN THE BALANCE

Scales 1, 2, and 3 are perfectly balanced. Determine how many triangles it takes to balance scale 4.

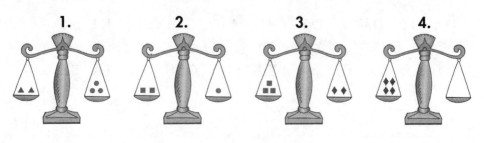

IN THE ABSTRACT

VISUAL ◆ SPATIAL

Fill in each section with one of the four symbols so no sections containing the same symbol touch. Four sections are already complete.

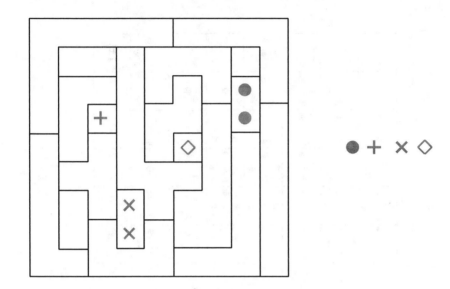

● + ✕ ◇

EASY PICKINGS

LANGUAGE

To solve, simply cross out one letter in each pair below. When the puzzle is completed correctly, the remaining letters will spell out a quote by singer Sophie Tucker.

IE ' OV ES   CB AE ET TN   RO SI CD HS

DA ON DV   OI ' VC AE   BV IE EI NF

PT RO OA RN ;   YR IM IC HG   IA TS

UB IE TY JT EL IR.

COUNTDOWN

Following the connecting lines, find the only route in this grid that passes through the numbers backward from 9 to 1 consecutively.

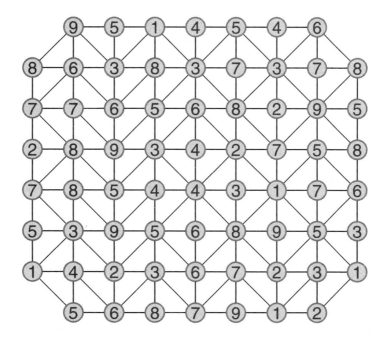

CODE WORD

Decipher a truism and the Code Word's eleven letters, represented by the numbers 1 through 11. So, if the Code Word were "FORMULATING," 1 in the quote would be F, 2 would be O, etc.

$$\overline{1} \ \ \overline{2} \ \ \overline{3} \ \ \overline{4} \ \ \overline{5} \ \ \overline{6} \ \ \overline{7} \ \ \overline{8} \ \ \overline{9} \ \ \overline{10} \ \ \overline{11}$$

W 3   F 3 3 6   M 5 4 H   W 10 R 1 3   B Y   8 H 3

4 10 11 8 3 M 2 8   10 F   F 10 10 6 1   8 H 7 11   B Y

8 H 3   6 5 K 3 W 7 R M   7 2 2 R 10 V 7 6   10 F

M 3 11   10 F   9 11 8 3 6 6 9 G 3 11 4 3 .

SUDOKU

LOGIC

Place a number into each box so each row across, column down, and small 9-box square within the larger square (there are 9 of these) contains 1 through 9.

			8					6
5			7	3			8	2
	8		5		2	4	7	
2	9			6			1	
			1	2	5			
	6			8			5	4
	7	1	2		8		9	
8	3			4	1			5
6					9			

GOING IN CIRCLES

LANGUAGE

In each circle, insert one letter into each empty space to form an 8-letter word. Words may read either clockwise or counterclockwise and may begin with any letter in the circle.

1.

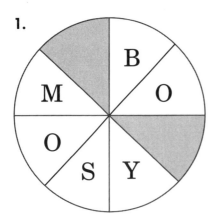

2.

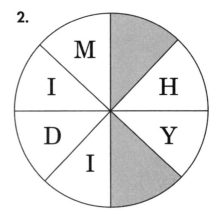

TRI, TRI AGAIN

Fit the nine triangles into the big one so six everyday words are spelled out reading across the arrows. Do not rotate the triangles.

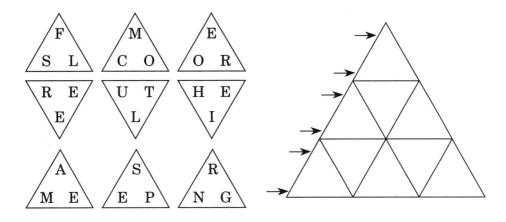

ANIMAL CHARADES

Each line contains a clue to a letter of the alphabet. These letters, in the given order, will spell out the name of an animal. The animal's identity is also hinted at in the last sentence of the Charade.

My FIRST is in SWAN and in WEAR;   _____

My SECOND is in PARROT and in PEAR;   _____

My THIRD is in DOLPHIN but not in DEPEND;   _____

My FOURTH is in TROUT but not in CONTEND;   _____

My FIFTH is in BLUEBIRD and in DOUBLE;   _____

My SIXTH is in SQUIRREL and in STUBBLE.   _____

My WHOLE is a critter with a mustache,
    Try to trim it and you might take a splash.

_____

MAGNIFIND

VISUAL ♦ SPATIAL

Figure out which area of the drawing has been enlarged.

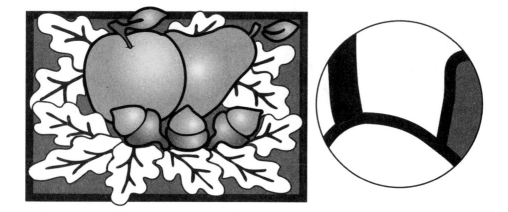

ALL IN A ROW

MATH

Which row below contains the most groups of consecutive numbers adding up to 13? Look carefully, because some groups may overlap. We've underlined an example of a group in each row to start you off.

A. 6 2 <u>1 2 4 6</u> 3 5 2 4 1 5 6 1 9 3 2 2 8 2 7 2 2 4

B. 3 3 3 4 4 9 8 1 1 <u>7 4 2</u> 3 6 3 8 2 5 1 7 9 1 6 2

C. 4 1 7 1 3 8 5 9 6 2 7 <u>3 4 6</u> 1 1 8 2 4 3 7 3 5 2

"Education is the best provision for old age."
— *Aristotle*

THE LINEUP

While scrutinizing the lineup of letters below, can you answer the five given questions correctly in five minutes or less?

F O X Y J S L I T W V G A R M E N T P D C R Y I N G K H B G M U S E Z

1. Which letter of the alphabet does not appear in the lineup? _____

2. What 7-letter word — with its letters in correct order and appearing together — can you find in the lineup? _____

3. Which letter of the alphabet appears exactly three times in the lineup? _____

4. What 6-letter word — with its letters in correct order and appearing together — can you find in the lineup? _____

5. Other than the answers to Questions 2 and 4, how many everyday words — with their letters in correct order and appearing together — of four or more letters can you find in the lineup? _____

QUICK FILL

Determine the 10-letter word from the clues. All the letters in the word are listed.

C   D   E   I   O   P   R   T   U   V

1. In the alphabet, letter 1 is somewhere before letter 2.

2. Letters 8, 6, and 10, in order, spell out a word meaning frozen cubes.

3. In the alphabet, letter 4 is somewhere before letter 3, which is a vowel.

4. In the alphabet, letter 7 is immediately before letter 5, which is immediately before letter 9.

$$\overline{1} \quad \overline{2} \quad \overline{3} \quad \overline{4} \quad \overline{5} \quad \overline{6} \quad \overline{7} \quad \overline{8} \quad \overline{9} \quad \overline{10}$$

ELIMINATION

LANGUAGE

Cross off the capitalized words below according to the instructions given. The remaining words, in order, will form a thought.

FEW IT DIG TURBAN GREAT YOUR CON VIED
HAPPENED WELL RENT BOWLER BEFORE CORD
ONE YOU TAIL BASKET ARE FEDORA NIGHT
THIRSTY DANE

Eliminate...

1. the words that, when put together, form a New Hampshire city.

2. each word that forms a new word when "cur" is placed before it.

3. names of headwear.

4. the word that contains the eleventh letter of the alphabet.

5. the word that becomes a new word when "sit" is inserted somewhere inside it.

6. the words that form the title of a Clark Gable-Claudette Colbert movie.

7. the words that might be a tongue-in-cheek description of a terrific person from Copenhagen.

LICENSE PLATES

LANGUAGE

Each box contains six letters of the first name and the last name of an actor born in the United Kingdom. The top three are a part of the first name and the bottom three are a part of the last name, in order.

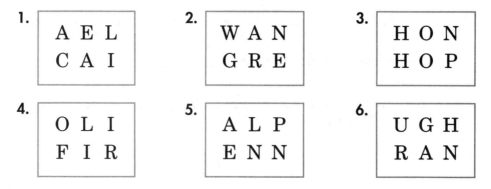

1.
A E L
C A I

2.
W A N
G R E

3.
H O N
H O P

4.
O L I
F I R

5.
A L P
E N N

6.
U G H
R A N

CARD SENSE

Five playing cards were shuffled and put in a pile, one on top of another. Using the clues, can you identify each card's position in the pile?

1. The colors alternate from top to bottom.

2. The sevens are adjacent and both are somewhere below the two.

3. The diamond is somewhere above the ace.

WORD HUNT

Find words by moving from one letter to any adjoining letter. You may start a word with any letter in the diagram. In forming a word you may return to a letter as often as you wish, but do not stand on a letter using it twice in direct succession. In this Word Hunt, you are searching for 4-letter words that end with OW (such as GLOW). We found 17 words, including GLOW.

S	G	R	V	A
M	C	H	O	T
E	O	W	S	N
R	P	L	K	J
Z	B	F	G	V

Your list of words:

ONLINE NETWORK

In each two-column group, take the letters in the left-hand column along the paths (indicated by the lines) and place them in their proper boxes in the right-hand column. When done, you'll find three words with similar meanings reading down each of the two right-hand columns.

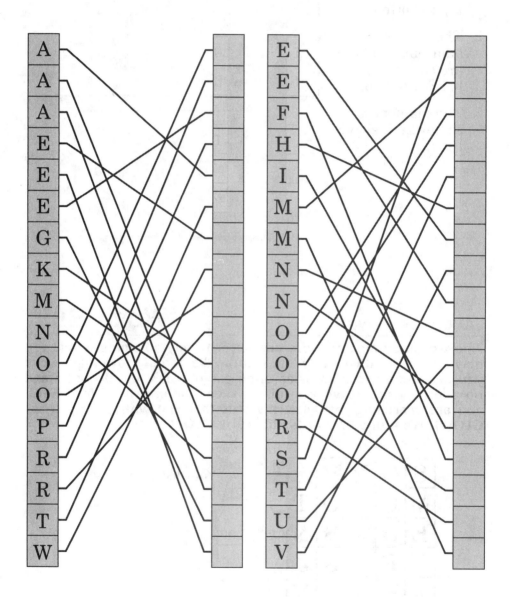

ROUND TRIP

When this puzzle has been completed correctly, you will have made a round trip through its set of dots. You must visit every dot exactly once, make no diagonal moves, and return to your starting point. Parts of the right path are shown; can you find the rest?

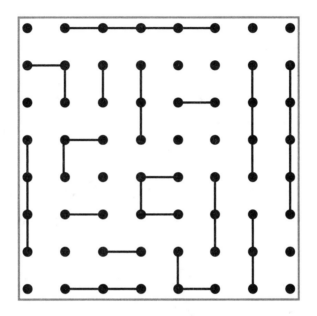

DOVETAILED WORDS

Two related words, with their letters in the correct order, are combined in each row of letters. Can you find both words? In a line like POBOOXDELER, or POboOxDeLEr, you can see the two words POODLE and BOXER.

1. C H O N I C D E E A L _____ _____

2. F C A I V L L I I N T G Y _____ _____

3. S H B E E L A L C H _____ _____

4. B N O O O V E K L _____ _____

5. P R R I E W Z A R E D _____ _____

ASSOCIATIONS

LANGUAGE

You'll find eight groups of three words that can be associated in some way with each other (example: mantel, fireplace, logs). Cross out each group as you find it. The initial letters of the remaining words will spell out the answer to the riddle:

WHAT WAS THE FIRST ARTIFICIAL FISH?

DUNE   AGONY   VERDICT   VERMONT   PRIOR

ERROR   DOUBT   LEMON   INTUITION   HILL   ARROW

CONNECTICUT   DIAMOND   SINGLE   QUESTION   SHIP

TRANCE   FEELING   INCH   RIDGE   CABINET   DECISION

RUBY   SELTZER   ROWBOAT   TREATY   MISTAKE

USUAL   DISPUTE   ROYAL   SENSE   SAPPHIRE

GRAMMAR   MASSACHUSETTS   EVENT   CATAMARAN

OMELET   BLUNDER   FINDING   NEPAL

BULL'S-EYE LETTER

LANGUAGE

Add the SAME single letter to each group of three letters, then rearrange the letters to form six everyday 4-letter words.

— — — —

— — — —

— — — —

— — — —

— — — —

— — — —

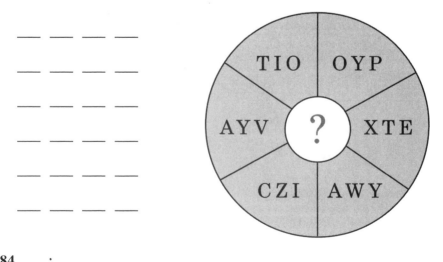

MISSING DOMINOES

In this game you use all 28 dominoes that are in a standard set. Each one has a different combination from 0-0, 0-1, 0-2, to 6-6. Domino halves with the same number of dots lie next to each other. To avoid confusion we have used an open circle to indicate a zero. Can you fill in the missing white dominoes to complete the board?

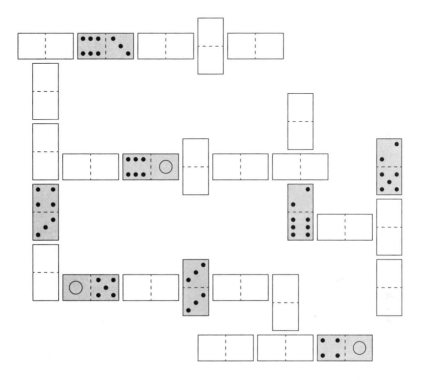

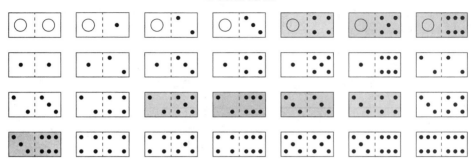

DOMINOES

SLIDE RULE

LANGUAGE

Slide each column of letters up or down in the box and form as many everyday 3-letter words as you can in the windows where BIT is now. We formed 24 words, including BIT.

Your list of words:

OVERLAY

VISUAL ◆ SPATIAL

When you overlay the three diagrams in the top row, which of the three lettered diagrams, A, B, or C, will be formed?

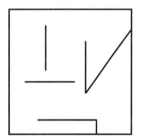
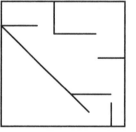
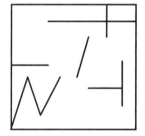

A.

B.

C.

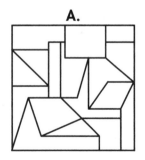
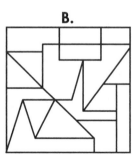
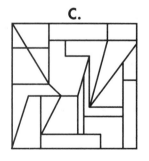

186

ARROW MAZE

Starting at the S and following the arrow up, see if you can find your way to F. When you reach an arrow, you MUST follow its direction and continue in that direction until you come to the next arrow. When you reach a two-headed arrow, you can choose either direction. It's okay to cross your own path.

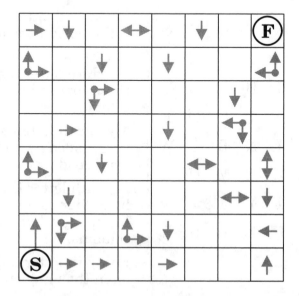

VISUAL ◆ SPATIAL

BLOCK PARTY

Study the different views of the block, and draw what should appear on the face that has a question mark.

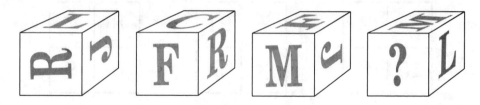

WORD CHARADE

LANGUAGE ◆ VISUAL

Find each letter in the diagram according to the instructions, and write each letter on its dash to spell out a 6-letter word.

My first letter is in the top four rows, but not in the bottom four rows.

E	Y	R	N	Y	Q	G	O
V	T	J	A	T	S	U	L
Z	M	C	I	H	L	M	T
L	F	H	W	T	D	O	F
Y	Q	S	I	N	B	C	W
D	V	A	L	E	M	U	L
G	L	H	I	V	J	I	Q
A	O	M	F	Z	L	S	R

My second letter is the only consonant in one of the four corners.

My third letter appears three times in one of the columns.

My fourth letter is surrounded by an 8-letter word reading clockwise.

My fifth letter is in the left-hand four columns, but not in the right-hand four columns.

My sixth letter appears more often than any other letter.

— — — — — —

WHAT'S YOUR NUMBER?

MATH ◆ LOGIC

Can you figure out the sequence of numbers in the boxes below and what missing number goes into the space with the question mark?

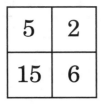

5	2
15	6

7	21
3	9

8	?
6	9

188

SQUARE LINKS

WEEK 27

Write one letter in each empty box so that an everyday 8-letter word is spelled out around each blue box. Each word may read either clockwise or counter-clockwise, and may start at any of its letters.

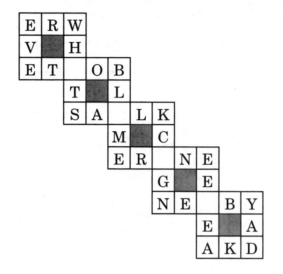

WORD EQUATIONS

Determine the three defined words in each equation. The third word is formed when the second is written directly after the first; for example, for "for each + shape = act in a play," you would respond "per + form = perform."

1. no longer alive + fishing wire = due date

2. tin container + performed = honest and frank

3. light-switch position + drink cubes = work area

4. book leaf + picnic pest = beauty contest

5. football official + employ = decline

"Learning is not attained by chance, it must be sought for with ardor and attended to with diligence." — *Abigail Adams*

TIPS OF THE ICEBERG

The chart shows the gratuities each waiter or waitress earned on a recent breakfast shift at the Iceberg Diner. All you have to do is some careful addition and then answer the following questions:

1. Who made the most in total tips?
2. Who made the least?
3. Which two waitpersons made exactly the same amount?

EMPLOYEE	TIP 1	TIP 2	TIP 3	TIP 4	TIP 5
Al	$2.10	$2.80	$2.25	$2.05	$2.00
Brenda	$1.70	$4.20	$4.20	$3.70	$2.05
Charlie	$2.10	$3.10	$2.10	$2.10	$2.90
Dena	$1.90	$1.90	$1.35	$6.60	$2.00
Ed	$3.00	$3.90	$2.00	$2.00	$3.75
Flora	$2.20	$2.40	$5.80	$1.55	$2.70
Greta	$2.00	$1.85	$2.05	$2.00	$2.80

VISION QUEST

Find the row or column that contains five DIFFERENT watercrafts.

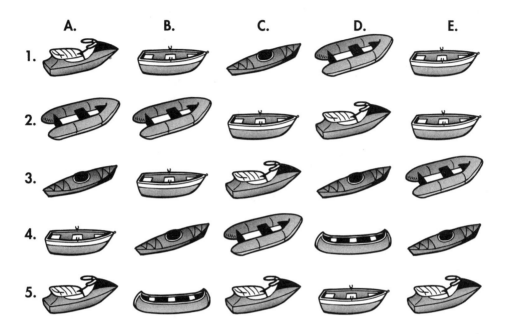

SKILLS TEST

MATH

Two bicyclists cover a distance of 15 miles in two hours. A motorcyclist goes twice as fast. What distance does the motorcyclist cover in one hour?

a. 10 miles   b. 15 miles   c. 20 miles   d. 25 miles   e. 30 miles

D COUNT

VISUAL

Here's an eye exam that's also a D exam! First, read the sentence below. Next, go back and read the sentence again, but this time count all of the D's. How many D's are there?

DID DEEDEE DADE DRIVE

DEIDRE DAVIDS TO DAVID

DUDLEY'S DAIRY, OR DID

DEIDRE DAVIDS DRIVE

DEEDEE DADE TO DOVER,

DELAWARE?

TARGET SHOOT

LANGUAGE

Find the two letters which, when entered into the center circle of each target, will form three 6-letter words reading across.

1.

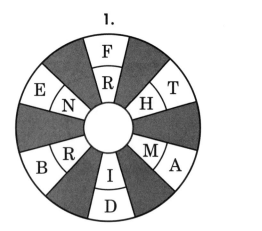

2.

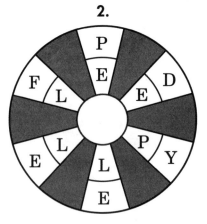

ALPHABET SOUP

Cross off each letter from the alphabet list that appears in the larger group of letters. Then rearrange the letters not crossed out to form the name of the state that entered the Union on March 15, 1820.

```
V S V S Y V S Y V S G U G U C G U C U G

C F V F C V P C F V J X J X Z J X J Z X

P K R K R P L R K P Z O Q Z Q O Z U Q Z

K L W L W K L W K L H D R D H S D R H S

Y X G X G Y X G Y X F B Q H B T Q F B T
```

A B C D E F G H I J K L M N O P Q R S T U V W X Y Z

State: _____

FUN WITH FACTS AND FIGURES

This puzzle tests you on several little facts and figures. Solve the quiz in the order given since each answer is used in the next statement. There are no fractions used here.

1. Take the number of the date that Christmas falls on in December and divide that by the number of sides on a pentagon. _____

2. Next, multiply by the number of seconds in four minutes. _____

3. Now, subtract the value of the Roman numeral M. _____

4. Add the number of musicians in eighty quintets. _____

5. Divide by the number of lungs in the human body. _____

Our answer is the number of points in a perfect game of bowling. *Is yours?*

ANAGRAM MAZE

LANGUAGE ◆ VISUAL

The diagram contains 36 words, 19 of which are anagrams of other everyday words. Start at the top arrow and anagram LIFE. While solving, move up, down, right, or left to the only adjacent word that can be anagrammed. Continue until you arrive at the bottom arrow. There is only one path through the maze.

1 LIFE	2 LILY	3 LESS	4 BAKE	5 EARL	6 NEON
— — — —	— — — —	— — — —	— — — —	— — — —	— — — —
7 RIOT	8 BEAU	9 BURY	10 BEAN	11 MALT	12 ABET
— — — —	— — — —	— — — —	— — — —	— — — —	— — — —
13 GEAR	14 CORK	15 PEST	16 CELL	17 MINK	18 DIRE
— — — —	— — — —	— — — —	— — — —	— — — —	— — — —
19 GRIT	20 FANG	21 WOOL	22 ATOM	23 MARE	24 FOAL
— — — —	— — — —	— — — —	— — — —	— — — —	— — — —
25 HAVE	26 AFAR	27 MAKE	28 SERF	29 OXEN	30 KNOW
— — — —	— — — —	— — — —	— — — —	— — — —	— — — —
31 TINY	32 MAZE	33 HOOT	34 BEAR	35 GUST	36 SPAN
— — — —	— — — —	— — — —	— — — —	— — — —	— — — —

COUNT ON IT!

LANGUAGE

Use the given letters to fill in the familiar saying, one letter per dash. All the letters following 1 are the first letters of each word, the letters following 2 are the second letters of each word, etc. It is up to you to determine which letter goes where.

1. O O O O S M   2. F I U F I U   3. G T N T

4. D H   5. T

$$\overline{}_{1}\ \overline{}_{2}\ \overline{}_{3}\quad \overline{}_{1}\ \overline{}_{2}\quad \overline{}_{1}\ \overline{}_{2}\ \overline{}_{3}\ \overline{}_{4}\ \overline{}_{5},$$

$$\overline{}_{1}\ \overline{}_{2}\ \overline{}_{3}\quad \overline{}_{1}\ \overline{}_{2}\quad \overline{}_{1}\ \overline{}_{2}\ \overline{}_{3}\ \overline{}_{4}.$$

194

LOOSE TILE

The tray on the right seemed the ideal place to store the set of loose dominoes. Unfortunately, when the tray was full, one domino was left over. Determine the arrangement of the dominoes in the tray and which is the Loose Tile.

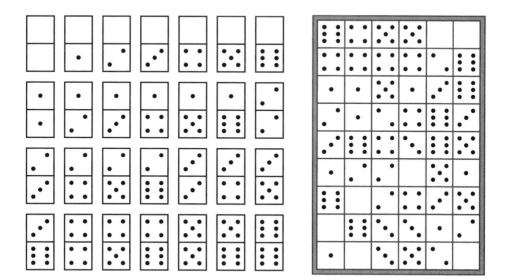

COMPOUND IT

Starting at #1, pick a word that will form a compound word with a word chosen in #2. Then with the word you've selected in #2, pick one from #3 to form another compound word. Continue in this manner to #10, so that you've formed nine compound words. In some instances more than one compound word can be formed, but there is only one path to get you to #10.

1. put, fort, day, needle

2. light, point, night, down

3. stand, hearted, wind, town

4. ship, blown, stiff, off

5. shoot, shore, board, shape

6. bird, line, walk, game

7. man, brain, bath, way

8. robe, tub, wave, house

9. hold, kind, tree, part

10. track, bay, label, over

GRAND TOUR

LANGUAGE ◆ VISUAL

Form a continuous chain of 5-letter words moving through the maze from START to FINISH. The second part of one word becomes the first part of the next word. This puzzle starts with TU-TOR-TE (tutor, torte).

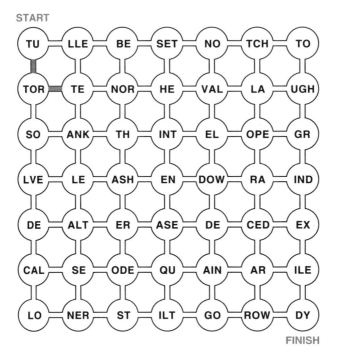

START

TU	LLE	BE	SET	NO	TCH	TO
TOR	TE	NOR	HE	VAL	LA	UGH
SO	ANK	TH	INT	EL	OPE	GR
LVE	LE	ASH	EN	DOW	RA	IND
DE	ALT	ER	ASE	DE	CED	EX
CAL	SE	ODE	QU	AIN	AR	ILE
LO	NER	ST	ILT	GO	ROW	DY

FINISH

WORD VISIBILITY

LANGUAGE ◆ LOGIC

There are six 5-letter words below. The first letter of the answer is found in the first pair of letters, and it is either the top or the bottom letter. Continue across each pair.

For example, the word GIRL would be found thus: G A R L
                                                    L I T X

1. G U L T E
   P O C S N

2. L A O E K
   B R T W R

3. S D O O H
   V N E R P

4. T A I N B
   I C Y O G

5. Y I U F E
   C O L N G

6. M Y O S T
   R A R N H

196

COUNT THE SQUARES

WEEK
28

To solve this puzzle, write down the four letters that describe each square (a figure with four EQUAL sides) in this figure. We found 18 squares; how many can you locate?

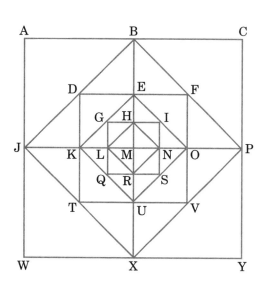

RINGERS

Each Ringer is composed of five rings. Use your imagination to rotate the rings so that you spell out four 5-letter words reading from the outside to the inside when all five rings are aligned correctly.

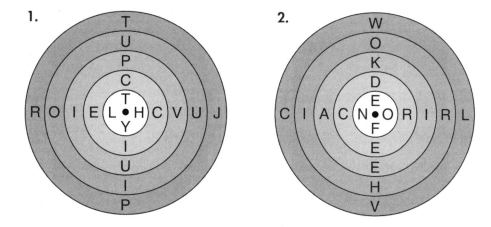

1.

2.

WAYWORDS

LANGUAGE

A 7-word thought can be found beginning with the word THE. Then, move to any adjacent box up, down, or diagonally for each following word.

METHOD	PRICE	CLOSED	SIGN
FEET	THE	VALUE	MOUTH
NO	PERCH	WILL	FOREVER
PORTION	GATHER	FELINE	JOURNEY

ANTONYMS QUIZ

LANGUAGE

An antonym is a word that is opposite in meaning to another word; for example, "cold" is the antonym of "hot." One of the words following each capitalized word is the antonym of that word.

1. LABORIOUS   a. luxurious   b. peculiar   c. simple

2. TURBULENT   a. calm   b. irate   c. foreign

3. SLIPSHOD   a. painstaking   b. belated   c. paltry

4. DIVERGENT   a. quarrelsome   b. parallel   c. hapless

5. MELANCHOLY   a. solid   b. swarming   c. jubilant

6. MISERLY   a. generous   b. astray   c. mocking

7. SERVITUDE   a. concord   b. freedom   c. stress

8. HEFTY   a. caustic   b. gaunt   c. wicked

SEVEN WORD ZINGER

Using each letter once, form seven everyday 3-letter words with the first letter coming from the center, the second from the middle, and the third from the outer circle. Your words may differ from ours.

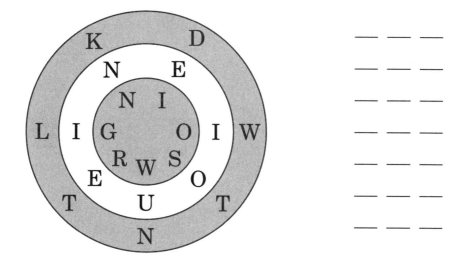

— — —

— — —

— — —

— — —

— — —

— — —

— — —

CIRCLE MATH

Each overlapping circle is identified by a letter having a different number value from 1 to 9. Where some circles overlap, there is a number: It is the SUM of the values of the letters in those overlapping circles. Can you figure out the correct values for the letters? As a starting help, B = 2.

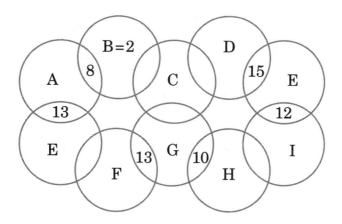

199

WEEK 29 | STACKED UP

VISUAL ◆ SPATIAL

The box on the left can be formed by three of the numbered boxes superimposed on top of each other; do not turn them in any way. Can you figure out which three work?

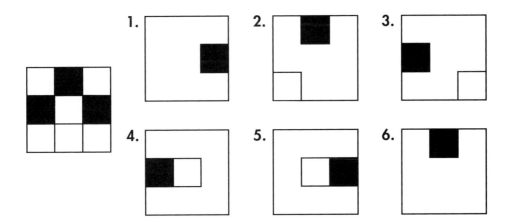

SUDOKU

LOGIC

Directions for solving are on page 176.

	6				2	3	8	9
	3	5	9		4		6	
7				3				
6				7	5			
	7	3		2		9	4	
			3	9				7
				1				4
	8		5		3	6	1	
4	1	2	8				9	

Ring Logic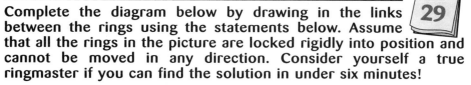

Complete the diagram below by drawing in the links between the rings using the statements below. Assume that all the rings in the picture are locked rigidly into position and cannot be moved in any direction. Consider yourself a true ringmaster if you can find the solution in under six minutes!

1. The diagram is symmetrical from left to right.

2. Each ring is linked to exactly two rings.

3. The right side of ring E is to the front.

4. The left side of ring C is to the front.

5. Ring L is behind ring J.

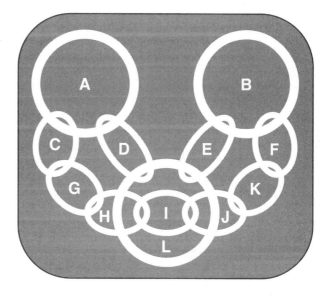

Circle Search

Move from circle to adjoining circle, horizontally and vertically only, to form 14 common, everyday words of at least three letters. Don't change the order of the letters in the circles that contain more than one letter. Proper names are not allowed.

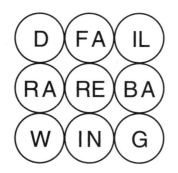

IN THE MONEY

How quickly can you convert each bag of money into dollars and cents and determine which one contains the greatest amount?

1. 22 quarters
2. 45 dimes
3. 583 pennies
4. 121 nickels

CROSS PATHS

Directions for solving are on page 173.

HOLE IN ONE

Directions for solving are on page 172. This time, the 4-digit number combination uses 6, 7, 8, and 9.

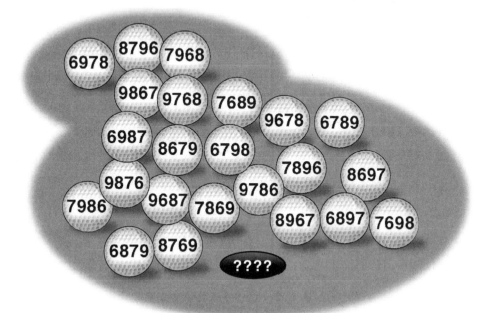

MATH ◆ LOGIC

IN THE BALANCE

Directions for solving are on page 173.

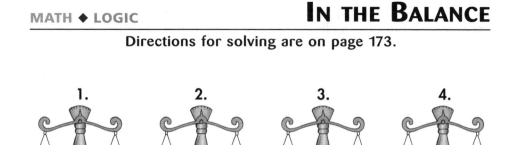

HEXAGON HUNT

VISUAL

In this diagram of six-sided figures, there are 10 "special" hexagons. These 10 are special because the six numbers around each one are all different from each other and the center. We've circled one of the 10. Can you find the other 9?

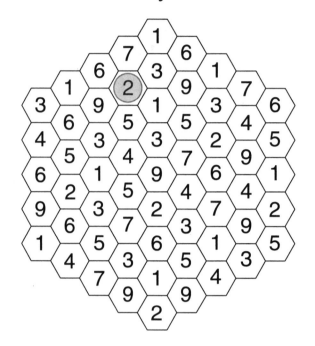

NEXT TO NOTHING

LANGUAGE ◆ VISUAL

In the first row below, the A is next to the number zero, and the Y is next to the letter O. First, circle all of the letters next to zeroes. Next, scramble the circled letters to spell out a woman's name.

A0	YO	VO	DO
LO	WO	HO	E0
UO	BO	I0	SO
GO	PO	RO	MO
KO	QO	FO	ZO
N0	C0	XO	J0

COUNT TO TEN

Examine the black cats and ghosts and then answer these questions: 1. Which row contains the most black cats? 2. Which row contains the most ghosts? 3. Which row contains an equal number of black cats and ghosts?

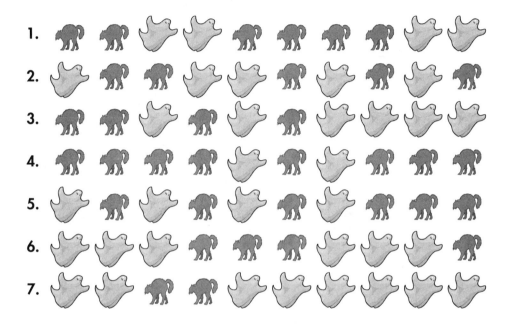

U.S. T'S

This list consists of the names of six U.S. States, but we've removed all of their letters except for the T's. Can you write one letter on each dash to complete the names of the states?

1. __ __ __ __ __ __ T __ __ __ T
2. __ __ __ T   __ __ __ __ __ __ __ __
3. __ __ __ T __ __ __
4. T __ __ __ __
5. __ T __ __
6. __ __ __ __ __ __ T

KEEP ON MOVING

VISUAL

The goal is to move from the shaded square to the asterisk. Since the shaded square has the number 3 in it, you must move three squares up, down, left, or right, but not diagonally. In the new square will be another number; move that number of squares up, down, left, or right, continuing in this way until you reach the asterisk. It's okay to cross your own path.

2	4	3	2	2	5
5	2	1	4	2	2
3	1	2	3	4	5
4	4	2	**3**	3	1
2	3	3	3	1	5
5	2	3	4	✳	2

STAR WORDS

VISUAL ◆ LOGIC

Only five of the eight words given will fit together in the diagram. Place them in the directions indicated by the arrows.

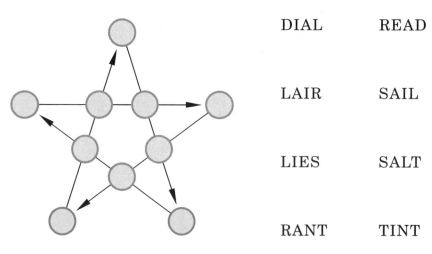

DIAL   READ

LAIR   SAIL

LIES   SALT

RANT   TINT

STACKED UP

WEEK 30

Directions for solving are on page 200.

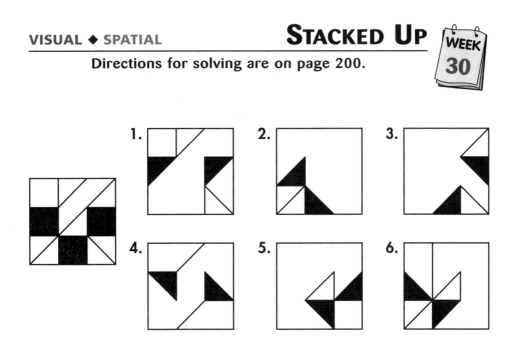

LOGIC

SUDOKU

Directions for solving are on page 176.

	6				4		1	
		7	8		6	5		4
	5	4				7		8
4	3	1	9					
	7		5		2		4	
					1	9	3	7
1		8				4	5	
7		5	4		9	3		
	4		2				7	

FILLING STATION

LANGUAGE

Place the given consonants on the dashes to form words. The vowels have already been placed for you, and as an additional help, each entry lists its category beside its given consonants.

1. D H H L L P P (city)

__ __ I __ A __ E __ __ __ I A

2. C M N R V V W (household sight)

__ I __ __ O __ A __ E   O __ E __

3. G H H L N N P S T T T (movie)

" __ __ E   E __ __ __ I __ __

__ A __ I E __ __ "

4. G H P S T T (food)

__ __ A __ __ E __ __ I

5. C H N R R S (animal)

__ __ I __ O __ E __ O __

MAGIC NUMBER SQUARES

MATH

Fill in the empty boxes so these groups add up to the number below each diagram: 1. each row; 2. each column; 3. each long diagonal; 4. the four center squares; 5. the four corner squares; and 6. each quarter of the diagram. A number will be used only once per diagram.

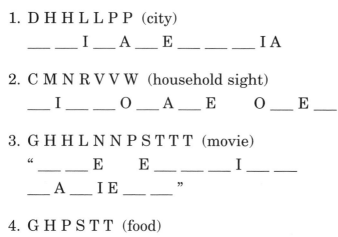

1.

18			21
13	15		
	20		9

54

2.

10	21	17	
	23		11
			25

70

WORD WHEEL

WEEK 30

Starting with the "M" at the arrow, see how many everyday words of three or more letters you can find going clockwise. Don't skip over any letters. For example, if you saw the letters C, A, R, E, D, you would form five words: CAR, CARE, CARED, ARE, RED. We found 30 words.

CHANGELINGS

Can you change the first word into the second word (in each set) by changing only one letter at a time? Do not rearrange the order of the letters with each change. Words beginning with a capital letter, slang, or obsolete words aren't allowed. The number in parentheses indicates the number of changes we used for that Changeling.

1. SOUP

_____

_____

_____

STIR
(4 changes)

2. VINE

_____

_____

_____

HANG
(4 changes)

3. LONG

_____

_____

_____

HIKE
(4 changes)

209

CODE WORD

Directions for solving are on page 175.

$$\overline{1}\ \overline{2}\ \overline{3}\ \overline{4}\ \overline{5}\ \overline{6}\ \overline{7}\ \overline{8}\ \overline{9}\ \overline{10}\ \overline{11}$$

4 2 9 3 1   10 9 9 10 S   3 2 9   10 7 N 9   B 11   W 7 8 9 N

W H 7   3 2 9   S 8 3 2 1   9 N 7 U 4 H   1 7   K N 7 W

1 H 9 11   6 3 N ,   7 2   1 7 7   5 4 N 7 2 3 N 1   1 7

1 H 5 N K   1 H 9 11   6 3 N N 7 1 .

IN THE ABSTRACT

Directions for solving are on page 174.

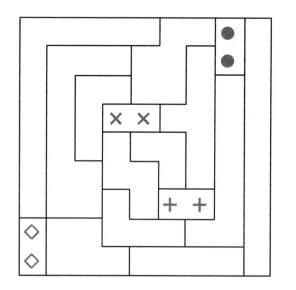

LETTER, PLEASE

WEEK
30

The numbers below stand for certain letters on the telephone dial. You will see that one number may stand for more than one letter — for example, 2 may be A, B, or C. By finding the correct letter for each number, you will have spelled out a truism.

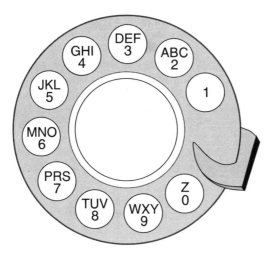

2   3 7 4 3 6 3

4 6   6 3 3 3

4 7   2   3 7 4 3 6 3

4 6 3 3 3 3.

PROGRESSION

How many of the numbered designs are identical to the one on the left?

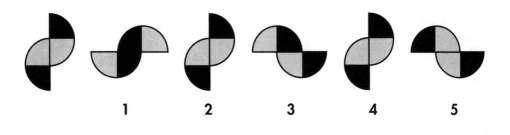

| 1 | 2 | 3 | 4 | 5 |

"Whoever ceases to be a student has never been a student."
— *George Iles*

COUNTDOWN

VISUAL

Directions for solving are on page 175.

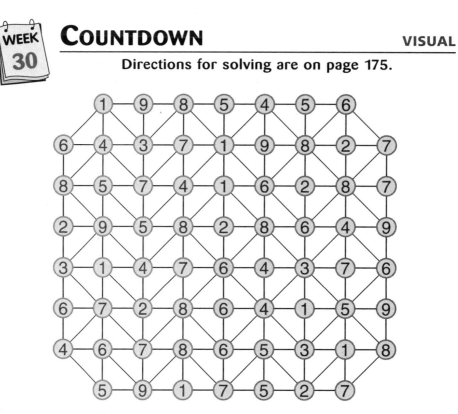

SYMBOL-ISM

DECODING

This is simply a Cryptogram that uses symbols instead of letters to spell out a truism. Each symbol stands for the same letter throughout. For this puzzle, we've already indicated that ☆ = O and ♣ = T.

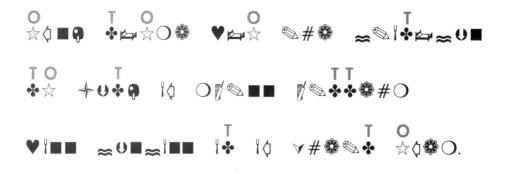

ONLINE NETWORK

WEEK 30

Directions for solving are on page 182.

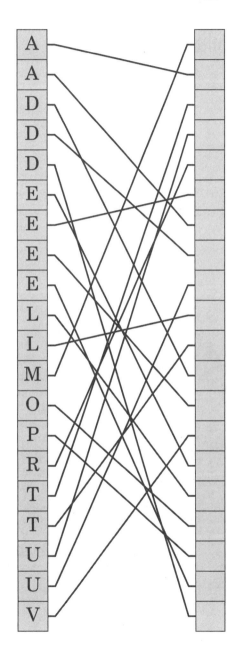

MARCHING ORDERS

MATH ◆ LOGIC

Using a different two-step sequence of addition and subtraction, can you make your way from Start to Finish in each puzzle by moving up, down, or diagonally? We've started the first one for you using the sequence +3 and −2; continue this sequence to reach Finish. You will not cross your own path or pass through any square twice.

1. FINISH ⬆

9	8	11	9	12	10
3	7	4	8	9	13
7	5	8	5	10	7
4	2	7	6	9	11
6	3	5	4	8	7
1	4	2	6	3	5

⬆ START

2. FINISH ⬆

10	6	16	12	17	13
12	11	15	14	10	12
8	9	10	9	13	11
5	6	7	4	8	12
8	2	9	6	7	9
3	4	5	10	11	16

⬆ START

QUICK FILL

LANGUAGE

Directions for solving are on page 179.

A D E E F G M N R T

1. In the alphabet, letter 6 is immediately before letter 1 and letter 5 is immediately before letter 7.

2. Letter 10 is from the first half of the alphabet.

3. Letters 7, 8 (which is a consonant), and 9, in some order, spell out the name of a number.

4. Letter 3 is a vowel and letter 2 is from the second half of the alphabet.

5. Letters 4, 5, and 6, in some order, spell out a word meaning an expensive stone.

$$\overline{1} \quad \overline{2} \quad \overline{3} \quad \overline{4} \quad \overline{5} \quad \overline{6} \quad \overline{7} \quad \overline{8} \quad \overline{9} \quad \overline{10}$$

214

GOING IN CIRCLES

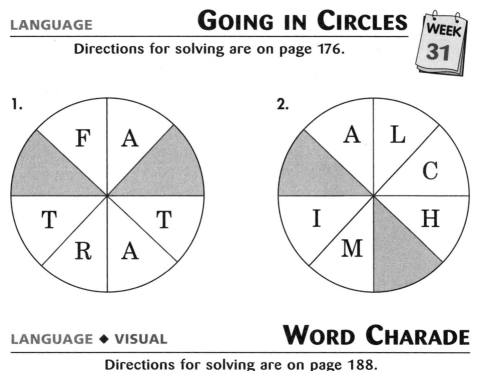

WEEK
31

Directions for solving are on page 176.

1.

2.

LANGUAGE ◆ VISUAL

WORD CHARADE

Directions for solving are on page 188.

My first letter is the only letter from the first half of the alphabet in one of the rows.

My second letter is the only vowel in one of the columns.

My third letter is in the third column, but not in the fourth column.

My fourth letter only appears to the immediate left or right of wherever my third letter appears.

My fifth letter is the sixth letter of a seven-letter word reading upward.

My sixth letter is not in the diagram.

M	W	P	I	Y	J	H	C
U	D	E	B	K	V	G	Y
A	H	K	P	E	D	S	R
W	X	T	R	U	M	V	T
H	L	I	K	Q	X	Z	L
V	F	D	E	S	V	O	U
L	Q	B	T	Z	P	G	O
E	D	R	K	L	B	J	P

— — — — — —

WHAT'S YOUR NUMBER?

MATH ◆ LOGIC

Can you figure out the sequence of numbers in the first two large circles and what missing number goes into the space with the question mark in the third large circle?

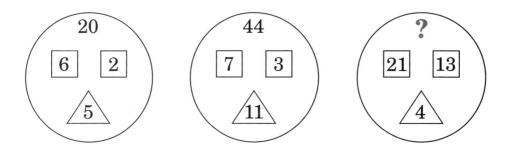

RELATIONSHIPS QUIZ

LANGUAGE

KENNEL is to DOG as STY is to PIG because a DOG lives in a kennel and a PIG lives in a STY. Each of the statements below is a relationship of some kind. Can you select the right word from the four following each?

1. POD is to PEA as HUSK is to _____.
   (a) corn   (b) voice   (c) bread   (d) foot

2. SCHOOL is to CLASSROOM as BOOK is to _____.
   (a) teacher   (b) bookshelf   (c) library   (d) chapter

3. FRANCE is to SPAIN as UNITED STATES is to _____.
   (a) Oklahoma   (b) Austin   (c) Mexico   (d) South America

4. LION is to PRIDE as GOOSE is to _____.
   (a) hoard   (b) pond   (c) swarm   (d) gaggle

5. MOZZARELLA is to ITALY as EDAM is to _____.
   (a) Netherlands   (b) Germany   (c) Egypt   (d) Denmark

216

ELIMINATION

Directions for solving are on page 180. Once again, the remaining words will form a thought.

PRIDE IF BOOK ALWAYS FIDDLE THE GOLDEN
GIVE PIERCE SHOE CREDIT GATE PACK WHERE
FITS PERUSE NATURE CREDIT WEAR CASE
BRIDGE IS BANANA GRANT FLOCK DUE IT

Eliminate…

1. the words that form the name of a San Francisco tourist attraction.

2. the words that are also the last names of Presidents.

3. the word that, when two of its letters are eliminated, forms the name of a South American country.

4. the words that are the names of animal groups.

5. the words that can follow "second."

6. the six words that form a saying that means "Should lower phalanges-covering raiment conform properly, don said article."

7. the two words that, when put together, can form a compound word no matter the order of the words.

EASY PICKINGS

To solve, simply cross out one letter in each pair below. When the puzzle is completed correctly, the remaining letters will spell out a quote by U.S. President Warren G. Harding.

SG TO AV EM CR NE MT GE NX TY

AR UF NT EH RI   AN ML LG

ID FS   EA   SV ER RM EY

SN KI MN PW LZ KE

TS VH GI UN GP .

ALPHABET SOUP

VISUAL ◆ LANGUAGE

Cross off each letter from the alphabet list that appears in the larger group of letters. Then rearrange the letters not crossed out to form the name of a country.

```
L U L U B L U L B U C V C V C N C V N V
O R O Z R O R O U B J L J L A J L J A L
V R V R V R M V R V A C N C A C N C A N
Q I Q I Q Z I Q Z I S W S F W F S W F S
X F M X M F X M F X K O H K S Q J D K D
```

A B C D E F G H I J K L M N O P Q R S T U V W X Y Z

Country: _____

DOVETAILED WORDS

LANGUAGE

Directions for solving are on page 183.

1. C D A E C S E T U R S T   _____   _____

2. V E L L I V N E E T N   _____   _____

3. Z H E O B R R S A E   _____   _____

4. B F E E D O R R E A T   _____   _____

5. P C E A A S N H E U W T   _____   _____

MISSING DOMINOES

WEEK
31

In this game you use all 28 dominoes that are in a standard set. Each one has a different combination from 0-0, 0-1, 0-2, to 6-6. Domino halves with the same number of dots lie next to each other. To avoid confusion we have used an open circle to indicate a zero. Can you fill in the missing white dominoes to complete the board?

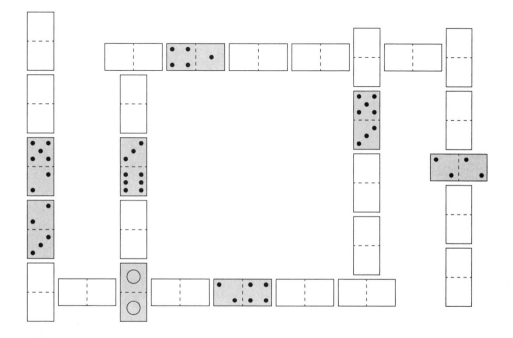

DOMINOES

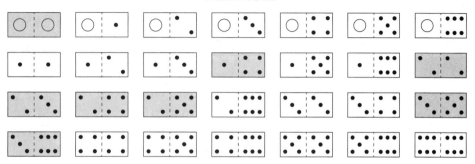

VISION QUEST

VISUAL

Find the row or column with five DIFFERENT bakery treats.

ANIMAL CHARADES

LANGUAGE

Directions for solving are on page 177.

My FIRST is in PORPOISE and in AROUSE; _____

My SECOND is in SHREW and in BROWSE; _____

My THIRD is in SALMON but not in LAMP; _____

My FOURTH is in TERRAPIN but not in STAMP; _____

My FIFTH is in REINDEER and in DESIRE; _____

My SIXTH is in GIRAFFE and in WILDFIRE; _____

My SEVENTH is in MINK but not in KNOW; _____

My EIGHTH is in BISON but not in BELOW; _____

My NINTH is in PANTHER and in TELEPHONE. _____

My WHOLE is a marine creature with a really long jawbone.

_____

TRI, TRI AGAIN

Directions for solving are on page 177.

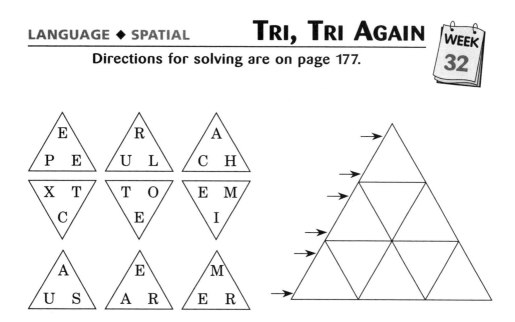

LANGUAGE # WAYWORDS

Directions for solving are on page 198. This time, you'll be looking for a 9-word thought beginning with TRY.

PREVENTS	TO	BEST	WANT
MAKE	BECOMES	TRY	ENEMY
JUSTICE	A	MAKING	AN
POINT	WITHOUT	LESSON	MANNER

"The beginning of knowledge is the discovery of something we do not understand."
— *Frank Herbert*

OVERLAY

VISUAL ◆ SPATIAL

Directions for solving are on page 186.

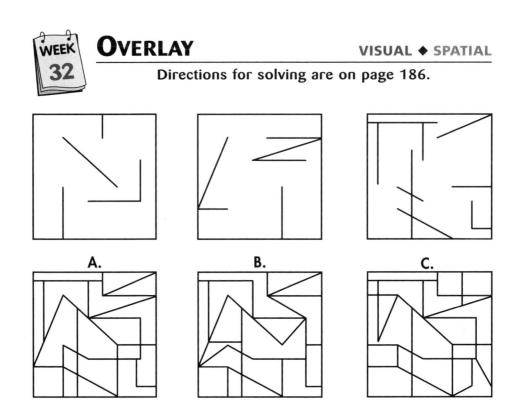

A.   B.   C.

CIRCLE SEARCH

LANGUAGE

Directions for solving are on page 201. Here you're looking to form 15 words. Proper names, plurals, and present-tense verbs ending in "s" are not allowed.

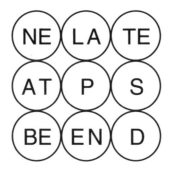

ROUND TRIP

WEEK
32

Directions for solving are on page 183.

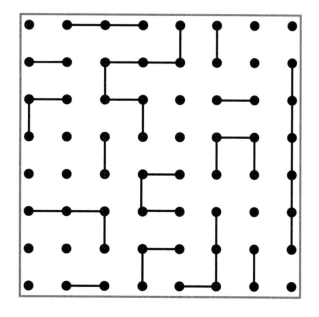

TARGET SHOOT

Directions for solving are on page 192.

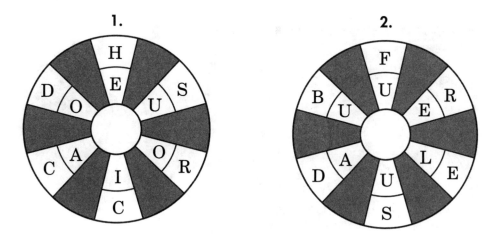

1.

2.

SUDOKU

LOGIC

Directions for solving are on page 176.

		2	8				9	4
	9		6		2			
6		8				2	7	
		6		5	7			8
	7						6	
2			3	1		9		
	2	9				4		3
			5		4		2	
4	6				3	8		

MAGNIFIND

VISUAL ◆ SPATIAL

Figure out which area of the drawing has been enlarged.

LOOSE TILE

The tray on the right seemed the ideal place to store the set of loose dominoes. Unfortunately, when the tray was full, one domino was left over. Determine the arrangement of the dominoes in the tray and which is the Loose Tile.

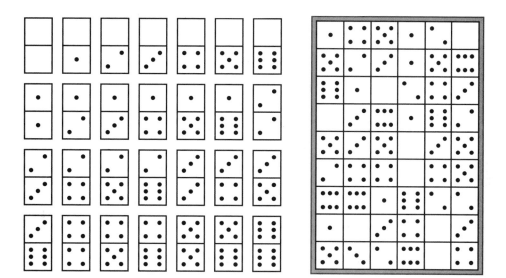

ASSOCIATIONS

Directions for solving are on page 184.

WHICH FOLKS BUY SHEET MUSIC FOR OBOES?

COLD JUNE PARSNIP INITIATE NIPPY ERADICATE
RIDDLE TACO OPERA UNUSUAL PUN PUNISH
START LEVER ODD BRISK CALCULUS EPIC JOKE
GEOMETRY WADDLE JULY BEGIN HONEST LION
ODOR BURRITO TIGER REACT AUGUST ENCHILADA
EMPIRE IRREGULAR JAGUAR ENTERTAIN DAILY
ALGEBRA

ANAGRAM MAZE

VISUAL ◆ SPATIAL

Directions for solving are on page 194. This time, there are 19 words to anagram, and the first one is OWLS.

1 JEST	2 BLOW	3 LACY	4 OWLS	5 WAIT	6 CULT
7 BUSH	8 WINE	9 CREW	10 PLUS	11 OOZE	12 PURR
13 VETS	14 ALOE	15 ICON	16 SCAR	17 GAPE	18 NEAT
19 CLAM	20 LIED	21 TILL	22 DECK	23 INTO	24 CAFE
25 BODY	26 FIVE	27 FALL	28 HUNT	29 ECRU	30 HUTS
31 WHIM	32 CUFF	33 NEST	34 MOPE	35 ACTS	36 FOIL

E COUNT

VISUAL

Directions for solving are on page 192. This time, see how many E's you can count in the sentence.

EVERY EGG THE CHEF FRIED

YESTERDAY NEEDED PEPPER;

NEVERTHELESS, HE CREATED

SEVENTY-THREE DELECTABLE

WESTERN OMELETS IN THE

PRECEDING WEEK.

SLIDE RULE

Directions for solving are on page 186. This time, we formed 29 4-letter words, including VAST.

Your list of words:

I		L	
M U A	N		
V A S T			
R E I Y			
J	R		

THE LINEUP

Directions for solving are on page 179.

SBWVOFRJACKPKNUCKLEZEXITMAGNETMADEHQK

1. Which letter of the alphabet does not appear in the lineup? _____

2. What 6-letter word — with its letters in correct order and appearing together — can you find in the lineup? _____

3. Which letter of the alphabet appears exactly three times in the lineup? _____

4. What 7-letter word — with its letters in correct order and appearing together — can you find in the lineup? _____

5. Other than the answers to Questions 2 and 4, how many everyday words — with their letters in correct order and appearing together — of four or more letters can you find in the lineup? _____

BULL'S-EYE LETTER

LANGUAGE

Directions for solving are on page 184.

_ _ _ _

_ _ _ _

_ _ _ _

_ _ _ _

_ _ _ _

_ _ _ _

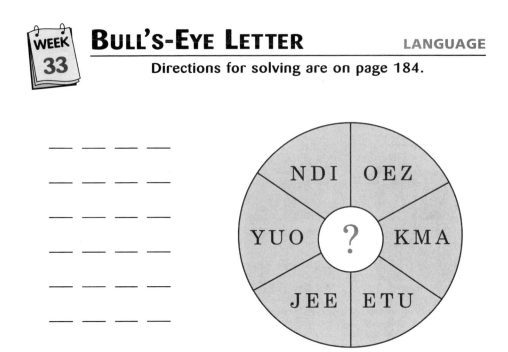

SQUARE LINKS

LANGUAGE

Directions for solving are on page 189.

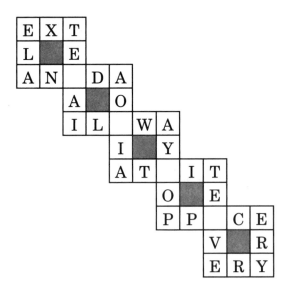

RING LOGIC

Directions for solving are on page 201.

1. The right side of ring B is to the front.

2. Ring C is linked to the back of ring A.

3. Rings D, H, and I are each linked to two rings.

4. Ring E is linked to three rings.

5. The left sides of rings F, K, L, and M are to the front.

6. Ring J is behind ring I and is linked to two rings.

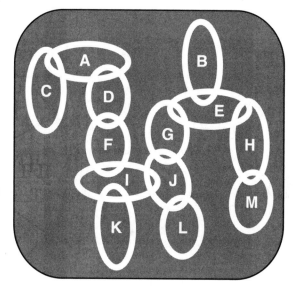

ALL IN A ROW

Directions for solving are on page 178. This time, look for the most groups of consecutive numbers adding up to 14.

A. 2 3 5 5 6 8 4 4 1 1 5 7 9 3 3 4 8 2 7 1 5 6 4 5

B. 8 3 5 1 2 1 5 9 7 3 2 4 1 8 3 6 2 1 2 9 4 7 7 3

C. 4 4 5 3 1 8 7 2 2 1 2 9 3 1 1 5 6 4 1 9 2 5 7 6

WHIRLIGIG

In each numbered section are five letters. Rearrange each group of letters so that when you add the "UP" from the middle of the diagram to the front of each group, you will form 12 common 7-letter words.

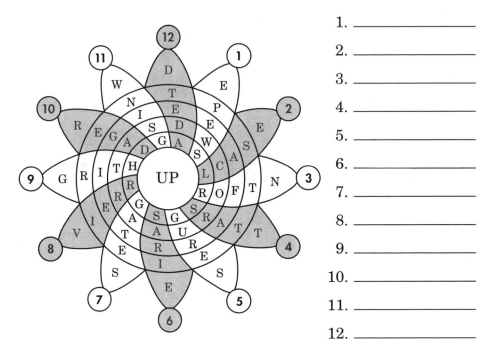

1. _____

2. _____

3. _____

4. _____

5. _____

6. _____

7. _____

8. _____

9. _____

10. _____

11. _____

12. _____

COMPOUND IT

Directions for solving are on page 195.

1. prize, bed, true, cross

2. rock, love, road, fight

3. work, block, runner, in

4. horse, load, down, room

5. shoe, power, fly, time

6. house, leaf, box, paper

7. back, trade, bound, boy

8. friend, fire, hood, ground

9. proof, wink, trap, swell

10. find, door, pace, luck

FUN WITH FACTS AND FIGURES

Directions for solving are on page 193.

1. Take the number of vowels in the word COLLAR and multiply it by the number of consonants in the word. _____

2. Next, add the number of nickels in two dollars. _____

3. Now subtract the number of U.S. states that border the Pacific Ocean. _____

4. Multiply by the number of letters in the name of the country that contains Tokyo and Kyoto. _____

5. Subtract the number halfway between ten and twenty. _____

The letters in our answer can be scrambled to form the phrase HUNTED WORD. Can yours?

HEXAGON HUNT

Directions for solving are on page 204.

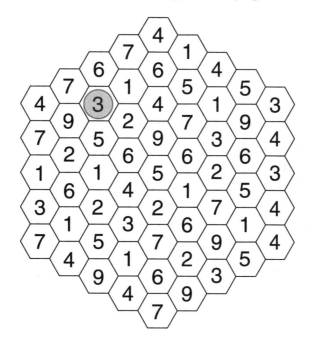

WORD EQUATIONS LANGUAGE

Directions for solving are on page 189.

1. sloped walkway + ripen = violent outburst

2. possessed + landing pier = food fish

3. church ringer + jump, bunny style = hotel worker

4. jogged + grocery bag = plunder

5. used a chair + wrath = ironic comedy

CARD SENSE  LOGIC

Directions for solving are on page 181.

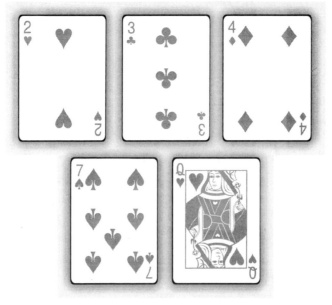

1. The bottom card is not red.

2. The three is directly between the hearts.

3. The diamond is adjacent to the queen.

4. The four is not on top.

232

CIRCLE MATH

Directions for solving are on page 199. We've started you off by telling you that C = 7.

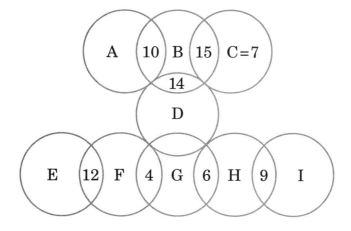

ANTONYMS QUIZ

Directions for solving are on page 198.

1. EXHAUST   a. refresh   b. fluster   c. grunt

2. OSTENTATIOUS   a. sullen   b. humble   c. responsive

3. PRUDENT   a. rash   b. valuable   c. chic

4. VENGEFUL   a. fortunate   b. moot   c. forgiving

5. INARTICULATE   a. boundless   b. eloquent   c. cardinal

6. LAUNCH   a. terminate   b. estimate   c. ratify

7. STEALTHY   a. shapely   b. ravenous   c. obvious

8. EXORBITANT   a. melodic   b. cheap   c. servile

CROSS-UPS

Using only the letters given above each diagram, fill in the boxes in such a way that an everyday compound word is formed, one part reading across and the other part reading down. The letter already in the diagram is a letter shared by both parts of the word. Note: Each part of the compound word is an entire word on its own.

1. A D H I L N

2. D N P R U W

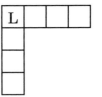

3. B C D H K N

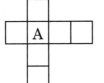

4. E F G I N O

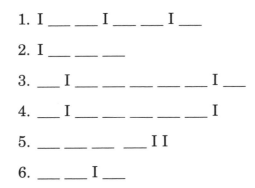

U.S. I'S

This list consists of the names of six U.S. States, but we've removed all of their letters except for the I's. Can you write one letter on each dash to complete the names of the states?

1. I __ __ I __ __ I __

2. I __ __ __

3. __ I __ __ __ __ __ I __

4. __ I __ __ __ __ __ I

5. __ __ __ __ I I

6. __ __ I __

234

SUDOKU

Directions for solving are on page 176.

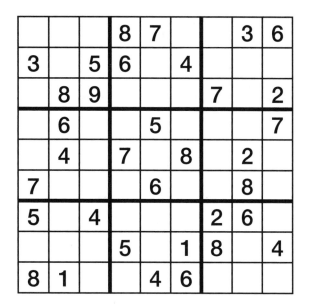

LANGUAGE ◆ SPATIAL

WORD HUNT

Directions for solving are on page 181. This time, you'll be searching for 5-letter words that begin with Q (such as QUEST). We found 14 words, including QUEST.

K	S	T	R	A	M
A	E	Q	U	I	L
C	U	R	O	T	E
I	K	I	Y	A	V

Your list of words:

KEEP ON MOVING

 VISUAL

WEEK 34

Directions for solving are on page 206. Here, start in the shaded square with the number 1.

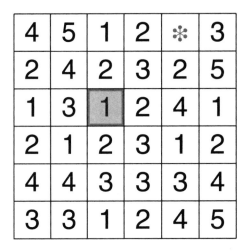

4	5	1	2	✳	3
2	4	2	3	2	5
1	3	1	2	4	1
2	1	2	3	1	2
4	4	3	3	3	4
3	3	1	2	4	5

ARROW MAZE

VISUAL

Directions for solving are on page 187. This time, you'll begin by moving to the right from the starting box.

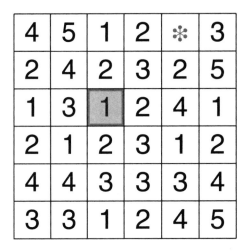

LICENSE PLATES

Each box contains three letters of a National Football League city and three letters of its team's name. The top three are a part of the city's name and the bottom three are a part of the team's, in order.

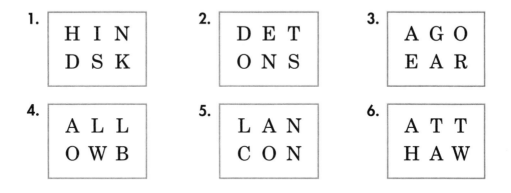

1.
H I N
D S K

2.
D E T
O N S

3.
A G O
E A R

4.
A L L
O W B

5.
L A N
C O N

6.
A T T
H A W

LANGUAGE ♦ SPATIAL

RINGERS

Directions for solving are on page 197.

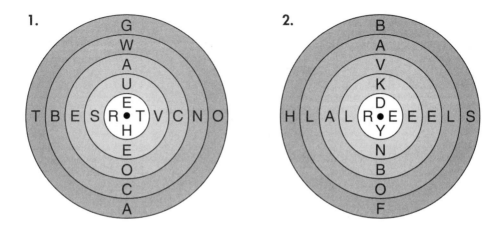

1.

2.

COUNT TO TEN

VISUAL ◆ MATH

WEEK 34

Examine the dodge balls and soccer balls and then answer these questions: 1. Which row contains the most dodge balls? 2. Which row contains the most soccer balls? 3. Which row contains an equal number of dodge balls and soccer balls?

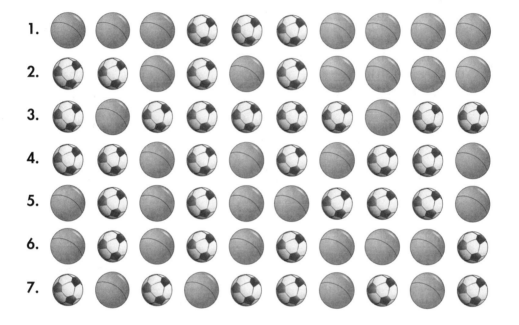

BLOCK PARTY

VISUAL ◆ SPATIAL

Directions for solving are on page 187.

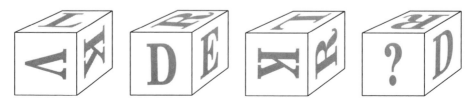

TIPS OF THE ICEBERG

We're back at the Iceberg Diner. After doing some careful addition, answer the following questions:

1. Who made the most in total tips?
2. Who made the least?
3. Which two waitpersons made exactly the same amount?

EMPLOYEE	TIP 1	TIP 2	TIP 3	TIP 4	TIP 5
Hank	$1.25	$1.25	$1.30	$1.10	$1.85
Inez	$1.10	$1.20	$1.20	$0.60	$1.00
Jack	$2.20	$2.10	$2.05	$0.45	$5.00
Ken	$1.50	$1.35	$1.25	$2.05	$4.00
Laura	$2.00	$2.35	$0.40	$0.85	$3.00
Marty	$2.60	$1.10	$1.00	$1.00	$2.00
Noel	$1.80	$0.85	$2.00	$1.10	$1.00

TRI, TRI AGAIN

LANGUAGE ◆ SPATIAL

Directions for solving are on page 177.

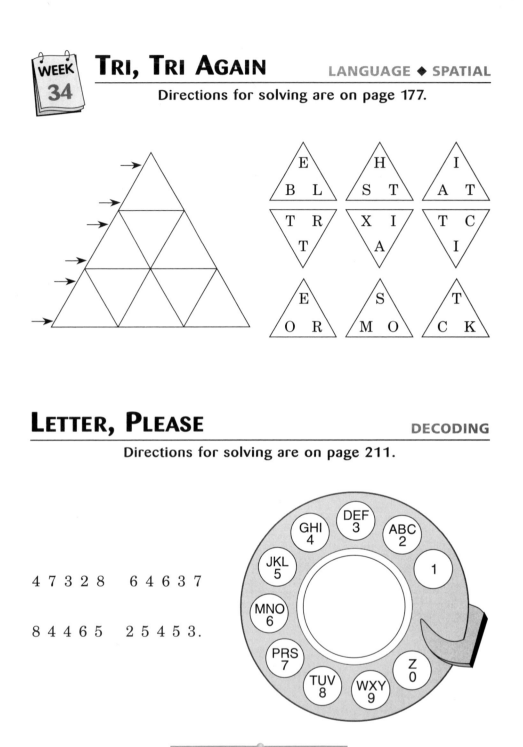

LETTER, PLEASE

DECODING

Directions for solving are on page 211.

4 7 3 2 8   6 4 6 3 7

8 4 4 6 5   2 5 4 5 3.

"Memory is a man's real possession…In nothing else is he rich, in nothing else is he poor."
— *Alexander Smith*

STAR WORDS

WEEK
35

Directions for solving are on page 206.

DANK   SEEK

DENT   TEES

KNEW   THAW

KNOT   WEED

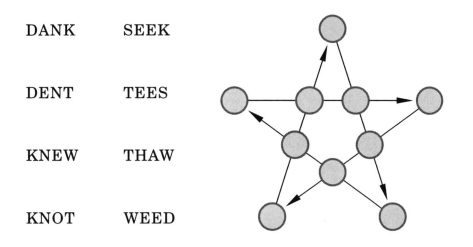

WORD VISIBILITY

Directions for solving are on page 196.

1. B R D K E
   F A I B M

2. M R U W T
   D E A F E

3. C I E B Y
   W H T T R

4. S L R G O
   E T Y A W

5. R U N S T
   P O O A D

6. H Y C G E
   V E D E F

WORD WHEEL

VISUAL ◆ SPATIAL

Directions for solving are on page 209. Beginning with the "R" at the top of the wheel, we formed 31 words of three or more letters.

SYMBOL-ISM

DECODING

Directions for solving are on page 212. For this puzzle, we've indicated that ▦ = R.

☀ⓘ◀ⓘ ⓘ⛟ ⒡★ⓘ ◀ⓘ☀☂ ⛟∅▦-▦ⓘ∅⋔★♡⚭⌘

∅⚭☯ ⓘ◇⋔♡⒡♡⚭⌘ ⓘ⌗ⓘ⚭⒡☀ ⓘ⛟ ⓘ⛗▦

✔♡⌗ⓘ☀ ∅▦♡☀ⓘ ⛟▦ⓘ◀ ⌂⚭ⓘ◇⊠ⓘ⋔⒡ⓘ☯

ⓘ⚭⋔ⓘ⌂⚭⒡⛗▦☀.

COUNT ON IT!

Directions for solving are on page 194.

1. M A I H C H   2. S A O A I   3. S M N S

4. E S T   5. L   6. E

$$\overline{}\ \ \overline{}\ \overline{}\ \overline{}\ \overline{}{}^{,}\ \ \ \overline{}\ \overline{}\ \overline{}\ \overline{}\ \ \ \overline{}\ \overline{}$$
$$\ 1\ \ \ \ \ 1\ \ 2\ \ 3\ \ 4\ \ \ \ \ 1\ \ 2\ \ 3\ \ 4\ \ \ \ \ 1\ \ 2$$

$$\overline{}\ \overline{}\ \overline{}\ \ \ \overline{}\ \overline{}\ \overline{}\ \overline{}\ \overline{}\ \overline{}.$$
$$1\ \ 2\ \ 3\ \ \ \ \ 1\ \ 2\ \ 3\ \ 4\ \ 5\ \ 6$$

RELATIONSHIPS QUIZ

Directions are on page 216.

1. CARPENTER is to HAMMER as JUDGE is to _____.
   (a) bench   (b) gavel   (c) lawyer   (d) robe

2. GALLON is to QUART as BUSHEL is to _____.
   (a) peck   (b) pound   (c) gill   (d) inch

3. DEAN is to COLLEGE as ABBOT is to _____.
   (a) Costello   (b) friar   (c) silence   (d) monastery

4. CALIFORNIA is to REDWOOD as VIRGINIA is to _____.
   (a) peach   (b) pine   (c) dogwood   (d) palm

5. MORTAR is to BRICKS as NAIL is to _____.
   (a) house   (b) lumber   (c) pestle   (d) saw

FILLING STATION

LANGUAGE

Directions for solving are on page 208.

1. B D M N N T (game)
   __ A __ __ I __ __ O __

2. B D L M N N R R (actor)
   __ A __ __ O __ 　 __ __ A __ __ O

3. D H P R S S S T V W (TV show)
   " __ E __ __ E __ A __ E 　 __ O U __ E __ I __ E __ "

4. C L M P P P R T T (thing)
   __ A __ __ O __ 　 __ O __ __ U __ E __

5. L R S T T V W (fictional character)
   O __ I __ E __ 　 __ __ I __ __

MARCHING ORDERS

MATH ◆ LOGIC

Directions for solving are on page 214. We've started the first one for you using the sequence +6 and −4.

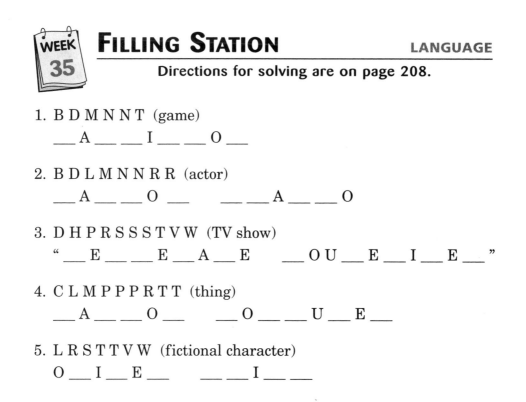

1. FINISH

11	17	8	16	21	17
15	12	13	19	15	20
9	5	11	7	13	19
3	4	13	15	14	13
7	5	9	10	17	12
1	6	11	15	11	10

START

2. FINISH

18	24	23	26	30	28
13	19	22	27	25	20
16	21	9	18	13	15
11	14	16	12	11	10
7	9	4	9	5	12
1	6	3	8	7	11

START

COUNT THE TRIANGLES

WEEK
35

To solve this puzzle, write down the three letters that describe each triangle (a figure with three sides) in this figure. We found 23 triangles; how many can you locate?

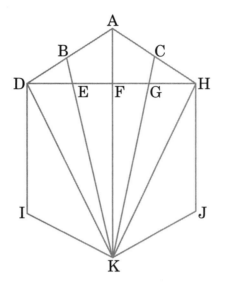

VISUAL ◆ LOGIC # SHIFTING GEARS

Can you determine which cogs will turn counterclockwise when cog A is turned in a clockwise direction?

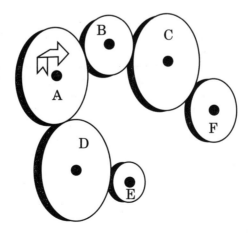

ELIMINATION

LANGUAGE

Directions for solving are on page 180. Once again, the remaining words will form a thought.

SOYBEAN USE HIS SCHNAPPS RAIN TASTEFUL SPRIGHTLY PIANO WORDS METHANE MONEY IN VIOLIN REIGN CASE CHEESE SOLDIER YOU GROWTHS ARE HAVE SAXOPHONE GARNET TO REIN FIELD EAT SOON SUBPOENA THEM PARTED

Eliminate…

1. the words that complete the proverb: "A fool and…"

2. the three words that end with the same three letters, in any order.

3. the words that contain four consonants grouped together.

4. the words that are names for musical instruments.

5. the words that form the name of where the Chicago Bears play home games.

6. the words that are all pronounced the same.

7. the two words that, when the letters are scrambled together, form the name of a southern European capital and its country.

PROGRESSION

LOGIC

Which of the numbered designs are identical to the one on the left?

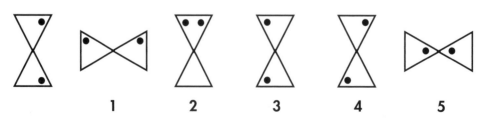

1   2   3   4   5

WHAT'S YOUR NUMBER?

Can you figure out the sequence of numbers in the left-hand, right-hand, and bottom spokes and what missing number goes into the space with the question mark on the top spoke?

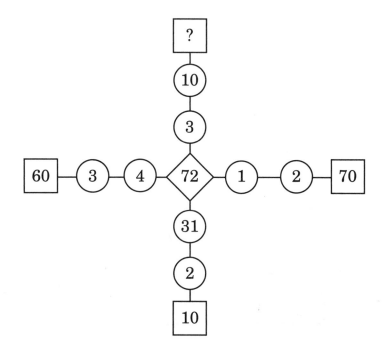

SKILLS TEST

MATH

Sam and Tom have 81 music CDs together. Sam has 23 more than Tom. How many CDs belong to Sam?

a. 52   b. 19   c. 41   d. 46   e. 27

IN THE ABSTRACT

VISUAL ◆ SPATIAL

Directions for solving are on page 174.

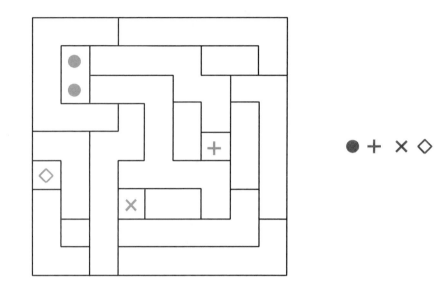

● + ✕ ◇

ARROW MAZE

VISUAL

Directions for solving are on page 187. This time, you'll begin by moving to the right from the starting box.

PRESIDENTIAL LIMITS

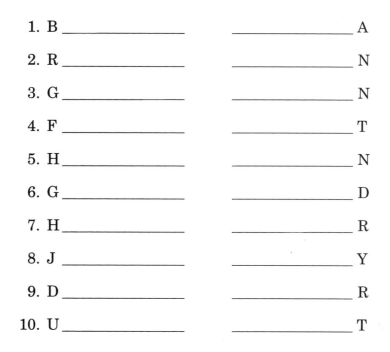

WEEK 36

The list below consists of the names of 10 U.S. Presidents, but we've removed all of the letters between the first and last ones. Can you complete the names of the Chief Executives?

1. B _____ _____ A

2. R _____ _____ N

3. G _____ _____ N

4. F _____ _____ T

5. H _____ _____ N

6. G _____ _____ D

7. H _____ _____ R

8. J _____ _____ Y

9. D _____ _____ R

10. U _____ _____ T

WAYWORDS

Directions for solving are on page 198. This time, you'll be looking for a 10-word joke beginning with SOME.

REASON	A	ACTUAL	CONTRITE
STORM	FEW	ARE	COVET
OF	TREES	SOME	PEOPLE
SHORT	A	FOREST	BELIEVE

SEVEN WORD ZINGER

LANGUAGE

Directions for solving are on page 199.

— — — —

— — — —

— — — —

— — — —

— — — —

— — — —

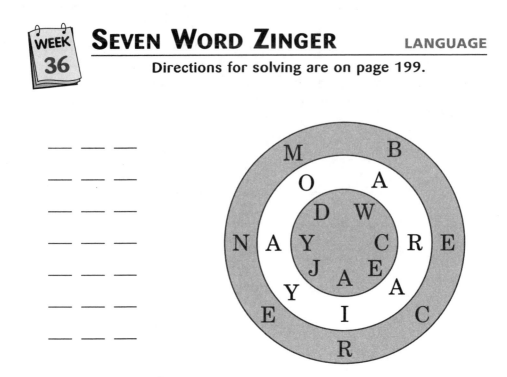

EASY PICKINGS

LANGUAGE

To solve, simply cross out one letter in each pair below. When the puzzle is completed correctly, the remaining letters will spell out a quote by playwright Friedrich Schiller.

SE VO TE GN   IW ES AE HK   DM DE NH

WT AH EK NE   AU NM TI TN IE DV

GA HR EF   PE DO WI XE DR FQ UN HL .

"The ability to focus attention on important things is a defining characteristic of intelligence."
— *Robert J. Shiller*

SUDOKU

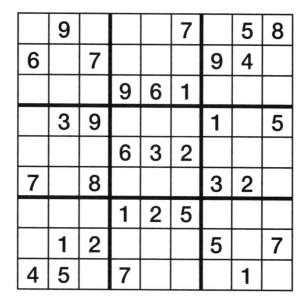

Directions for solving are on page 176.

SWITCHEROO

In each group, for the first word and its number equivalent given, determine what the number equivalent is for the second word.

1. LEAN is to 3175 as LANE is to:
   (a) 3751 (b) 3157 (c) 3517 (d) 5173

2. RIDE is to 8462 as DIRE is to:
   (a) 6842 (b) 4862 (c) 6482 (d) 2468

3. NONE is to 9573 as NEON is to:
   (a) 9537 (b) 7359 (c) 7953 (d) 7593

4. BUST is to 1329 as STUB is to:
   (a) 2931 (b) 2139 (c) 2913 (d) 3291

5. MEAT is to 8024 as TEAM is to:
   (a) 4082 (b) 4208 (c) 2048 (d) 4028

6. STEP is to 5786 as PEST is to:
   (a) 6785 (b) 6875 (c) 8657 (d) 6857

ASSOCIATIONS

LANGUAGE

Directions for solving are on page 184.

WHAT DID THE LIGHTHOUSE KEEPER HAVE FOR BREAKFAST?

ATLANTA SUAVE BUNNY THIN HAPPY ETHIOPIA

DEBONAIR   HARVARD   APPLE   MONTGOMERY

SLENDER CANDY MERRY PRINCETON OPINION

SENIOR NAVIGATE ORIGINAL URBANE AVERAGE

JOYFUL NOVEL NURTURE YEAR JUNIOR DEPRIVE

NASHVILLE EJECT DECADE SLIM GAS UNIQUE

GRAVEL CENTURY SOPHOMORE SHELF YALE

SLIDE RULE

LANGUAGE

Directions for solving are on page 186. We formed 45 4-letter words, including HEAD.

Your list of words:

ANAGRAM MAZE

Directions for solving are on page 194. This time, there are 21 words to anagram and the first is CAME.

1 SLIT	2 FETE	3 DOSE	4 TIED	5 UNDO	6 CAME
7 SEWN	8 WISH	9 CLAP	10 SPAR	11 PACE	12 THAW
13 KEEN	14 COLA	15 LYRE	16 FOUL	17 TERM	18 BANG
19 BATH	20 MICE	21 CHUM	22 PROD	23 RAID	24 LOUT
25 CLIP	26 TINY	27 LOOK	28 ZINC	29 HARE	30 JUMP
31 WENT	32 STUN	33 FATS	34 NAVE	35 PIER	36 DANK

ALL IN A ROW

Directions for solving are on page 178. This time, look for the most groups of consecutive numbers adding up to 15.

A. 3 2 1 5 4 3 8 2 5 3 8 4 3 7 1 6 2 7 2 1 5 7 6 2

B. 6 3 6 8 2 5 1 7 8 3 2 1 2 3 4 5 5 4 1 3 2 7 6 8

C. 4 1 9 2 3 1 1 9 1 4 6 4 2 3 8 2 5 2 2 3 3 8 6 9

COUNTDOWN

Following the connecting lines, find the only route in this grid that passes through the numbers backward from 9 to 1 consecutively.

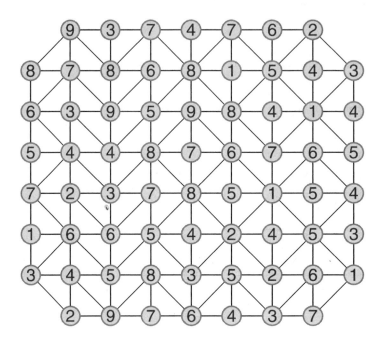

QUICK FILL

Determine the 10-letter word from the clues. All the letters in the word are listed.

A B D E E L L O P R

1. Letter 7 is a vowel.

2. Letter 9 appears elsewhere in the word.

3. Letters 8, 10, and 1, in order, spell out something to sleep on.

4. Letter 6 is from the second half of the alphabet.

5. Letters 3, 5, 4, and 2, in order, spell out a resident of Warsaw.

$$\overline{1}\ \ \overline{2}\ \ \overline{3}\ \ \overline{4}\ \ \overline{5}\ \ \overline{6}\ \ \overline{7}\ \ \overline{8}\ \ \overline{9}\ \ \overline{10}$$

SUDOKU

Place a number into each box so each row across, column down, and small 9-box square within the larger square (there are 9 of these) contains 1 through 9.

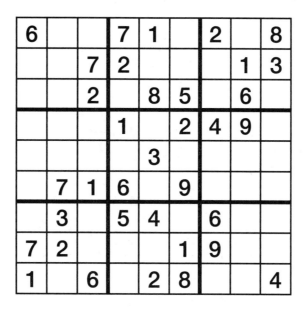

VISUAL

A COUNT

Here's an eye exam that's also an A exam! First, read the sentence below. Next, go back and read the sentence again, but this time count all of the A's. How many are there?

AS ALWAYS, ALAN ADAMS

ASKED FOR ASPARAGUS A LA

CARTE, AND ALAN'S AUNTS

ANNA AND AGATHA ATE AN

AROMATIC BAKED ALASKA.

HEXAGON HUNT

VISUAL

In this diagram of six-sided figures, there are 10 "special" hexagons. These 10 are special because the six numbers around each one are all different from each other and the center number. We've circled one of the 10. Can you find the other 9?

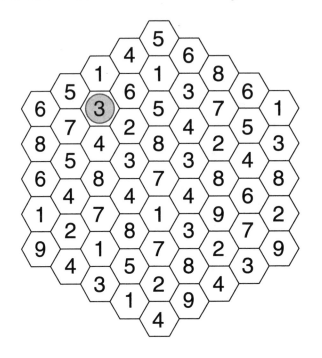

CODE WORD

DECODING

Decipher a quote and the Code Word's eleven letters, represented by the numbers 1 through 11. So, if the Code Word were "THUNDERCLAP," 1 in the quote would be T, 2 would be H, etc.

$$\overline{1}\ \overline{2}\ \overline{3}\ \overline{4}\ \overline{5}\ \overline{6}\ \overline{7}\ \overline{8}\ \overline{9}\ \overline{10}\ \overline{11}$$

2 7 8 11 L 4 5 8 5 2 2 4 6 8 9 F 8 11 2 10 4 N 1 6 8 9 5 4 N

11 4 3 8 5 10 5 W 7 8 N 7 8 4 9 5 7 8 F 10 L L 5 4 U 2

1 N 8 3 6 L 4 Y 3 8 N 2 1 6 6 L 10 11 1 2 10 4 N .

EASY PICKINGS

WEEK 37

To solve, simply cross out one letter in each pair below. When the puzzle is completed correctly, the remaining letters will spell out a quip.

ME NO TD EN YS TE SY   IW SR

HF MO RD   ET HI DO TS ED   WR FH RO

HX AF GV SE   BN OG

TX AD SL SE NM CT.

LANGUAGE ◆ VISUAL

ANAGRAM MAZE

The diagram contains 36 words, 19 of which are anagrams of other everyday words. Start at the top arrow and anagram LEFT. While solving, move up, down, right, or left to the only adjacent word that can be anagrammed. Continue until you arrive at the bottom arrow. There is only one path through the maze.

1 CULT	2 WINE	3 LEFT	4 RIDE	5 BAKE	6 WAIT
7 CREW	8 FALL	9 OOZE	10 HUNT	11 PEST	12 CLAY
13 VEIL	14 LISP	15 SILT	16 INTO	17 PLUS	18 RIPE
19 BUST	20 FIVE	21 PALE	22 LIED	23 SURF	24 MASH
25 CAPE	26 PURR	27 CUFF	28 FOIL	29 WHIM	30 DECK
31 HATE	32 NONE	33 DISK	34 OVER	35 BODY	36 JUMP

WORD CHARADE

VISUAL ◆ LANGUAGE

Find each letter in the diagram according to the instructions, and write each letter on its dash to spell out a 6-letter word.

My first letter appears directly below an H and to the immediate left of a J.

E	A	D	N	L	Q	H	M
G	G	U	V	K	W	Z	P
B	I	L	G	H	A	S	J
Z	M	Q	H	M	T	C	U
A	H	Z	L	J	F	Q	K
C	O	X	A	E	C	E	U
T	N	E	I	D	E	B	O
U	V	Y	O	I	N	Z	J

My second letter is a corner letter from the second half of the alphabet.

My third letter appears in the second column but not in the fourth column.

My fourth letter is the second letter of an 8-letter word reading right to left.

My fifth letter is the only vowel in one of the columns.

My sixth letter does not appear in the diagram.

— — — — — —

ALL IN A ROW

MATH

Which row below contains the most groups of consecutive numbers adding up to 9? Look carefully, because some groups may overlap. We've underlined an example of a group in each row to start you off.

A. 4 1 3 1 2 5 6 7 1 1 4 1 2 8 3 5 6 2 1 3 1 4 5 2

B. 6 1 4 8 2 2 5 7 3 3 1 2 1 4 1 7 3 1 6 5 5 3 4 1

C. 7 3 2 2 1 2 2 6 4 1 5 8 1 4 3 7 1 5 3 6 2 4 7 1

TARGET SHOOT

Find the two letters which, when entered into the center circle of each target, will form three 6-letter words reading across.

1.

2.

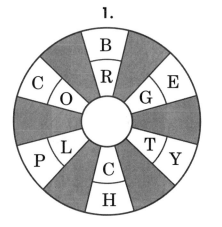

IN THE ABSTRACT

Fill in each section with one of the four symbols so no sections containing the same symbol touch. Four sections are already complete.

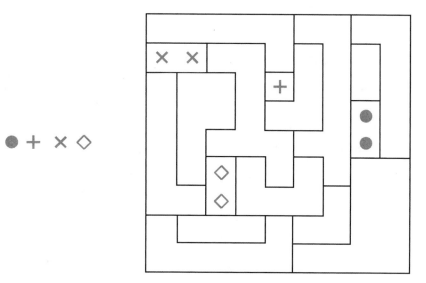

LICENSE PLATES

LANGUAGE

Each box contains six letters of the first and last name of a member of the Basketball Hall of Fame. The top three are a part of the first name and the bottom three are a part of the last name, in order.

1.
```
H A R
A R K
```

2.
```
S I A
T H O
```

3.
```
I L L
U S S
```

4.
```
A R R
I R D
```

5.
```
H A E
O R D
```

6.
```
I L T
H A M
```

COUNT TO TEN

MATH ◆ VISUAL

Examine the ladybugs and dragonflies and then answer these questions: 1. Which row contains the most ladybugs? 2. Which row contains the most dragonflies? 3. Which row contains an equal number of ladybugs and dragonflies?

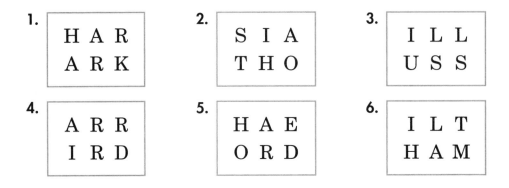

1.
2.
3.
4.
5.
6.
7.
8.
9.
10.

BULL'S-EYE LETTER

Add the SAME single letter to each group of three letters, then rearrange the letters to form six everyday 4-letter words.

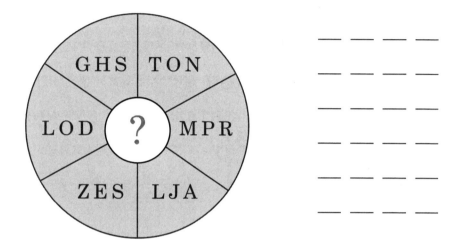

— — — —

— — — —

— — — —

— — — —

— — — —

— — — —

WAYWORDS

A 7-word thought can be found beginning with the word A. Then, move to any adjacent box up, down, or diagonally for each following word.

FRIENDLY	POOR	FOOLISH	SIMPLE
FOOLISH	A	TIME	LEADER
OTHERS	GRACE	WILL	SHOULD
OPTIONS	MAKE	CORNER	FEW

CIRCLE SEARCH

LANGUAGE

Move from circle to adjoining circle, horizontally and vertically only, to form 14 common words of at least three letters. Don't change the order of the letters in the circles that contain more than one letter. Proper names are not allowed.

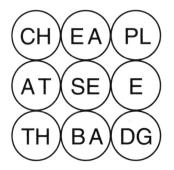

RING LOGIC

LOGIC

Complete the diagram by drawing in the links between the rings using the statements. Assume that all the rings in the picture are locked rigidly into position and cannot be moved in any direction. Consider yourself a true ringmaster if you can find the solution in under six minutes!

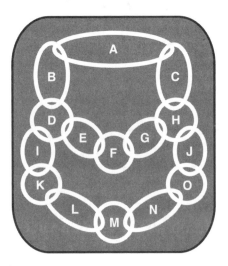

1. The pattern is symmetrical from left to right.

2. Each ring is linked at least twice.

3. The bottom of rings A and G are to the front.

4. The right side of rings C and I are to the front.

5. The top of ring N is to the front.

ARROW MAZE

Starting at the S and following the arrow to the right, see if you can find your way to F. When you reach an arrow, you **MUST** follow its direction and continue in that direction until you come to the next arrow. When you reach a two-headed arrow, you can choose either direction. It's okay to cross your own path.

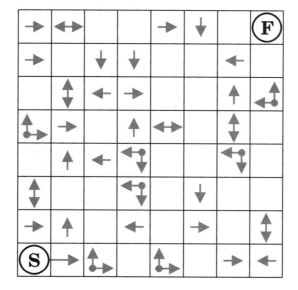

LANGUAGE

DOVETAILED WORDS

Two related words, with their letters in the correct order, are combined in each row of letters. Can you find both words? In a line like POTEORDRLEIER, or POteOrDrLEier, you can see the two words POODLE and TERRIER.

1. F P I H L O T M O   _____ _____

2. B G R R O I O D M E   _____ _____

3. T P U A N R C T D U A Y L _____ _____

4. B S A T T O I C N K   _____ _____

5. S S C A A R R O N F G   _____ _____

ONLINE NETWORK

In each two-column group, take the letters in the left-hand column along the paths (indicated by the lines) and place them in their proper boxes in the right-hand column. When done, you'll find three related words reading down each of the two right-hand columns.

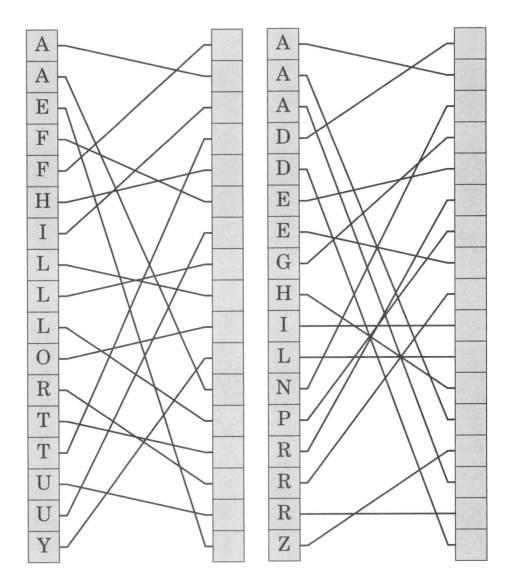

LOOSE TILE

The tray on the right seemed the ideal place to store the set of loose dominoes. Unfortunately, when the tray was full, one domino was left over. Determine the arrangement of the dominoes in the tray and which is the Loose Tile.

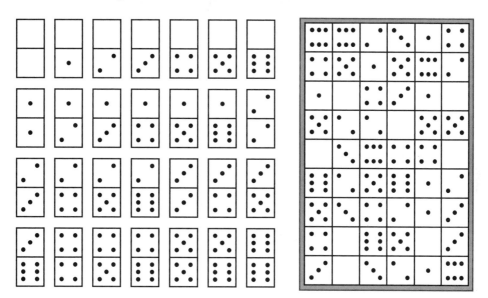

GOING IN CIRCLES

In each circle, insert one letter into each empty space to form an 8-letter word. Words may read either clockwise or counter-clockwise and may begin with any letter in the circle.

1.

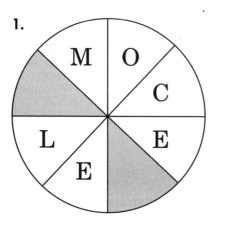

2.

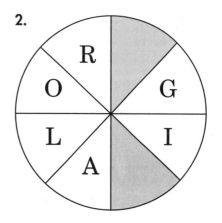

FUN WITH
FACTS AND FIGURES

MATH

This puzzle tests you on a lot of little facts and figures. Solve the quiz in the order given since each answer is used in the next statement. There are no fractions used here.

1. Take the number of the date that New Year's Eve falls on in December and subtract the number of doughnuts in a baker's dozen. _____

2. Next, add the number of dimes in five dollars. _____

3. Now, divide by the value of the Roman numeral XXXIV. _____

4. Multiply by the number of letters in the name of the country that contains Berlin and Munich. _____

5. Subtract the number of lives that a cat is reputed to have. _____

Our answer is the number of human senses. Is yours?

COMPOUND IT

LANGUAGE

Starting at #1, pick a word that will form a compound word with a word chosen in #2. Then with the word you've selected in #2, pick one from #3 to form another compound word. Continue in this manner to #10, so that you've formed nine compound words. In some instances more than one compound word can be formed, but there is only one path to get you to #10.

1. honey, stone, air, treat

2. brush, fare, dew, wall

3. well, board, back, work

4. load, horse, fleet, spring

5. radish, shoe, let, back

6. fire, drop, string, ground

7. water, cloth, power, storm

8. way, bound, proof, house

9. boat, less, hold, time

10. age, over, person, mold

DEDUCTION PROBLEM

Penelope and two friends went to the local pizzeria. Each ordered a slice of pizza with one meat topping and one vegetable topping (one person requested mushrooms). From this information and the clues below, can you determine each person's two toppings?

1. Malcolm didn't request onions or sausage.

2. Jessica ordered bacon, but she didn't get peppers.

3. No one had pepperoni and peppers together.

SEVEN WORD ZINGER

Using each letter once, form seven everyday 3-letter words with the first letter coming from the center, the second from the middle, and the third from the outer circle. Your words may differ from ours.

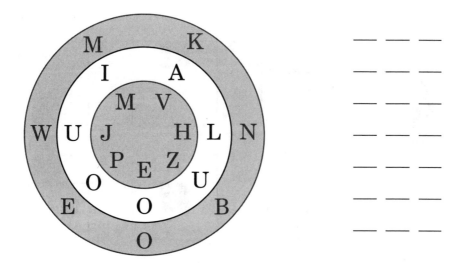

— — —

— — —

— — —

— — —

— — —

— — —

— — —

TRI, TRI AGAIN

LANGUAGE ◆ SPATIAL

Fit the nine triangles into the big one so six everyday words are spelled out reading across the arrows. Do not rotate the triangles.

STACKED UP

VISUAL ◆ SPATIAL

The box on the left can be formed by three of the numbered boxes superimposed on top of each other; do not turn them in any way. Can you figure out which three work?

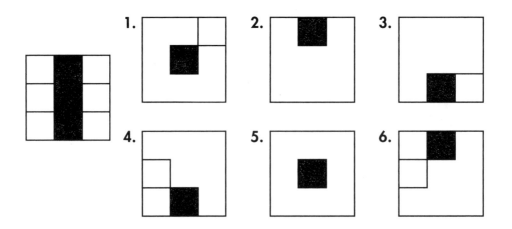

268

ANIMAL CHARADES

WEEK
39

Each line contains a clue to a letter of the alphabet. These letters, in the given order, will spell out the name of an animal. The animal's identity is also hinted at in the last sentence of the Charade.

My FIRST is in GUPPY and in GRAPE;   _____

My SECOND is in CHEETAH and in SCRAPE;   _____

My THIRD is in RHINOCEROS but not in MISER;   _____

My FOURTH is in TURKEY but not in GEYSER;   _____

My FIFTH is in PYTHON and in HONEY;   _____

My SIXTH is in CHAMELEON and in MONEY;   _____

My SEVENTH is in KANGAROO but not in SNACK.   _____

My WHOLE is a feline with fur that is black.

KEEP ON MOVING

The goal is to move from the shaded square to the asterisk. Since the shaded square has the number 2 in it, you must move two squares up, down, left, or right, but not diagonally. In the new square will be another number; move that number of squares up, down, left, or right, continuing in this way until you reach the asterisk. It's okay to cross your own path.

4	4	2	2	5	2
4	4	2	2	4	1
1	5	4	2	4	4
5	2	3	1	2	3
2	4	*	2	1	2
3	4	1	1	5	2

CARD SENSE

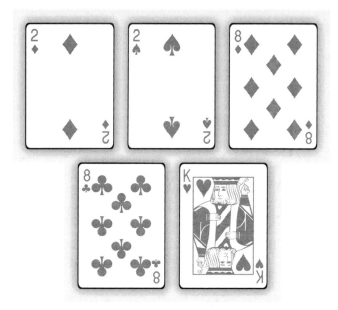

Five playing cards were shuffled and put in a pile, one on top of another. Using the clues, can you identify each card's position in the pile?

1. The king is above the club but below both diamonds.

2. The twos are adjacent but neither is on top of the pile.

3. The diamonds aren't adjacent.

SLIDE RULE

LANGUAGE

Slide each column of letters up or down in the box and form as many everyday 3-letter words as you can in the windows where RIB is now. We formed 37 words, including RIB.

Your list of words:

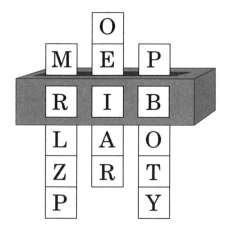

270

TIPS OF THE ICEBERG

The chart shows the gratuities each waiter or waitress earned on a recent breakfast shift at the Iceberg Diner. All you have to do is some careful addition and then answer the following questions:

1. Who made the most in total tips?
2. Who made the least?
3. Which two waitpersons made exactly the same amount?

EMPLOYEE	TIP 1	TIP 2	TIP 3	TIP 4	TIP 5
Al	$2.10	$1.80	$1.10	$1.05	$1.00
Brenda	$1.70	$4.10	$2.10	$2.75	$1.90
Charlie	$1.20	$3.10	$1.15	$1.10	$1.95
Dena	$4.90	$1.90	$1.35	$6.65	$1.00
Ed	$1.05	$3.90	$2.00	$1.05	$3.80
Flora	$1.10	$3.90	$4.80	$1.05	$1.70
Greta	$1.00	$1.85	$1.00	$3.00	$1.85

WORK 39 — WORD HUNT

LANGUAGE ♦ SPATIAL

Find words by moving from one letter to any adjoining letter. You may start a word with any letter in the diagram. In forming a word you may return to a letter as often as you wish, but do not stand on a letter using it twice in direct succession. In this Word Hunt, you are searching for 4-letter words that end with O. We found 19 words, including ZERO. Hyphenated words are not allowed

Your list of words:

O	T	E	P	Y
D	N	S	O	T
U	J	I	L	G
H	E	R	A	H
Z	M	O	T	U

SUDOKU

LOGIC

Directions for solving are on page 255.

6		7				4		
1			7	6				5
	5	8			1	3	7	
5	8		2	9				
4		6				5		8
			5	8			2	4
	1	2	4			9	5	
7				3	9			2
		9				6		1

MISSING DOMINOES

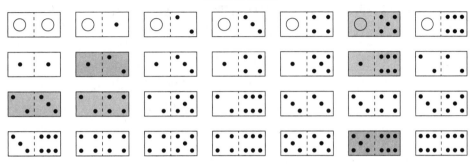

WEEK 39

In this game you use all 28 dominoes that are in a standard set. Each one has a different combination from 0-0, 0-1, 0-2, to 6-6. Domino halves with the same number of dots lie next to each other. To avoid confusion we have used an open circle to indicate a zero. Can you fill in the missing white dominoes to complete the board?

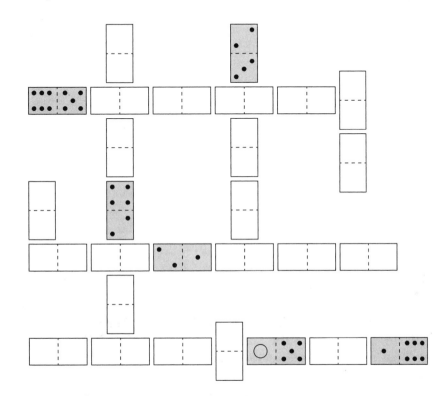

DOMINOES

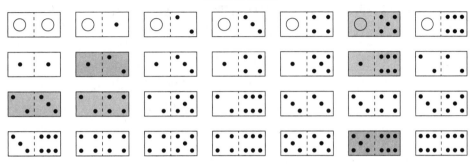

GETTING IN SHAPE

VISUAL

Which two boxes contain the same nine shapes?

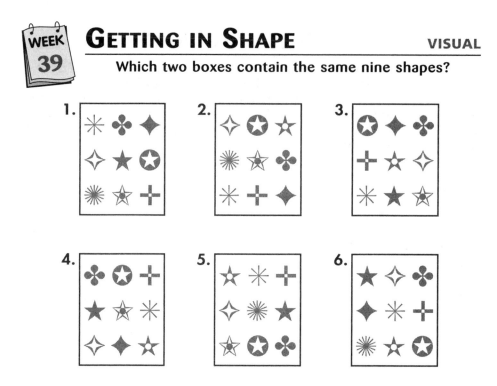

RELATIONSHIPS QUIZ

LANGUAGE

KENNEL is to DOG as STY is to PIG because a DOG lives in a KENNEL and a PIG lives in a STY. Each of the statements below is a relationship of some kind. Can you select the right word from the four following each?

1. HEAD is to HAT as FOOT is to _____.
   (a) toe (b) shoe (c) ankle (d) inch

2. MOTHER is to DAUGHTER as MARE is to _____.
   (a) zebra (b) foal (c) kid (d) filly

3. PENCIL is to ERASER as HOUSE is to _____.
   (a) door (b) paint (c) roof (d) kitchen

4. TRANSCRIBE is to WRITE as DICTATE is to _____.
   (a) speak (b) think (c) judge (d) type

5. NURSERY is to SHRUB as SCHOOL is to _____.
   (a) district (b) principal (c) pupil (d) college

GRAND TOUR

WEEK
40

Form a continuous chain of 5-letter words moving through the maze from START to FINISH. The second part of one word becomes the first part of the next word. This puzzle starts with AM-BLE-AT (amble, bleat).

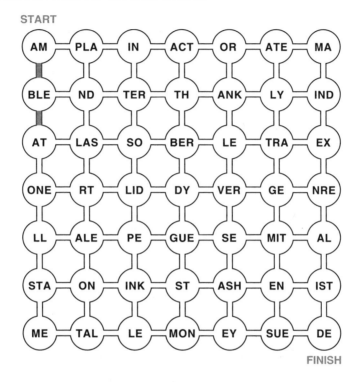

SYMBOL-ISM

DECODING

This is simply a Cryptogram that uses symbols instead of letters to spell out a truism. Each symbol stands for the same letter throughout. For this puzzle, we've already indicated that ✳ = G and ▲ = S.

ASSOCIATIONS

LANGUAGE

You'll find eight groups of three words that can be associated in some way with each other (example: mantel, fireplace, logs). Cross out each group as you find it. The initial letters of the remaining words will spell out the answer to the riddle:

WHAT'S WORSE THAN RAINING CATS AND DOGS?

MONTREAL PREY HAPPY ABANDON SHIELD

AGENT SPUR ITALIAN CALGARY RELINQUISH

PROTECT LACE HELICOPTER SEDUCE IRRITATE

PICK NAKED VICTIM LURE GOAD CHOOSE

GRAPE ENTICE QUARRY TAPESTRY SURRENDER

ASPARAGUS AIRPLANE SELECT XENON GUARD

PROD INNOCENT TORONTO STRANGE DIRIGIBLE

WORD VISIBILITY

LANGUAGE

There are six 5-letter words below. The first letter of the answer is found in the first pair of letters, and it is either the top or the bottom letter. Continue across each pair.

For example, the word GIRL would be found thus: <u>G</u> A <u>R</u> <u>L</u>
                                                    L <u>I</u> T X

1. W L R T Y
   M U G K O

2. C R E S N
   K H A M E

3. S P U R B
   T I O C E

4. G H X U M
   M A E I R

5. F O W D A
   C U B R G

6. D E O M L
   A R T P A

COUNT THE RECTANGLES

To solve this puzzle, write down the four letters that describe each rectangle in this figure. We found 38 rectangles; how many can you locate?

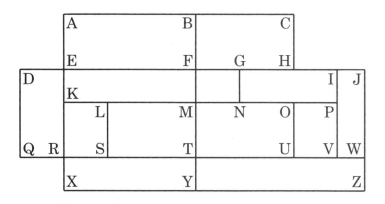

THE LINEUP

While scrutinizing the lineup of letters, can you answer the five questions correctly in five minutes or less?

PRFJESTVNTHUDWSUGGESTCSLUDGEKFEXAMZYQOIGT

1. Which letter of the alphabet does not appear in the lineup? _____

2. What 7-letter word — with its letters in correct order and appearing together — can you find in the lineup? _____

3. Which letter of the alphabet appears exactly three times in the lineup? _____

4. What 6-letter word — with its letters in correct order and appearing together — can you find in the lineup? _____

5. Other than the answers to Questions 2 and 4, how many everyday words — with their letters in correct order and appearing together — of four or more letters can you find in the lineup? _____

STAR WORDS

VISUAL ◆ LOGIC

Only five of the eight words given will fit together in the diagram. Place them in the directions indicated by the arrows.

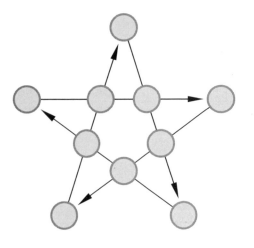

DUAL   SANG

GAIT   SNUG

LIES   TAIL

LINT   TEND

MAGNIFIND

VISUAL ◆ SPATIAL

Figure out which area of the drawing has been enlarged.

ALPHABET SOUP

WEEK **40**

Cross off each letter from the alphabet list that appears in the larger group of letters. Then rearrange the letters not crossed out to form the name of a fruit.

```
H W Y H C D O I V Y C H D A W Y E R J X Y

D V W A Q H C D I J E D A J Q X I F Y G J S

R W H V A I G Z X Y F B R K D N J T Z K T
```

```
A B C D E F G H I J K L M N O P Q R S T U V W X Y Z
```

ELIMINATION

Cross off the capitalized words according to the instructions given. The remaining words, in order, will form a thought.

SUPPORT DOUGH HE ABLE-BODIED BRIDGE WHO CHICKENS TORSO BREAD CHURCH HESITATES BEFORE CABBAGE IS SHORT-LIVED RUSTY TEMPLE BREAK OFTEN THEY QUICK-WITTED THE ARE PRONOUN HEARTS MOSQUE WISEST HATCHED

Eliminate…

1. slang words for money.

2. the five words that follow: "Do not count your…"

3. the words with letters only from the second half of the alphabet.

4. hyphenated words.

5. places of worship.

6. the word that can precede "down," "fast," "neck," and "through."

7. the names of card games.

ANTONYMS QUIZ   LANGUAGE

An antonym is a word that is opposite in meaning to another word; for example, "cold" is the antonym of "hot." One of the words following each capitalized word is the antonym of that word.

1. RIDICULE   a. praise   b. revolt   c. signify

2. COPIOUSNESS   a. guidance   b. scarcity   c. bravery

3. FORFEIT   a. disdain   b. acquire   c. hasten

4. ABOMINABLE   a. virtuous   b. mutinous   c. recurrent

5. AGGRIEVED   a. habitual   b. restive   c. happy

6. VERBOSE   a. pithy   b. devout   c. giddy

7. ADDLE   a. empower   b. rivet   c. enlighten

8. HALLOW   a. convene   b. defile   c. provoke

WHAT'S YOUR NUMBER?   MATH ◆ LOGIC

Can you figure out the relationship of the three numbers in the first two rectangles and, based on that, what missing number goes into the space with the question mark?

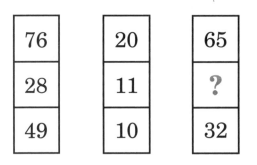

76		20		65
28		11		?
49		10		32

MARCHING ORDERS

Using a different two-step sequence of addition and/or subtraction, can you make your way from Start to Finish in each puzzle? We've started the first one for you using the sequence +2 and +3; continue this sequence to reach Finish. You will not cross your own path or pass through any square twice.

1.　　FINISH

24	25	29	31	34	36
18	13	26	21	19	35
9	12	24	18	22	16
8	3	7	11	14	19
5	6	9	12	14	17
4	7	8	10	11	16

START

2.　　FINISH

14	17	18	21	28	34
12	13	16	22	23	33
8	7	10	11	25	30
6	9	12	24	26	29
5	3	8	9	20	18
2	4	7	10	14	16

START

RINGERS

Each Ringer is composed of five rings. Use your imagination to rotate the rings so that you spell out four 5-letter words reading from the outside to the inside when all five rings are aligned correctly.

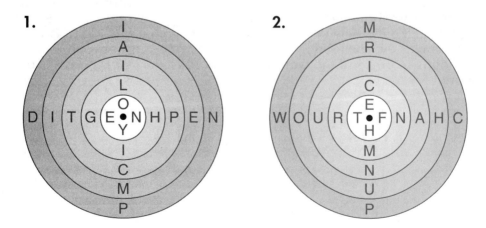

281

CROSS PATHS

VISUAL

Start at the arrow. There are two circles in that box, so move two boxes, either across or up. Each time you land in a box, move the number of dots in that box in only one direction, up, down, or across until you reach Finish (F). You may cross your own path, but do not retrace it.

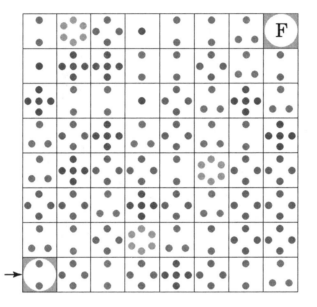

POP!

LANGUAGE

The balloons in a dart game are arranged so their letters spell out the word "PLANETS." To win, you must pop six different balloons with six different darts, but after each pop the remaining letters must spell out a new word reading across from left to right. Do not rearrange the balloons. Can you determine the order of the balloons to pop and the words formed? Your words may differ from ours.

IN THE BALANCE

Scales 1, 2, and 3 are perfectly balanced. Determine how many triangles it takes to balance scale 4.

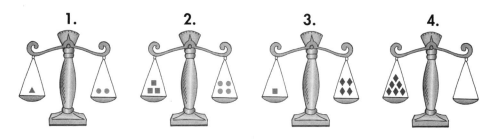

LOGIC

HOLE IN ONE

Twenty-four golfers entered a hole-in-one contest. Each golfer was given a ball with a different 4-digit number combination using the numbers 3, 5, 7, and 8 on it. Looking at the 23 balls still on the green, can you figure out what combination is on the ball that won the contest?

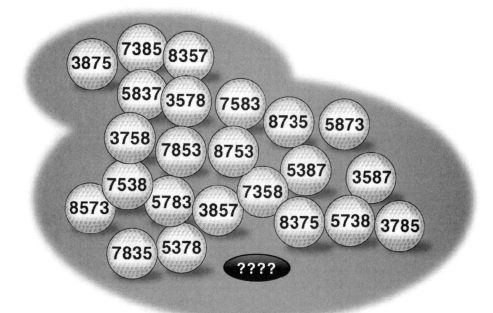

TRIANGULAR SQUARE

MATH ◆ SPATIAL

Place the nine numbered squares into the diagram so that the four numbers in each of the diagram's four large triangles equal the number outside of it. The patterns have to match and you may not rotate the squares.

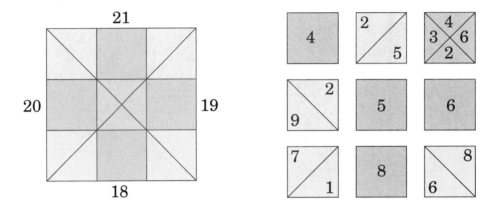

CROSS PATHS

VISUAL

Directions for solving are on page 282.

HOLE IN ONE

Directions for solving are on page 283. This time, the 4-digit number combination uses 2, 3, 8, and 9.

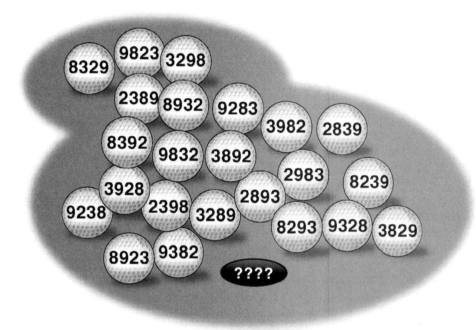

LANGUAGE

POP!

Directions for solving are on page 282. This time, you'll be using the letters in the word "CHEATED."

BLOCK PARTY

VISUAL ◆ SPATIAL

Study the different views of the block, and draw what should appear on the face that has a question mark.

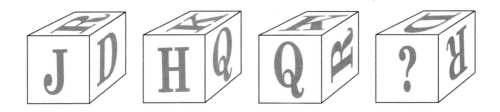

OVERLAY

VISUAL ◆ SPATIAL

When you overlay the three diagrams in the top row, which of the three lettered diagrams, A, B, or C, will be formed?

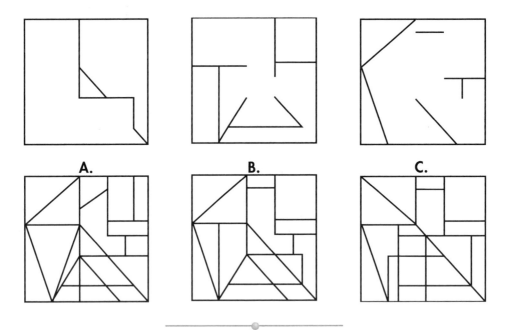

"Common sense in an uncommon degree is what the world calls wisdom."
— *Samuel Taylor Coleridge*

MAGIC NUMBER SQUARE

Fill in the boxes with the numbers 1 through 25 (one number per box) so that each row, each column, and each long diagonal adds up to 65. Each number is used only once; those already entered in the diagram have been crossed off the number list.

1 2 3 4 5 6 7 8 9 10 11 12 13 14 15 16 17 18 19 20 21 22 23 24 25

3		9		15
		21	14	
7			1	19
		5	18	
11		17		23

QUICK FILL

Directions for solving are on page 254.

C C E E I L N O R T

1. In the alphabet, one letter separates letter 2 and letter 8, in some order.

2. Letter 7 is a vowel.

3. Letters 2, 3 (which is a vowel), and 10 are from the first half of the alphabet.

4. In the alphabet, letter 6 is somewhere before letter 5.

5. Letters 9, 4, and 1, in order, spell out a word meaning frozen water.

$\overline{1}$ $\overline{2}$ $\overline{3}$ $\overline{4}$ $\overline{5}$ $\overline{6}$ $\overline{7}$ $\overline{8}$ $\overline{9}$ $\overline{10}$

CALL TO ORDER

VISUAL ◆ LOGIC

WEEK 42

In what order should these figures be placed so that they are arranged from simplest to the most complete?

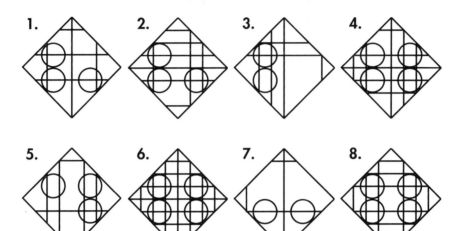

ROUND TRIP

VISUAL ◆ LOGIC

When this puzzle has been completed correctly, you will have made a round trip through its set of dots. You must visit every dot exactly once, make no diagonal moves, and return to your starting point. Parts of the right path are shown; can you find the rest?

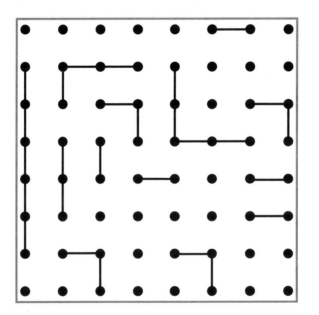

ALL IN A ROW

Directions for solving are on page 258. This time, look for the most groups of consecutive numbers adding up to 10.

A. 1 2 3 9 7 1 2 6 1 9 2 2 2 2 2 5 3 1 1 6 1 8 1 2

B. 1 1 1 7 2 5 3 3 3 3 1 8 2 5 9 2 8 1 3 3 4 4 1 1

C. 1 9 2 9 1 8 1 5 6 2 1 1 6 7 2 2 2 4 1 3 4 6 5 5

VISUAL ◆ SPATIAL

COUNT THE TRIANGLES

To solve this puzzle, write down the three letters that describe each triangle in this figure. We found 50 triangles; how many can you locate?

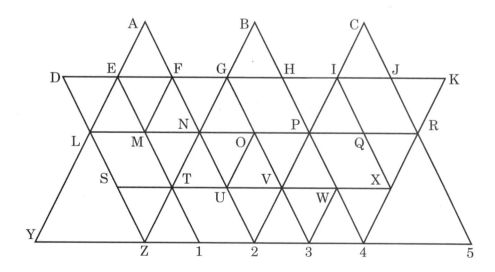

EASY PICKINGS

LANGUAGE

Solving directions are on page 257. This time the remaining letters will spell out a thought.

HO AO EM ER   NI ST   TR EH EC

SJ OW NE EH RT EA MS TE   TB RY PA EI

ON SF   HT ME AW ZV EI VN.

ELIMINATION

LANGUAGE

Directions for solving are on page 279. Once again, the remaining words will form a thought.

MASTERPIECE AS PRINCESS APARTMENT DUCK
WE SUSCEPTABLE COAT TOOTHBRUSH CHASE
SOUP CURIOSITY DORMITORY JOY JACKET
HORSE KILLED WE EARL HOUSE MANUEVER MAY
BOOKSHELF FEATHERS RUN THE PARKA PAST
INNOCULATION HAPPINESS BARON CAT

Eliminate…

1. compound words.

2. words that are outer garments.

3. the words that form the saying that means "inquisitiveness dispatched a particular feline member."

4. titles of British royalty.

5. misspelled words.

6. places to reside in.

7. a two-word Marx Brothers movie and then another two-word movie also with the Marx Brothers.

STACKED UP

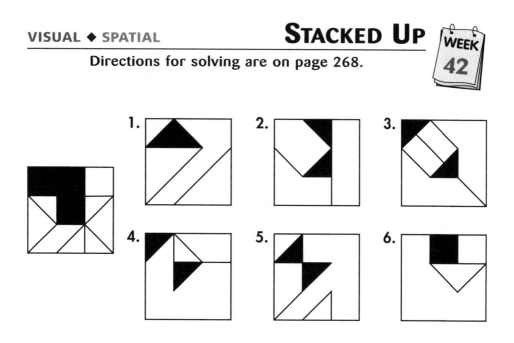

Directions for solving are on page 268.

WEEK 42

LANGUAGE

WORD WHEEL

Starting with the "P" at the arrow, see how many everyday words of three or more letter you can find going clockwise. Don't skip over any letters. For example, if you saw the letters C, A, R, E, D, you would form five words: CAR, CARE, CARED, ARE, RED. We found 28 words.

ONLINE NETWORK

Directions for solving are on page 264.

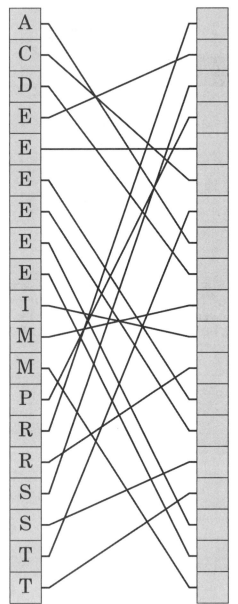

ASSOCIATIONS

Directions for solving are on page 276.

HOW DO RABBITS TRAVEL?

LIME   RADICAL   BALLET   IMPAIR   YOGA   THUMB

HEAVY   SYDNEY   ARTICLE   LEMON   FOREFINGER

RADIANT   SLEEPY   DEFEAT   ETCH   EXTREME   PINKIE

PASTURE   COLLAPSE   DAMAGE   VANQUISH   INJURE

DROWSY   LUCKY   PERTH   AVERAGE   ORANGE   CRASH

NATURE   CONQUER   TIRED   CANBERRA   ULTRA

EMPTY   FALL

DEDUCTION PROBLEM

Three neighbors have companion canines that they care for. Each person has a different dog. The pets have their favorite toys that they like to chew on and play with; no two enjoy the same kind of plaything (one often has a doll clutched between its teeth). Also, each critter wears a different colored collar. From this information and the clues below, can you determine each dog's owner, plaything, and collar color?

1. The beagle likes to chew on a piece of rope.

2. Andrew's dog does not play with an old shoe.

3. The three dogs are the one owned by Sarah, the critter with the red collar, and the collie.

4. The collie does not have a green collar.

5. Lisa (whose dog does not wear a brown collar) does not own a terrier.

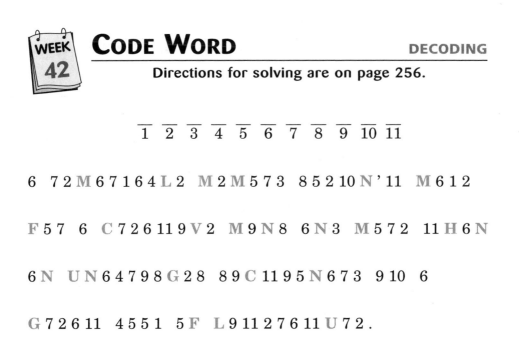

CODE WORD

DECODING

Directions for solving are on page 256.

$$\overline{1} \ \overline{2} \ \overline{3} \ \overline{4} \ \overline{5} \ \overline{6} \ \overline{7} \ \overline{8} \ \overline{9} \ \overline{10} \ \overline{11}$$

6 7 2 M 6 7 1 6 4 L 2 M 2 M 5 7 3 8 5 2 10 N ' 11 M 6 1 2

F 5 7 6 C 7 2 6 11 9 V 2 M 9 N 8 6 N 3 M 5 7 2 11 H 6 N

6 N U N 6 4 7 9 8 G 2 8 8 9 C 11 9 5 N 6 7 3 9 10 6

G 7 2 6 11 4 5 5 1 5 F L 9 11 2 7 6 11 U 7 2 .

FUN WITH FACTS AND FIGURES

MATH

Directions for solving are on page 266.

1. Take the number of consonants in the word PATROL and divide by the number of vowels in the word. _____

2. Next, multiply by the number of legs on a spider. _____

3. Now, add the number gamblers aim for in a game of blackjack. _____

4. Subtract the number of babies in a group that is comprised of three sets of twins, two sets of triplets, and two sets of quadruplets. _____

5. Add the only number between 30 and 40 that is divisible by seven. _____

Our answer is the number of weeks in a year. *Is yours?*

ARROW MAZE

Directions for solving are on page 263.

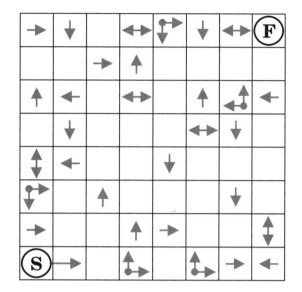

LANGUAGE

DOVETAILED WORDS

Directions for solving are on page 263.

1. C M I E D N D T L E E R _____ _____

2. T S A L R M O O U N T _____ _____

3. A S F G H H A A W N L _____ _____

4. D S H E E P R U T I F Y F _____ _____

5. L T U A D R L E E E N _____ _____

"There are two worlds: the world that we can measure with line and rule, and the world that we feel with our hearts and imaginations."
— *Leigh Hunt*

CIRCLE MATH

MATH

Each overlapping circle is identified by a letter having a different number value from 1 to 9. Where some circles overlap, there is a number: It is the SUM of the values of the letters in those overlapping circles. Can you figure out the correct values for the letters? As a starting help, E = 6.

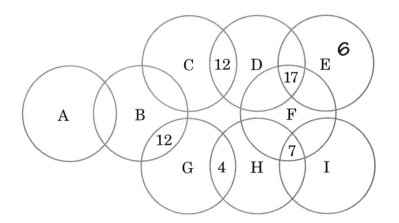

WHAT'S YOUR NUMBER?

MATH ◆ LOGIC

Can you figure out the relationship of each word and number group and, based on that, what missing number goes into the space with the question mark?

SEVEN	TEN	ELEVEN
5	3	6

SEVENTY	FOUR	FOURTEEN
7	4	?

ANAGRAM MAZE

Directions for solving are on page 257. This time, there are 17 words to anagram and the first word you'll be anagramming is ROSE.

1 BEAN	**2** ROSE	**3** UNDO	**4** WISH	**5** ZINC	**6** JUMP
7 BOSS	**8** CLAP	**9** TERM	**10** CASK	**11** DIET	**12** POLE
13 DUES	**14** COLA	**15** FOUL	**16** NEST	**17** MICE	**18** FARE
19 PIGS	**20** INCH	**21** HOSE	**22** APES	**23** DANK	**24** MUSH
25 CLIP	**26** BANG	**27** LOOK	**28** WHOM	**29** CORK	**30** MEAT
31 FERN	**32** HURT	**33** MUSE	**34** KIWI	**35** BUSH	**36** LOOM

WORD VISIBILITY

Directions for solving are on page 276.

1. D E W O T
   T I B I M

2. C O P R F
   H L A D D

3. F L N S O
   P E I N Y

4. B H G C T
   R U O L E

5. V I B V H
   C E R W E

6. P O T P K
   R A U O R

VISION QUEST

VISUAL

Find the row or column that contains
five DIFFERENT train cars.

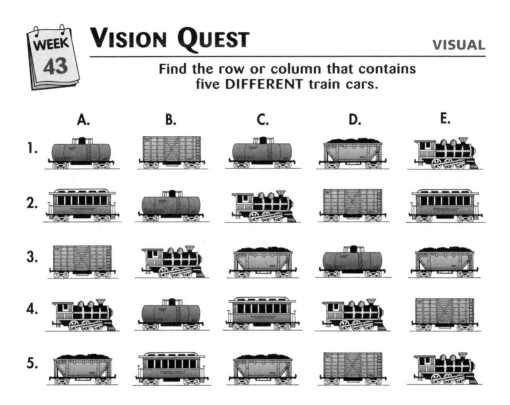

SEVEN WORD ZINGER

LANGUAGE

Directions for solving are on page 267.

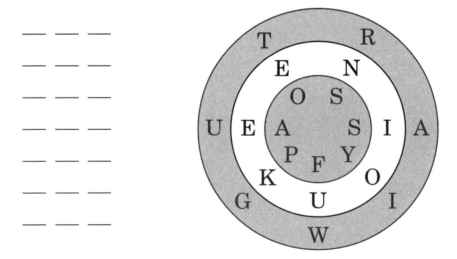

WAYWORDS

Directions for solving are on page 261. This time you'll be looking for a 9-word thought beginning with SAY.

VARIETY	PLEASURE	SHOULD	WHAT
OTHERS	WHAT	NOT	YOU
YOU	AND	SAY	JUST
CONSIST	MUST	NOTHING	GROUND

LANGUAGE

WORD CHARADE

Directions for solving are on page 258.

My first letter is surrounded by an 8-letter word, reading clockwise, composed of letters from the second half of the alphabet.

My second letter appears three times in one of the columns.

My third letter is to the immediate left or immediate right of my second letter wherever it appears.

My fourth letter appears only in the top half of the diagram.

My fifth letter is the only letter from the first half of the alphabet in one of the rows.

My sixth letter is directly below an L and to the immediate right of a W.

J	V	A	Y	K	Q	G	B
K	P	U	C	M	O	B	D
R	W	L	Z	V	X	P	U
O	M	R	N	S	P	F	A
G	K	B	U	C	R	J	Y
D	X	M	O	N	O	M	S
M	O	C	L	Z	B	K	N
F	A	W	Y	Q	O	M	V

— — — — — —

FIGURE FUN

VISUAL ◆ MATH

Each of the four geometric figures equals a number. Can you figure out which number each represents?

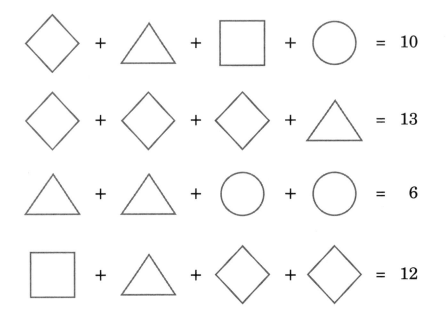

SLIDE RULE

LANGUAGE

Directions for solving are on page 270. Here, you're to form 4-letter words. We found 21 words, including MATE.

Your list of words:

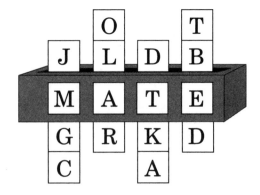

ALPHABET CIRCLE MAZE

Start at A at the bottom, continue through the alphabet only once, and finish at the Z in the center. You will pass through other letters when going from one letter to the next, but move in only one direction, either around a circle or along a spoke. Don't enter or cross through the Z until you are finished.

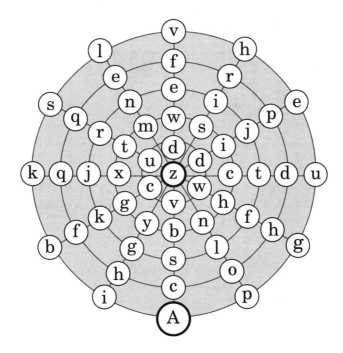

COMPOUND IT

Directions for solving are on page 266.

1. sun, grand, boy, tree

2. shine, house, father, friend

3. land, ship, boat, nap

4. slide, lord, mate, mark

5. down, crash, point, show

6. stream, turn, wind, vane

7. mill, fall, pipe, stop

8. stone, day, load, out

9. board, field, doors, let

10. pad, course, room, zone

SUDOKU

LOGIC

Directions for solving are on page 255.

9	3		4			8		
	5		7				3	
				1	3	9		5
	7				9	3		4
		3		6		5		
8		1	3				2	
3		7	5	8				
	2				1		5	
		9			4		8	7

IN THE ABSTRACT

VISUAL ◆ SPATIAL

Directions for solving are on page 259.

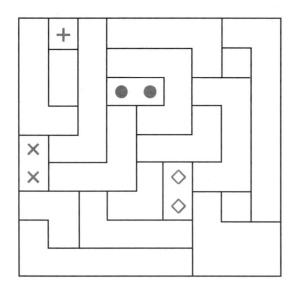

302

GOING IN CIRCLES

Directions for solving are on page 265.

1.

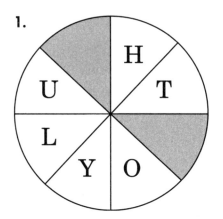

2.

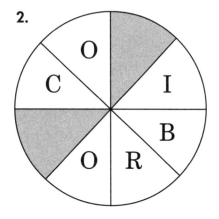

HEXAGON HUNT

Directions for solving are on page 256.

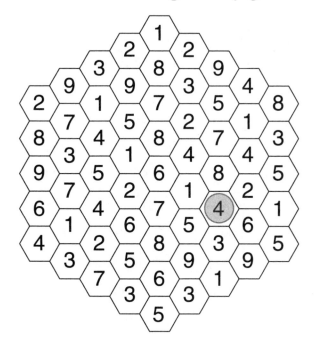

LETTER, PLEASE

DECODING

The numbers below stand for certain letters on the telephone dial. You will see that one number may stand for more than one letter — for example, 3 may be D, E, or F. By finding the correct letter for each number, you will have spelled out a thought.

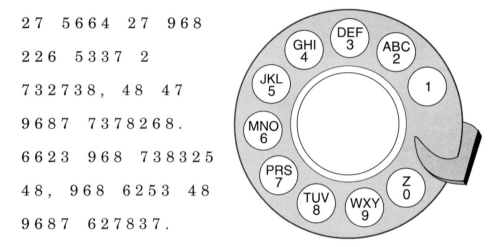

27   5664   27   968

226   5337   2

732738,   48   47

9687   7378268.

6623   968   738325

48,   968   6253   48

9687   627837.

CROSS EXAMINATION

LANGUAGE

In each set, cross out three groups of letters, so that the remaining four groups, in order, spell out a word.

1. PA   CLAD   REN   THES   ONE   IS   EL
2. BUSH   EL   ON   EC   OLA   TRI   CIAN
3. THER   ULT   MO   VERN   AT   ME   TER
4. HAR   DENT   IM   PSI   CH   AIN   ORD
5. CAT   HERN   AS   IC   TRO   PHE   NET
6. ST   AG   ELO   RIC   ULT   IRAN   URE
7. ME   SA   TROP   PER   OLIT   ICE   AN
8. PA   IN   DETA   VE   STI   RON   GATE

RELATIONSHIPS QUIZ

Directions for solving are on page 274.

1. HARSH is to GENTLE as BENEATH is to _____.
   (a) behind   (b) over   (c) under   (d) after

2. WATER is to HYDROGEN as SALT is to _____.
   (a) oxygen   (b) pepper   (c) sodium   (d) sailor

3. SCALES is to SNAKE as KEYS is to _____.
   (a) open   (b) exam   (c) fingers   (d) piano

4. DELICATESSEN is to SANDWICH as BOUTIQUE is to
   _____.
   (a) skirt   (b) spaghetti   (c) layer   (d) trendy

5. RUSTIC is to COUNTRY as URBAN is to _____.
   (a) cosmopolitan   (b) farm   (c) skyscraper   (d) city

VISUAL ◆ LOGIC

STAR WORDS

Directions for solving are on page 278.

DRUM   MEAT

FARM   REAM

FUEL   TEAR

LAUD   TURF

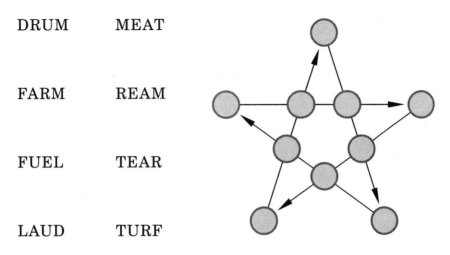

ANIMAL CHARADES

LANGUAGE

Directions for solving are on page 269.

My FIRST is in JACKAL and in CLASS;   _____

My SECOND is in GOLDFISH and in GLASS;   _____

My THIRD is in FLAMINGO but not in GAME;   _____

My FOURTH is in LION but not in NAME;   _____

My FIFTH is in IGUANA and in MAGIC;   _____

My SIXTH is in WOMBAT and in TRAGIC;   _____

My SEVENTH is in EGRET but not in DRUG;   _____

My EIGHTH is in TROUT but not in SHRUG;   _____

My NINTH is in PORCUPINE and in DROUGHT.   _____

My WHOLE is a reptile with a considerable snout.

_____

CHANGELINGS

LANGUAGE

Can you change the first word into the second word by changing only one letter at a time? Do not rearrange the order of the letters with each change. Each change must result in an everyday word, and words beginning with a capital letter, slang, or obsolete words aren't allowed.

1. GOLD

2. HARD

3. PULL

_____   _____   _____

_____   _____   _____

_____   _____   _____

FOIL   SEAT   HAIR
(4 changes)   (4 changes)   (4 changes)

TARGET SHOOT

WEEK 44

Directions for solving are on page 259.

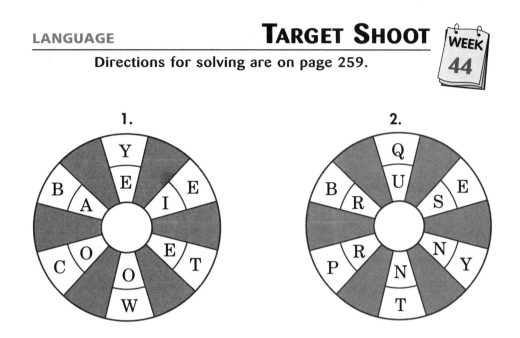

1.

2.

SYMBOL-ISM

Directions for solving are on page 275. For this puzzle, we've indicated that ← = F.

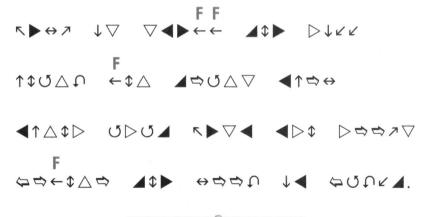

"Learning sleeps and snores in libraries, but wisdom is everywhere, wide awake, on tiptoe." — Josh Billings

CIRCLE SEARCH

LANGUAGE

Directions for solving are on page 262. Here you're looking to form 15 words of at least three letters.

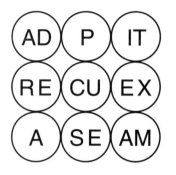

SWITCHEROO

DECODING

In each group, for the first word and its number equivalent given, determine what the number equivalent is for the second word.

1. LAST is to 1324 as SALT is to:
   (a) 2341 (b) 3214 (c) 2314 (d) 2134

2. MALE is to 6345 as LAME is to:
   (a) 5364 (b) 4635 (c) 3465 (d) 4365

3. WANE is to 5790 as ANEW is to:
   (a) 7905 (b) 9705 (c) 7095 (d) 7950

4. BEAN is to 8213 as BANE is to:
   (a) 8123 (b) 8213 (c) 8231 (d) 8132

5. GORE is to 6395 as OGRE is to:
   (a) 3965 (b) 3695 (c) 6395 (d) 9635

6. NUTS is to 7503 as STUN is to:
   (a) 3075 (b) 3507 (c) 3057 (d) 3750

7. HEAR is to 6918 as HARE is to:
   (a) 6189 (b) 6981 (c) 6198 (d) 6819

8. ATOM is to 5032 as MOAT is to:
   (a) 3250 (b) 2305 (c) 2530 (d) 2350

TIPS OF THE ICEBERG

WEEK 45

We're back at the Iceberg Diner. After doing some addition, answer the following questions:

1. Who made the most in total tips?
2. Who made the least?
3. Which two waitpersons made exactly the same amount?

EMPLOYEE	TIP 1	TIP 2	TIP 3	TIP 4	TIP 5
Hank	$2.10	$2.85	$1.50	$1.60	$1.80
Inez	$1.15	$2.95	$2.10	$2.60	$2.00
Jack	$1.80	$1.80	$1.75	$2.45	$1.00
Ken	$2.50	$2.35	$2.15	$2.05	$2.00
Laura	$1.00	$4.35	$0.90	$0.85	$4.00
Marty	$2.60	$1.35	$1.90	$2.00	$2.00
Noel	$0.90	$1.85	$1.80	$1.40	$3.00

WEEK 45 ZANY ZONES

LANGUAGE

Rearrange the letters in each nonsensical phrase to form a U.S. capital and its state.

1. AXIS ATE NUTS   _____ _____

2. SOAKS TEAK PAN   _____ _____

3. EMU SAT IGUANA   _____ _____

4. NOBLE YANK WARY   _____ _____

5. HEAT LONE MANNA   _____ _____

6. WINS DISCO MANSION   _____ _____

7. LIKE THAT CASUALTY   _____ _____

8. SHOUTS COMBAT ASSENTS   _____ _____

THE LINEUP

LANGUAGE

Directions for solving are on page 277.

XYBJTUCKPCLARINETZVIEWGSHOULDQMATH

1. Which letter of the alphabet does not appear in the lineup? _____

2. What 8-letter word — with its letters in correct order and appearing together — can you find in the lineup? _____

3. Which letter of the alphabet appears exactly three times in the lineup? _____

4. What 6-letter word — with its letters in correct order and appearing together — can you find in the lineup? _____

5. Other than the answers to Questions 2 and 4, how many everyday words — with their letters in correct order and appearing together — of four or more letters can you find in the lineup? _____

TRI, TRI AGAIN

WEEK 45

Directions for solving are on page 268.

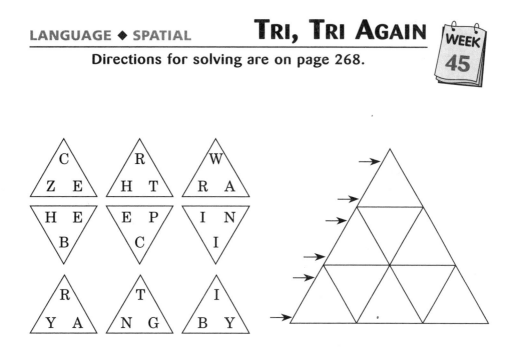

WORD HUNT

Directions for solving are on page 272. This time, you'll be searching for 4-letter words that begin with V (such as VINE). We found 24 words, including VINE.

I	M	S	N	T
N	A	T	E	E
L	W	V	O	R
Y	A	E	I	L
B	R	N	D	T

Your list of words:

RINGERS

Directions for solving are on page 281.

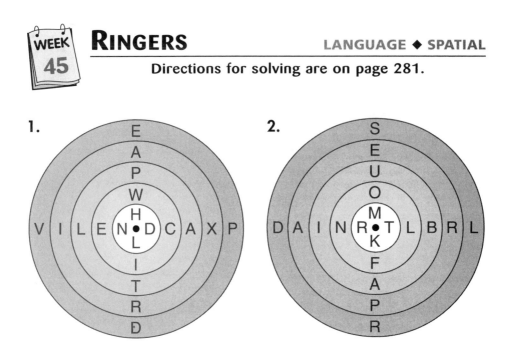

1.

2.

ROUND TRIP

Directions for solving are on page 288.

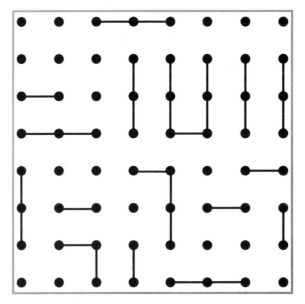

ALPHABET SOUP

Cross off each letter from the alphabet list that appears in the larger group of letters. Then rearrange the letters not crossed out to form the name of a country.

U	F	P	R	N	O	F	R	U	O	Z	P	N	R	U	Z
R	Z	N	D	K	X	D	O	F	W	C	F	N	P	X	C
W	P	C	F	S	V	R	Z	D	W	X	M	F	V	K	O
M	Z	K	D	Q	V	B	G	W	H	C	J	Q	B	E	N

A B C D E F G H I J K L M N O P Q R S T U V W X Y Z

Country: _____

LANGUAGE

SLIDE RULE

Directions for solving are on page 270. Here, you're to form 4-letter words. We found 28 words, including TRAP.

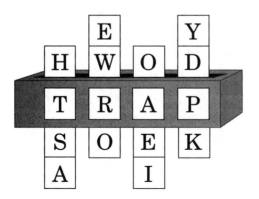

Your list of words:

COUNT TO TEN

VISUAL ◆ MATH

Examine the snowflakes and raindrops and then answer these questions: 1. Which row contains the most snowflakes? 2. Which row contains the most raindrops? 3. Which row contains an equal number of snowflakes and raindrops?

1.
2.
3.
4.
5.
6.
7.
8.
9.
10.

RING LOGIC

LOGIC

Directions for solving are on page 262.

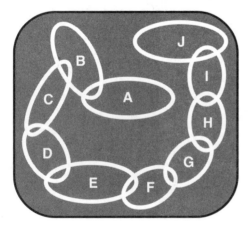

1. Rings A and J are linked once and every other ring is linked twice.

2. The bottom of rings A and E are to the front.

3. The left side of ring H is to the front.

WORD CHARADE

Directions for solving are on page 258.

WEEK 45

My first letter appears only in the third, fourth, and fifth rows.

My second letter appears once in each row and column.

My third letter appears more often than any other letter.

My fourth letter appears only in the fifth column.

My fifth letter appears only once in the diagram.

K	E	C	N	A	S	E	E
D	N	L	E	B	M	C	W
F	Q	I	C	D	N	D	J
C	Z	E	W	X	I	E	T
E	G	I	D	C	A	F	X
Z	O	S	E	Q	K	E	C
X	M	Z	D	B	C	L	F
W	C	N	E	T	J	G	M

My sixth letter is the only letter from the second half of the alphabet in one of the rows.

—— —— —— —— —— ——

WORD VISIBILITY

Directions for solving are on page 276.

1. F I E C N
   B R N L H

2. C H A I O
   P U R M B

3. N D W E M
   I A I O D

4. S R I N Y
   Y A C G T

5. A W K D L
   V O F U G

6. L N F S C
   D O E T Y

MISSING DOMINOES

VISUAL ◆ LOGIC

Directions for solving are on page 273.

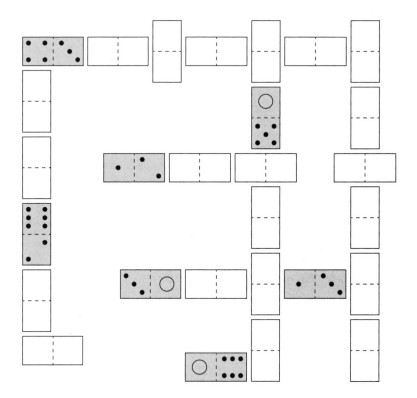

DOMINOES

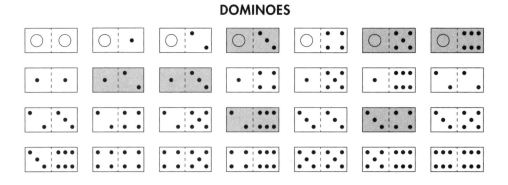

316

LOOSE TILE

WEEK 46

The tray on the right seemed the ideal place to store the set of loose dominoes. Unfortunately, when the tray was full, one domino was left over. Determine the arrangement of the dominoes in the tray and which is the Loose Tile.

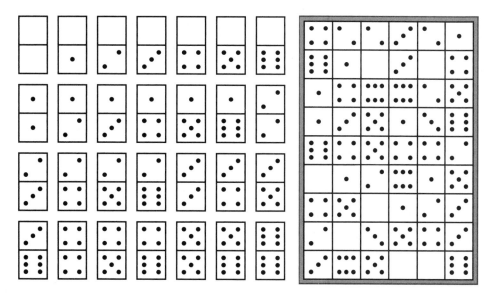

LANGUAGE

LICENSE PLATES

Each box contains six letters of the first and last name of a celebrity chef. The top three are a part of the first name and the bottom three are a part of the last name, in order.

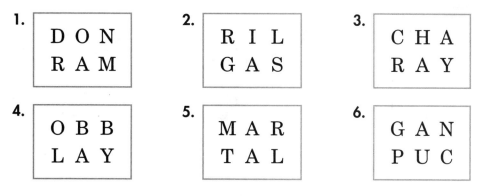

1.
D O N
R A M

2.
R I L
G A S

3.
C H A
R A Y

4.
O B B
L A Y

5.
M A R
T A L

6.
G A N
P U C

CARD SENSE

LOGIC

Directions for solving are on page 270.

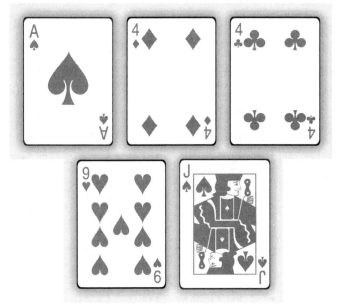

1. All three black cards are above the red cards.

2. The fours are adjacent.

3. The ace isn't on top of the pile.

WHAT'S YOUR NUMBER?

MATH ◆ LOGIC

Can you figure out the relationship of each group of numbers and, based on that, what missing number goes into the space with the question mark?

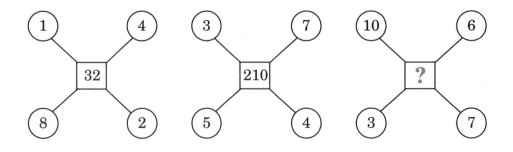

ANAGRAM MAZE

WEEK
46

Directions for solving are on page 257. This time, there are 19 words to anagram and the first word you'll be anagramming is DUST.

1 DUST	2 ONCE	3 NODE	4 LEAK	5 CHAR	6 MALT
7 LILY	8 LESS	9 BEAU	10 CELL	11 WARY	12 HAVE
13 GRIT	14 FANG	15 ISLE	16 COAT	17 VEER	18 MAKE
19 AFAR	20 LIFE	21 TILL	22 TINY	23 KNOW	24 OXEN
25 MINK	26 VOTE	27 MAZE	28 WHAT	29 ANTE	30 SALT
31 HOOT	32 ODES	33 ROBE	34 LEGS	35 WOOL	36 BOWL

LANGUAGE

WAYWORDS

Directions for solving are on page 261. This time you'll be looking for an 11-word thought beginning with EVERY.

IS	PERSON	EVERY	BEST
A	PROBLEM	OUR	LATE
CHANCE	WOBBLE	US	DO
DESIST	FOR	FROWN	TO

BULL'S-EYE LETTER

LANGUAGE

Directions for solving are on page 261.

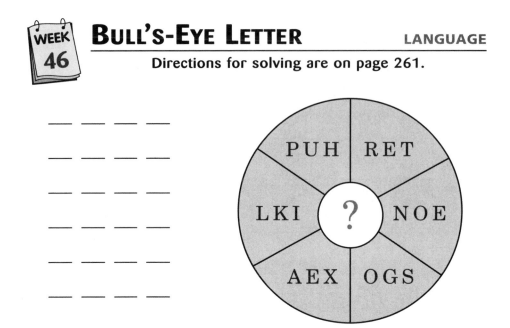

PUH | RET
LKI | ? | NOE
AEX | OGS

VISION QUEST

VISUAL

Find the row or column that contains five DIFFERENT hair care products.

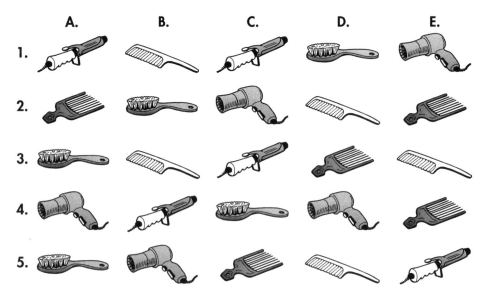

A.   B.   C.   D.   E.

1.
2.
3.
4.
5.

GETTING IN SHAPE

Which two boxes contain the same 12 shapes?

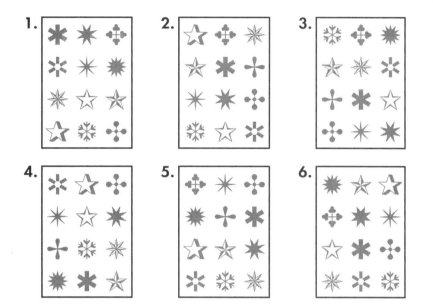

SEVEN WORD ZINGER

Directions for solving are on page 267.

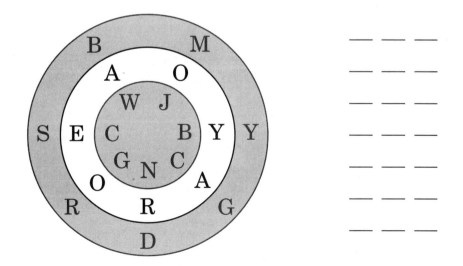

ANTONYMS QUIZ

LANGUAGE

Directions for solving are on page 280.

1. TEDIUM   a. plentitude   b. probity   c. excitement

2. EXQUISITE   a. crude   b. languorous   c. prospective

3. FORTHRIGHT   a. devious   b. thriving   c. fetching

4. DISHEVELED   a. hostile   b. dapper   c. forlorn

5. AVID   a. indifferent   b. aggregate   c. versant

6. IMPARTIALITY a. profusion   b. injunction   c. bias

7. PROGRESSIVE   a. enthralling   b. decorous   c. conventional

8. PREVALENT   a. rare   b. vehement   c. brash

BLOCK PARTY

VISUAL ◆ SPATIAL

Directions for solving are on page 286.

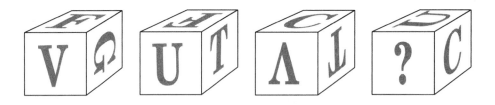

"It is important that students bring a certain ragamuffin, barefoot irreverence to their studies; they are not here to worship what is known, but to question it."

— *Jacob Bronowski*

MAGNIFIND

WEEK 47

Figure out which areas of the drawing have been enlarged.

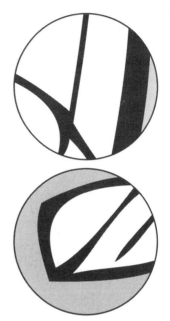

QUICK FILL

Directions for solving are on page 254.

A   A   E   E   G   I   N   R   T   V

1. Letter 1 is a consonant.
2. In some order, letters 3, 7, and 9 (which is a vowel) spell out a word meaning a tattered cloth.
3. Letter 4 appears elsewhere in the word.
4. In the alphabet, letter 7 is four letters after letter 10.
5. Letters 6, 5, and 2, in order, spell out a word meaning consumed food.
6. Letter 8 is a vowel.

$$\overline{1} \; \overline{2} \; \overline{3} \; \overline{4} \; \overline{5} \; \overline{6} \; \overline{7} \; \overline{8} \; \overline{9} \; \overline{10}$$

Z COUNT

VISUAL

Directions for solving are on page 255. This time, see how many Z's you can count in the sentence.

DIZZY LIZZIE BUZZI IS

DAZZLED AND FRAZZLED

BY THE PIZAZZ OF OZZIE ABRUZZI'S

JAZZY PUZZLES AND

SNAZZY QUIZZES IN THE

ZANZIBAR GAZETTE.

LETTER, PLEASE

DECODING

Directions for solving are on page 304.

2 626 946 92687

86 4283 447

326459 8733

872233 746853

5878 46 4686

76548427 263

4283 447

677663687 36

48 367 446.

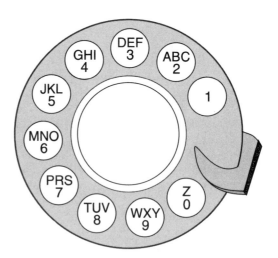

ONLINE NETWORK

Directions for solving are on page 264.

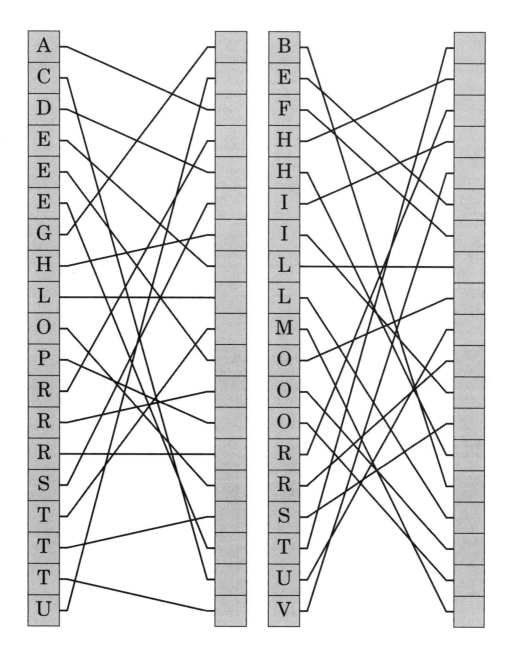

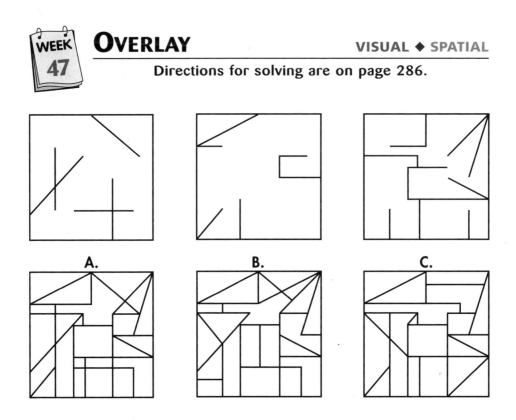

OVERLAY

VISUAL ◆ SPATIAL

Directions for solving are on page 286.

A.   B.   C.

MAGIC NUMBER SQUARE

MATH

Directions for solving are on page 287. Once again, fill in the rows, columns, and diagonals so that each one adds up to 65.

1 2 3 4 5 6 7 8 9 10 11 12 13 14 15 16 17 18 19 20 21 22 23 24 25

6	10			2
			14	19
17	21		5	
	12			
24			16	20

326

MATH

ALL IN A ROW

WEEK
47

Directions for solving are on page 258. This time, look for the most groups of consecutive numbers adding up to 11.

A. 6 2 2 3 5 7 1 2 1 9 1 3 6 1 8 4 4 5 3 9 6 2 1 2

B. 4 8 2 6 5 1 9 3 4 1 3 7 4 5 1 2 8 1 9 3 5 3 4 6

C. 1 1 2 6 3 4 8 2 5 4 1 1 7 6 2 4 8 1 4 2 4 5 3 1

VISUAL

COUNTDOWN

Directions for solving are on page 254.

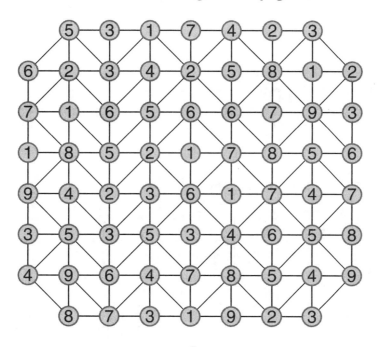

"The soul without imagination is what an observatory would be without a telescope."
                                    — *Henry Ward Beecher*

HEXAGON HUNT

VISUAL

Directions for solving are on page 256.

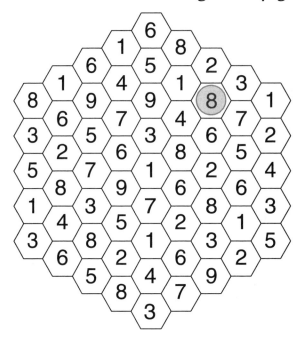

KEEP ON MOVING

VISUAL

Directions for solving are on page 269. Here, start in the shaded square with the number 4.

5	2	5	5	1	4
4	2	3	2	4	3
3	2	1	1	3	1
✳	2	2	3	2	4
2	1	3	4	4	3
3	3	1	1	5	4

EASY PICKINGS

To solve, simply cross out one letter in each pair below. When the puzzle is completed correctly, the remaining letters will spell out a truism.

PR EO OG AP DR DL WL EI ST HS

OG FC   TA OH ER   PS AE AS ET,

YN SO EU   MT NA YA   RH AW MV EC

HA   SI IP VO TR GL EG SA YS

FH GU GT US GR ED.

LANGUAGE ◆ VISUAL

GRAND TOUR

Directions for solving are on page 275. This time, you'll be look-ing for a chain of 5-letter words, start-ing with UN-CLE-AN (uncle, clean).

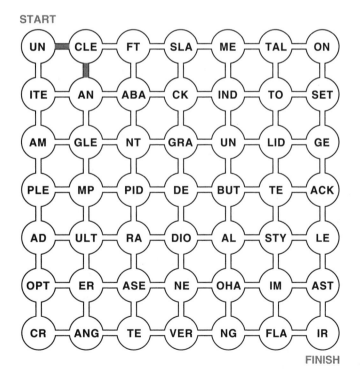

ASSOCIATIONS

VISUAL ◆ SPATIAL

Directions for solving are on page 276.

WHAT'S THE BEST CURE FOR INSOMNIA?

ANGER SKILLFUL GRACE AVOID CAFE OPULENT

LAOS OVEN SHUN TERRIBLE DRINK KING

NEGATIVE EMPHASIZE EVADE ITCH RUBBISH

GRASS STRESS EMPEROR HAMSTER THAILAND

TRICK DREADFUL CAMBODIA STEEPLE TRASH

EXPERT SCAMPER ACCENTUATE LAZY CZAR

EPIC RESTAURANT AWFUL EAGLE GARBAGE

PROFICIENT PARTNER DINER

IN THE ABSTRACT

VISUAL ◆ SPATIAL

Directions for solving are on page 259.

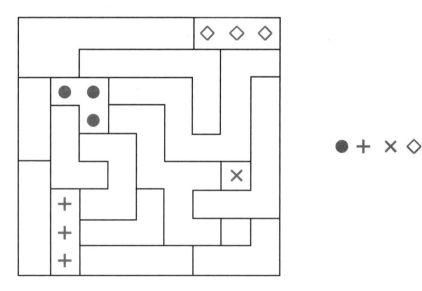

QUOTATION MARKS

Enter the capital letters in the diagram as indicated by the number-letter combinations to form a quote by Jerry Seinfeld. For example, one of the D's should be placed in the box where column 3 and row f intersect.

	1	2	3	4	5	6	7	8	9	10	11	12
a												
b												
c												
d												
e												
f												
g												
h												
i												

A: 7a, 9a, 5b, 12b, 5d, 9d, 12f, 3g, 6g, 12g, 8i

C: 1h

D: 3f, 11f

E: 10b, 11c, 12d, 9e, 5f, 7f, 10g, 1i, 4i, 10i

F: 8c, 6h

G: 1b

H: 4b, 9b, 4d, 8d, 8e, 12h

I: 3a, 11a, 4e, 7h

L: 2f, 4g, 3h

M: 8a, 1c

N: 12a, 4c, 10c, 1e, 5e, 3i

O: 2c, 7c, 12e

P: 10d, 11d, 7i, 9i

R: 1f, 8f, 11i

S: 5a, 1d, 2e, 8g, 9h, 6i

T: 4a, 3b, 6b, 8b, 5c, 3d, 6d, 7e, 2h, 8h, 11h

U: 3c

V: 6f

W: 12c, 11e, 5g, 5i

X: 11g

Y: 9f, 1g, 7g, 4h

Z: 10a

ARROW MAZE

VISUAL

Directions for solving are on page 263.

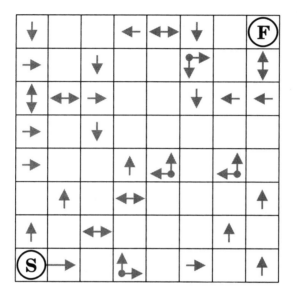

CODE WORD

DECODING

Directions for solving are on page 256.

$$\overline{1} \ \overline{2} \ \overline{3} \ \overline{4} \ \overline{5} \ \overline{6} \ \overline{7} \ \overline{8} \ \overline{9} \ \overline{10} \ \overline{11}$$

H 8 M 6 10 6 1 11   69   4   V 6 R 1 8 2   1 H 4 1   M 4 3 11

M 4 11   P R 2 4 5 H   4 3 D   F 2 W   W 6 10 10

P R 4 5 1 6 5 2;   H 7 W 2 V 2 R,   6 1 ' 9   9 7 M 2 1 H 6 3 G

1 H 4 1   2 V 2 R 1 1 7 3 2   69   H 4 P P 11   1 7   H 2 4 R

1 H 4 1   7 1 H 2 R 9   P 7 9 9 2 9 9.

CROSS-UPS

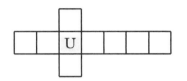
WEEK
48

Using only the letters given above each diagram, fill in the boxes in such a way that an everyday compound word is formed, one part reading across and the other part reading down. The letter already in the diagram is a letter shared by both parts of the word. Note: Each part of the compound word is an entire word on its own.

1. A D D L P R S T

2. B E G H S T T R

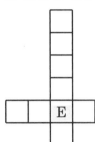

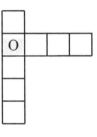

3. E E P R R V W

4. A E M P O T T R

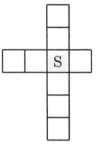

DOVETAILED WORDS

Directions for solving are on page 263.

1. Q P R U O O V T E E R B   _____ _____

2. D C R O A M M E A D Y   _____ _____

3. P T R O E P N U L D A Y R   _____ _____

4. Z B I P U P T E T O R N   _____ _____

5. O T U R L C H I I D P   _____ _____

"Tell me and I'll forget; show me and I may remember; involve me and I'll understand." — *Chinese proverb*

333

COMPOUND IT

 LANGUAGE

Directions for solving are on page 266.

1. take, mouse, count, flood

2. gate, water, trap, down

3. weight, front, color, melon

4. blind, fast, less, gift

5. more, bet, side, basket

6. step, swipe, track, neat

7. ladder, mother, brush, child

8. proof, like, hood, meat

9. read, wink, wise, canal

10. person, crack, need, sign

ELIMINATION

LANGUAGE

Directions for solving are on page 279. Once again, the remaining words will form a thought.

APPLE MAKE GRUDGES DEPOT EURO NORTH POTATO AND DAY TENOR HAY SALAD ANGER PESO BY DOCTOR FRIED ONLY PONDER WHILE CHICKEN AWAY GROW THE LIGHT WITH YEN SUN COLD NORTHWEST CONSTANT RODENT SHINES POUND CARE CUTS

Eliminate...

1. the four words that, when placed on the dashes, turn the following into a saying: "An — a — keeps the — —."

2. the words that are formed only from the letters in PORTEND.

3. the words that are the names of money from around the world.

4. the three two-word food items that are often served at picnics.

5. the three-word title of a Cary Grant movie.

6. the word that can follow "stop," "flash," "day," and "lime."

7. the six words that form a saying that means "fabricate provender during a particular span when solar productivity abounds."

CIRCLE MATH

Directions for solving are on page 296. As a starting help, F = 2.

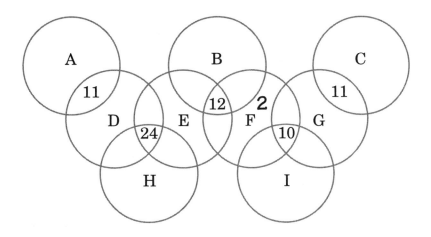

SUDOKU

Directions for solving are on page 255.

	4			7	2			1
		3		6	5			2
7	2							6
	7	9			8		2	
			2		7			
	8		5			9	3	
5							8	4
2			8	5		7		
9			7	1			5	

VISION QUEST

VISUAL

Find the row or column that contains five DIFFERENT lunch items.

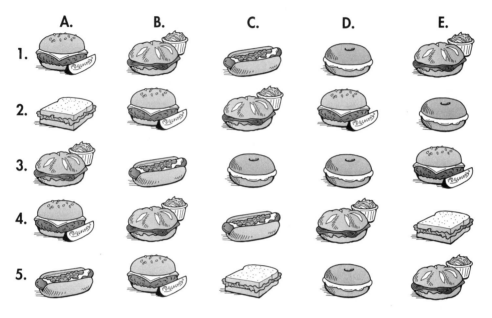

QUICK FILL

LANGUAGE

Determine the 10-letter word from the clues. All the letters in the word are listed.

C C E L M O O R T Y

1. Letter 8 is a consonant and letter 4 is a vowel.

2. In the alphabet, letter 5 is two letters before letter 3, and letter 3 is five letters before letter 7.

3. Letters 10, 9, and 1, in order, spell out the name of a backyard tree.

4. Letter 6 is from the first half of the alphabet and letter 2 is from the second half of the alphabet.

$$\overline{1} \quad \overline{2} \quad \overline{3} \quad \overline{4} \quad \overline{5} \quad \overline{6} \quad \overline{7} \quad \overline{8} \quad \overline{9} \quad \overline{10}$$

ONLINE NETWORK

In each two-column group, take the letters in the left-hand column along the paths (indicated by the lines) and place them in their proper boxes in the right-hand column. When done, for each puzzle you'll find three related words reading down the right-hand column.

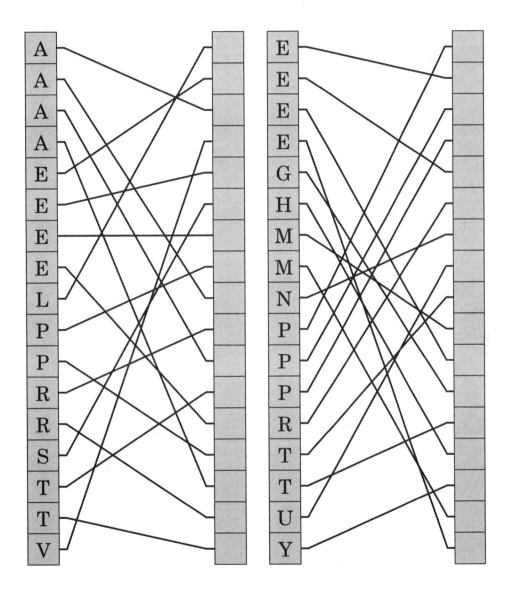

WEEK 49

COUNT TO TEN

 VISUAL ◆ MATH

Examine the chicks and eggs and then answer these questions: 1. Which row contains the most chicks? 2. Which row contains the most eggs? 3. Which row contains an equal number of chicks and eggs?

1.
2.
3.
4.
5.
6.
7.
8.
9.
10.

EASY PICKINGS

LANGUAGE

To solve, simply cross out one letter in each pair below. When the puzzle is completed correctly, the remaining letters will spell out a fact.

ST HN TE   MC AY WP SI TA EA LV

OU MF   DN ET IW   DY OA BR FK

IE HS   CA LG JB AB NX YH.

338

SUDOKU

WEEK 49

Place a number into each box so each row across, column down, and small 9-box square within the larger square (there are 9 of these) contains 1 through 9.

5		6	1				2	
		4		2	3	5	8	
8			5					
	2	1		7	9		5	
				5				
	9		6	3		7	1	
					5			2
	5	8	9	6		4		
	4				8	9		5

LICENSE PLATES

Each box contains six letters of the first and last name of an actor born in Ireland. The top three are a part of the first name and the bottom three are a part of the last name, in order.

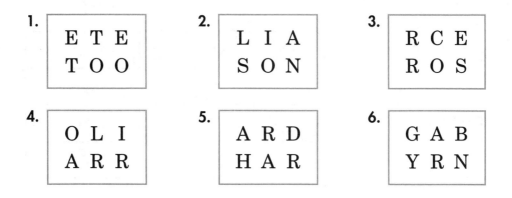

1.
E T E
T O O

2.
L I A
S O N

3.
R C E
R O S

4.
O L I
A R R

5.
A R D
H A R

6.
G A B
Y R N

MAGNIFIND

VISUAL ◆ SPATIAL

Figure out which area of the drawing has been enlarged.

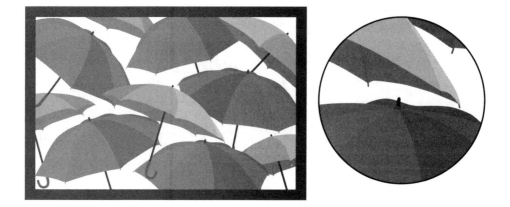

WAYWORDS

LANGUAGE

An 8-word thought can be found beginning with the word **THE**. Then, move to any adjacent box up, down, or diagonally for each following word.

GREATEST	FELLOW	WHO	PROUD
ERROR	THE	SIGHT	UP
EVEN	IN	IS	GIVING
PLEASANT	TRUST	LIFE	DETECT

HEXAGON HUNT

WEEK 49

In this diagram of six-sided figures, there are 10 "special" hexagons. These 10 are special because the six numbers around each one are all different from each other and the center. We've circled one of the 10. Can you find the other 9?

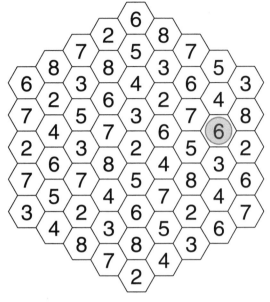

LANGUAGE ◆ VISUAL

ALPHABET SOUP

Cross off each letter from the alphabet list that appears in the larger group of letters. Then rearrange the letters not crossed out to form the name of a fruit.

R	W	K	R	P	W	R	K	P	N	K	P	W	N	R	K
K	Q	K	B	O	R	S	P	G	N	P	W	Q	N	K	U
H	C	Z	C	N	P	Z	H	C	V	G	N	P	W	R	H
T	O	F	X	T	D	A	Z	X	T	O	F	J	Y	Z	Q

A B C D E F G H I J K L M N O P Q R S T U V W X Y Z

Fruit: _____

FUN WITH FACTS AND FIGURES

MATH

This puzzle tests you on a lot of little facts and figures. Solve the quiz in the order given since each answer is used in the next statement. There are no fractions used here.

1. Take the number of wings on a duck and add to that a perfect score in bowling. _____

2. Next, subtract the number of quarters in 50 dollars. _____

3. Now, divide by the number it takes to tango in a familiar expression. _____

4. Multiply by the number of musicians in a quintet. _____

5. Add the value of the Roman numeral CXI. _____

Our answer is the number of days in a leap year. *Is yours?*

TRI, TRI AGAIN

LANGUAGE ◆ SPATIAL

Fit the nine triangles into the big one so six everyday words are spelled out reading across the arrows. Do not rotate the triangles.

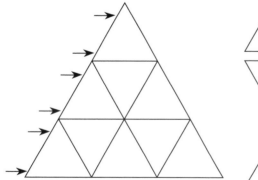
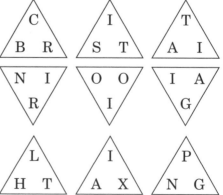

IN THE ABSTRACT

Fill in each section with one of the four symbols so no sections containing the same symbol touch. Four sections are already complete.

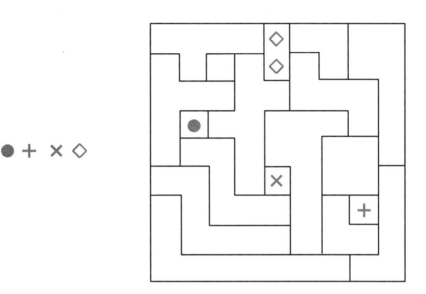

DECODING

CODE WORD

Decipher a truism and the Code Word's eleven letters, represented by the numbers 1 through 11. So, if the Code Word were "THUNDERCLAP," 1 in the truism would be T, 2 would be H, etc.

$$\overline{1}\ \overline{2}\ \overline{3}\ \overline{4}\ \overline{5}\ \overline{6}\ \overline{7}\ \overline{8}\ \overline{9}\ \overline{10}\ \overline{11}$$

11 O M 9   1 9 O 1 L 9   W 6 L L   G 9 3   C 10 9 8 6 3

5 O 10   4 2 V 6 7 G   7 6 C 9   1 9 10 11 O 7 2 L 6 3 6 9 11

W 4 9 7   3 4 9 Y   2 10 9   M 9 10 9 L Y   1 10 O U 8

O 5   3 4 9 6 10   3 9 9 3 4 .

GRAND TOUR

VISUAL ◆ LANGUAGE

Form a continuous chain of 5-letter words moving through the maze from START to FINISH. The second part of one word be-comes the first part of the next word. This puzzle starts with CA-BIN-GO (cabin, bingo).

START

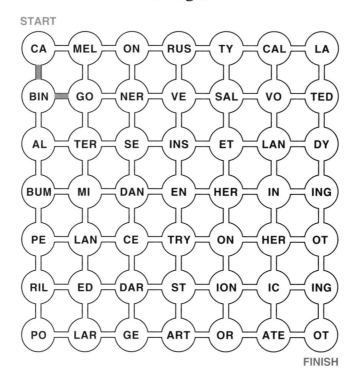

FINISH

SYMBOL-ISM

DECODING

This is simply a Cryptogram that uses symbols instead of letters to spell out a truism. Each symbol stands for the same letter throughout. For this puzzle, we've already indicated that ◇ = R and ✦ = L.

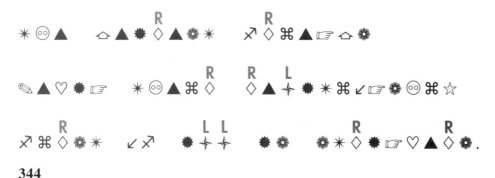

344

TIPS OF THE ICEBERG

WEEK 50

The chart shows the gratuities each waiter or waitress earned on a recent breakfast shift at the Iceberg Diner. All you have to do is some careful addition and then answer the following questions:

1. Who made the most in total tips?
2. Who made the least?
3. Which two waitpersons made exactly the same amount?

EMPLOYEE	TIP 1	TIP 2	TIP 3	TIP 4	TIP 5
Hank	$0.90	$1.95	$1.50	$1.95	$1.10
Inez	$1.20	$1.20	$1.20	$1.80	$1.60
Jack	$0.50	$1.10	$1.10	$2.85	$0.95
Ken	$1.60	$1.00	$1.30	$1.20	$2.00
Laura	$1.00	$2.00	$0.30	$1.45	$0.65
Marty	$1.80	$1.60	$1.20	$1.20	$1.20
Noel	$0.90	$1.10	$2.55	$1.60	$1.00

LOOSE TILE

VISUAL ◆ SPATIAL

The tray on the left seemed the ideal place to store the set of loose dominoes. Unfortunately, when the tray was full, one domino was left over. Determine the arrangement of the dominoes in the tray and which is the Loose Tile.

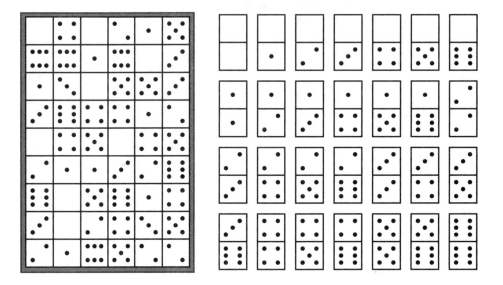

R COUNT

VISUAL

Here's an eye exam that's also an R exam! First, read the sentence below. Next, go back and read the sentence again, but this time count all of the R's. How many are there?

FORTY-THREE OR FORTY-FOUR WARRIORS

REARRANGED THEIR RAGGED ROPES,

COPPER SPEARS, AND IRON ARMOR

BEFORE HURRYING TOWARD THE

SECRET, SHELTERED FORT.

SEVEN WORD ZINGER

Using each letter once, form seven everyday 3-letter words with the first letter coming from the center, the second from the middle, and the third from the outer circle. Your words may differ from ours.

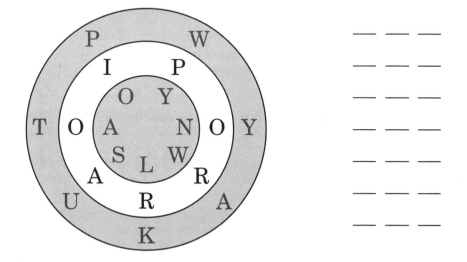

— — —

— — —

— — —

— — —

— — —

— — —

— — —

WHAT'S YOUR NUMBER?

Can you figure out the relationship of the numbers in the figures below and, based on that, what missing number goes into the space with the question mark?

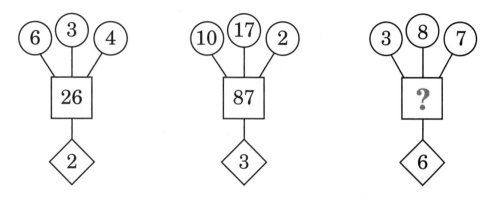

THE LINEUP

LANGUAGE

While scrutinizing the lineup of letters, can you answer the five questions correctly in five minutes or less?

VNZYAXLELIMEWCONNECTEDFITTINGKHJUMPQRST

1. Which letter of the alphabet does not appear in the lineup? _____

2. What 9-letter word — with its letters in correct order and appearing together — can you find in the lineup? _____

3. Which letter of the alphabet appears exactly three times in the lineup? _____

4. What 7-letter word — with its letters in correct order and appearing together — can you find in the lineup? _____

5. Other than the answers to Questions 2 and 4, how many everyday words — with their letters in correct order and appearing together — of four or more letters can you find in the lineup? _____

SKILLS TEST

LANGUAGE

Rearrange each group of letters below to spell out the name of a European nation.

1. AIRMOAN _____

2. ABAILRUG _____

3. MILEBUG _____

4. INABALA _____

5. AIRCOAT _____

U.S. A's

The list below consists of the names of six U.S. states, but we've removed all of their letters except for the A's. Can you write one letter on each dash to complete the names of the states?

1. __ __ __ A __ A

2. __ __ __ A

3. __ A __ __ __ A __ __

4. __ __ __ A __ __ __ A

5. __ A __ __ __

6. __ __ A __ __

ASSOCIATIONS

You'll find eight groups of three words that can be associated in some way with each other (example: mantel, fireplace, logs). Cross out each group as you find it. The initial letters of the remaining words will spell out the answer to the riddle:

WHAT'S SMARTER THAN A TALKING BIRD?

HELP   PRICE   AVERAGE   RECEIVE   COST   SQUIRT

SUITABLE   BERLIN   PANCAKE   AID   COLLEGE

MUNICH ELOPE KITCHEN FLAW LADY UNIVERSITY

BATHROOM   LEVER   DEFECT   GET   INCH   SCHOOL

PROPER   NERVOUS   ASSIST   FRANKFURT   GLAD

EXPENSE BARGAIN BASEMENT ENOUGH ACQUIRE

BLEMISH   FITTING   EXILE

ARROW MAZE

VISUAL

Starting at the S and following the arrow up, see if you can find your way to F. When you reach an arrow, you MUST follow its direction and continue in that direction until you come to the next arrow. When you reach a two-headed arrow, you can choose either direction. It's okay to cross your own path.

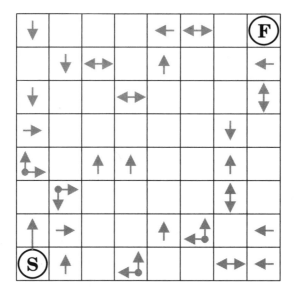

WORD VISIBILITY

LANGUAGE

There are six 5-letter words below. The first letter of the answer is found in the first pair of letters, and it is either the top or the bottom letter. Continue across each pair.

For example, the word GIRL would be found thus: G A R L
                                                 L I T X

1. R H E O N
   P A Z G R

2. F R S E N
   E I O W L

3. O D I P T
   A R O C A

4. J E R L P
   Q U L M Y

5. D L A P E
   S F O Y N

6. M U W B E
   Q I O T M

STACKED UP

The box on the left can be formed by three of the numbered boxes superimposed on top of each other; do not turn them in any way. Can you figure out which three work?

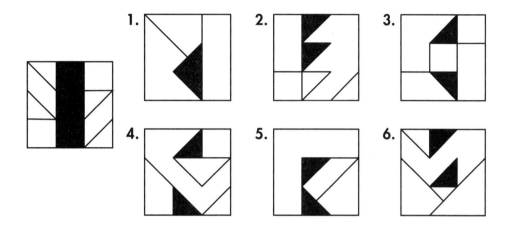

DOVETAILED WORDS

Two related words, with their letters in the correct order, are combined in each row of letters. Can you find both words? In a line like POTEORDRLEIER, or POteOrDrLEier, you can see the two words POODLE and TERRIER.

1. R B A O I O S S E T _____ _____

2. F S R N O O S W T _____ _____

3. J F O U R N E G S L E T _____ _____

4. P S E L T I I G H T T E _____ _____

5. P B A A N M D B O A O _____ _____

"A man begins cutting his wisdom teeth the first time he bites off more than he can chew."
— Herb Caen

COUNTDOWN

VISUAL

Following the connecting lines, find the only route in this grid that passes through the numbers backward from 9 to 1 consecutively.

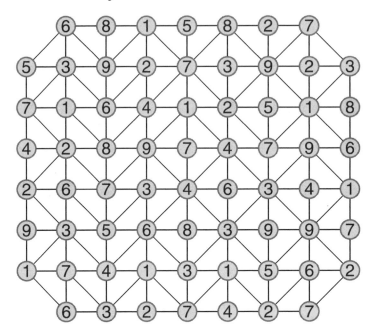

CHANGELINGS

LANGUAGE

Can you change the first word into the second word by changing only one letter at a time? Do not rearrange the order of the letters with each change. Each change must result in an everyday word, and words beginning with a capital letter, slang, or obsolete words aren't allowed.

1. PICK

_____

_____

_____

PEAS
(4 changes)

2. NAVY

_____

_____

_____

YARD
(4 changes)

3. WISE

_____

_____

_____

DADS
(4 changes)

SQUARE LINKS

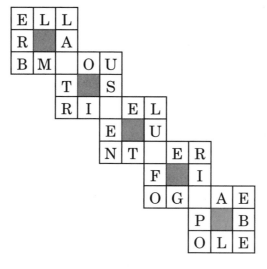

WEEK **51**

Write one letter in each empty box so that an everyday 8-letter word is spelled out around each blue box. Each word may read either clockwise or counter-clockwise, and may start at any of its letters.

WORD WHEEL

Starting with the "B" at the arrow, see how many everyday words of three or more letters you can find going clock-wise. Don't skip over any letters. For example, if you saw the letters C, A, R, E, D, you would form five words: CAR, CARE, CARED, ARE, RED. We found 32 words.

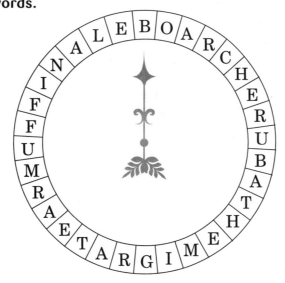

ELIMINATION

LANGUAGE

Cross off the capitalized words below according to the instructions given. The remaining words, in order, will form a thought.

STRANGERS TRY DORMANT NONE POEM ANIMAL ARE PERMANENT SO CHIC EMPTY STEM IN AS NOVEL RODEO THOSE THE FARM FULL MANICURE CHIN OF ESSAY AGO ORDINARY THEMSELVES FACIAL NIGHT

Eliminate the...

1. words that are written works.

2. four words that form the title of a Frank Sinatra song.

3. names of services one might receive at a beauty salon.

4. two words that, when put together, form the name of an Illinois city.

5. three words that will form three new words when an A is inserted somewhere in each one.

6. three words that begin with the same three letters, in some order.

7. two words that form the title of a book by George Orwell.

COMPOUND IT

LANGUAGE

Starting at #1, pick a word that will form a compound word with a word chosen in #2. Then with the word you've selected in #2, pick one from #3 to form another compound word. Continue in this manner to #10, so that you've formed nine compound words. In some instances more than one compound word can be formed, but there is only one path to get you to #10.

1. water, long, hat, corn

2. horn, meal, proof, check

3. read, pipe, up, time

4. worn, hold, line, out

5. backer, pouring, jump, over

6. kill, start, bite, power

7. less, house, joy, green

8. stew, stick, fall, bank

9. law, pin, foul, ball

10. park, giver, mouthed, dream

ANAGRAM MAZE

WEEK
51

The diagram contains 36 words, 21 of which are anagrams of other everyday words. Start at the top arrow and anagram BARE. While solving, move up, down, right, or left to the only adjacent word that can be anagrammed. Continue until you arrive at the bottom arrow. There is only one path through the maze.

1 BAND	2 BARE	3 FELT	4 SHOE	5 FOUR	6 MARK
7 BODY	8 FANG	9 FILM	10 LAKE	11 YAPS	12 IDLE
13 VETO	14 SILO	15 PEAS	16 PILL	17 WAIT	18 PAST
19 LACY	20 PACK	21 SMUG	22 RACE	23 GRIN	24 VASE
25 TILL	26 WISH	27 DISC	28 MILL	29 ZOOS	30 LARD
31 HARE	32 TEND	33 CORK	34 GLUE	35 ARMS	36 BALL

ALL IN A ROW

Which row below contains the most groups of consecutive numbers adding up to 10? Look carefully, because some groups may overlap. We've underlined an example of a group in each row to start you off.

A. 3 6 2 4 1 8 5 1 3 1 4 2 2 1 6 <u>7 3</u> 4 5 2 1 6 9 4

B. <u>7 1 2</u> 8 5 4 8 1 3 2 4 4 8 1 3 2 3 2 6 5 1 7 2 3

C. 5 1 4 7 6 2 4 4 1 8 1 5 9 2 3 1 1 3 4 <u>8 1</u> 1 3 4

TARGET SHOOT

LANGUAGE

Find the two letters which, when entered into the center circle of each target, will form three 6-letter words reading across.

1.   **2.**

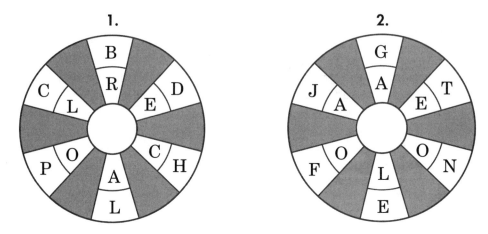

DEDUCTION PROBLEM

LOGIC

One of the most popular events at the Highland County Fair is the Heavy Hen contest, where farmers and poultry lovers from all over the county compete to see who can raise the heaviest hen. Henry Hooper had to harvest his hops early this year and, much to his dismay, missed the contest. However, his best friend Harvey had managed to attend, and Henry asked Harvey the results. Harvey, in a huff, gave Henry the following list of statements and told him that Henry could figure out the results himself with the information. Henry read the list and quickly determined the order, by weight, of the five finalists. Can you do the same?

1. Hen D weighed more than Hen E, but less than Hen C.

2. Hen E was heavier than Hen A.

3. Hen C weighed less than Hen B.

BULL'S-EYE LETTER

WEEK 52

Add the SAME single letter to each group of three letters then rearrange the letters to form six everyday 4-letter words.

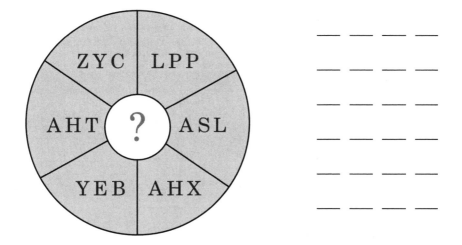

__ __ __ __

__ __ __ __

__ __ __ __

__ __ __ __

__ __ __ __

__ __ __ __

LANGUAGE # FILLING STATION

Place the given consonants on the dashes to form words. The vowels have already been placed for you, and as an additional help, each entry lists its category beside its given consonants.

1. C K R R S S (fabric)

__ E E __ __ U __ __ E __

2. G M N N P R S T Y (insect)

__ __ A __ I __ __   __ A __ __ I __

3. K L N R S (country)

__ __ I   __ A __ __ A

4. C D L M N R (television program)

"A __ E __ I __ A __   I __ O __"

5. B L N N S T T (game)

__ A __ __ E   __ E __ __ I __

357

MISSING LINKS

LANGUAGE

Using only the letters below, fill the diagram with everyday words. Be careful — this puzzle isn't as easy as it may look, so a little extra thought will be needed.

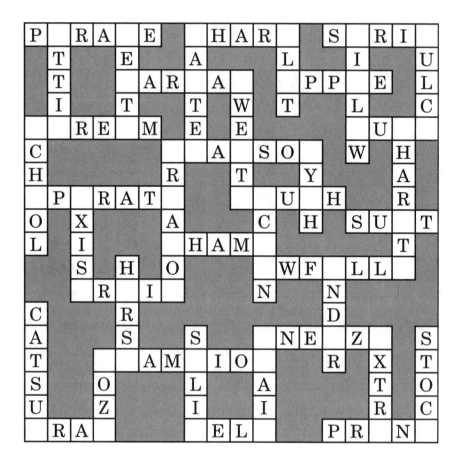

```
AAAAAA  CCC  D  EEEEE  F  G  HH  II  K
LLL  M  NNN  OOO  PPP  R  SSS  TTTTT  U
W  YYY
```

CARD SENSE

Five playing cards were shuffled and put in a pile, one on top of another. Using the clues, can you identify each card's position in the pile?

1. The black cards are adjacent.

2. The three is somewhere above both the club and the queen.

3. Neither heart is on the bottom.

4. The seven is not second from the top.

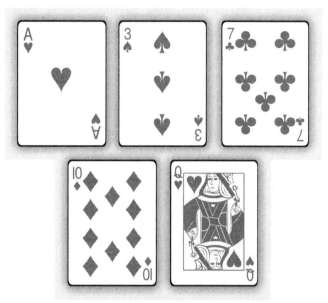

DOVETAILED WORDS

Two related words, with their letters in the correct order, are combined in each row of letters. Can you find both words? In a line like POTEORDRLEIER, or POteOrDrLEier, you can see the two words POODLE and TERRIER.

1. E S A O R I T H L   _____ _____

2. S H C I I S E T N O R C E Y   _____ _____

3. P P O A R T I C O H   _____ _____

4. S G P A O R M E T   _____ _____

5. C D I A N N G O H Y E   _____ _____

COUNT THE DIAMONDS

VISUAL ◆ SPATIAL

To solve this puzzle, write down the four letters that describe each diamond (a four-sided figure with two parallel sides) in this figure. We found 34 diamonds; how many can you locate?

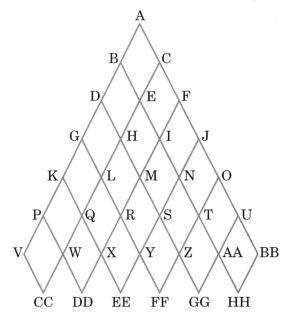

STAR WORDS

VISUAL ◆ LOGIC

Only five of the eight words given will fit together in the diagram. Place them in the directions indicated by the arrows.

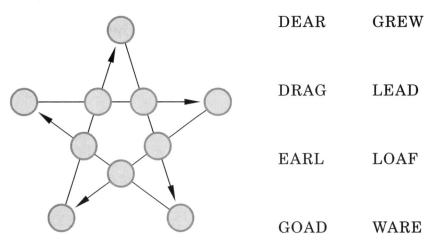

DEAR   GREW

DRAG   LEAD

EARL   LOAF

GOAD   WARE

CIRCLE MATH

WEEK 52

Each overlapping circle is identified by a letter having a different number value from 1 to 9. Where some circles overlap, there is a number: It is the SUM of the values of the letters in those overlapping circles. Can you figure out the correct values for the letters? As a starting help, E = 3.

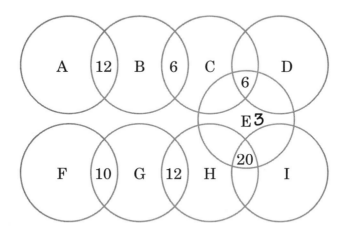

LANGUAGE   **SUDOKU**

Directions for solving are on page 339.

		5		3			8	
4		8	7				6	1
	7	9			2			
	2	4		5			7	
			9	6	4			
	8			7		4	5	
			6			7	4	
7	6				9	3		8
	4			8		1		

MISSING DOMINOES

VISUAL ◆ LOGIC

In this game use all 28 dominoes that are in a standard set. Each one has a different combination from 0-0, 0-1, 0-2, to 6-6. Domino halves with the same number of dots lie next to each other. To avoid confusion we have used an open circle to indicate a zero. Can you fill in the missing white dominoes to complete the board?

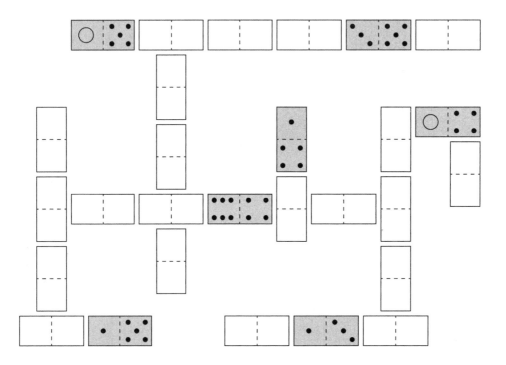

DOMINOES

ANSWERS

MAGNIFIND (Week 1)

EASY PICKINGS (Week 1)

If the shoe fits, you're not allowing for growth.

COUNT THE TRIANGLES (Week 1)

There are nine triangles: ABD, AGI, BCE, BDH, BGH, CDF, CEF, DHI, and EFH.

ANTONYMS QUIZ (Week 1)

1. a; 2. c; 3. c; 4. b; 5. a; 6. c; 7. c; 8. a.

SUDOKU (Week 1)

2	3	9	8	4	1	7	6	5
1	6	4	5	7	9	3	8	2
5	8	7	2	3	6	4	9	1
7	2	5	4	9	8	1	3	6
3	4	1	6	2	5	9	7	8
6	9	8	3	1	7	2	5	4
9	7	6	1	8	2	5	4	3
8	1	3	7	5	4	6	2	9
4	5	2	9	6	3	8	1	7

TRI, TRI AGAIN (Week 1)

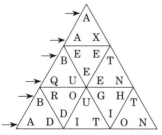

TIPS OF THE ICEBERG (Week 1)

1. Brenda ($6.30); 2. Greta ($3.70); 3. Dena and Flora ($5.25).

IN THE ABSTRACT (Week 1)

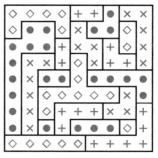

CODE WORD (Week 1)

Code Word: motherlands. The test of freedom is less in what we are free to do than in what we are free not to do.

WHAT'S YOUR NUMBER? (Week 1)

Six. The bottom number is one more than five times the top number.

RELATIONSHIPS QUIZ (Week 1)

1. b; 2. c; 3. b; 4. d; 5. b.

COUNTDOWN (Week 2)

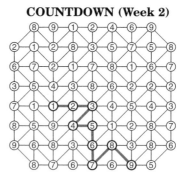

SYMBOL-ISM (Week 2)

I've found that happiness will add and multiply itself whenever you have divided it with others.

ROUND TRIP (Week 2)

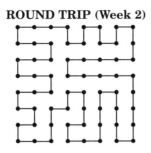

FUN WITH FACTS AND FIGURES (Week 2)

1. $17 + 8 = 25$; 2. $25 \times 30 = 750$; 3. $750 - 500 = 250$; 4. $250 \div 25 = 10$; 5. $10 + 18 = 28$.

ANAGRAM MAZE (Week 2)

	2	3	4	5	6
					12
13	14	15	16		18
19			22	23	24
25	26	27			
		33	34	35	

The path through the maze, with only one anagram given for each, is 2. mugs; 3. apes; 4. sack; 5. oils; 6. lied; 12. last; 18. coal; 24. vote; 23. much; 22. robe; 16. clay; 15. rock; 14. news; 13. lilt; 19. rage; 25. brag; 26. hear; 27. care; 33. pots; 34. dent; 35. ring.

ALL IN A ROW (Week 2)

Row B. Row A contains five groups: 551, 164, 3332, 29, and 812. Row B contains six groups: 74, 821, 56, 641, 173, and 38. Row C contains four groups: 236, 3611, 6212, and 92.

ONLINE NETWORK (Week 2)

Brutal honesty is a kind of compliment.

MAGIC NUMBER SQUARES (Week 2)

1.

14	4	18
16	12	8
6	20	10

2.

19	5	15
9	13	17
11	21	7

THE LINEUP (Week 2)

1. B; 2. straight; 3. T; 4. rifles; 5. west, omen, vein.

COUNT TO TEN (Week 2)

1. the second row; 2. the ninth row; 3. the eighth row.

WAYWORDS (Week 2)

Any change feels like it's wrong at first.

GRAND TOUR (Week 2)

unity, typos, posse, serum, rumba, baste, steel, elope, opera, radio, diode, décor, corgi, giant, antsy, syrup, rupee, eerie.

BLOCK PARTY (Week 2)

LOOSE TILE (Week 3)

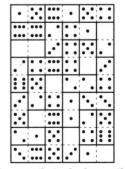

The 1-3 tile is the loose tile.

ASSOCIATIONS (Week 3)

speak, say, verbalize; distribute, allocate, apportion; Canberra, Sydney, Adelaide; categorize, group, rank; end, terminate, finish; heap, pile, stack; ginger, cinnamon, nutmeg. A reign coat.

HEXAGON HUNT (Week 3)

SLIDE RULE (Week 3)

cab, can, cat, cay, cry, cub, cue, cut, jab, jay, jib, jut, ran, rat, ray, rib, rub, rue, run, rut, sat, say, she, shy, sib, sin, sit, sub, sue, sun, wan, way, why, win, wit, wry.

SEVEN WORD ZINGER (Week 3)

cue, elk, lag, now, oat, pie, urn.

STACKED UP (Week 3)

Boxes 1, 4, and 6.

CIRCLE SEARCH (Week 3)

angel, anger, are, era, ink, kin, length, orang, orange, rang, range, ranger, rare, rarer, thin, think.

ELIMINATION (Week 3)

1. aghast, blast, caste, past; 2. and, tide, wait, for, no ("Time and tide wait for no man"); 3. gosh, egad, blimey; 4. great, expectations ("Great Expectations"); 5. guard, center, tackle; 6. alliteration, haiku, protagonist; 7. twelfth. Some people have delusions of adequacy.

TARGET SHOOT (Week 3)

1. ZZ: pizzas, puzzle, buzzer; 2. LT: sultan, filter, halted.

DOVETAILED WORDS (Week 3)

1. farm, ranch; 2. above, under; 3. ginger, garlic; 4. modern, retro; 5. plastic, rubber.

RING LOGIC (Week 3)

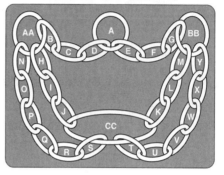

NEXT TO NOTHING (Week 3)
France.

ARROW MAZE (Week 3)

WORD VISIBLITY (Week 3)

1. worth; 2. chive; 3. media; 4. amble; 5. solar; 6. lyric.

LICENSE PLATES (Week 4)

1. Cate Blanchett; 2. Rachel Griffiths; 3. Judy Davis; 4. Naomi Watts; 5. Nicole Kidman; 6. Toni Collette.

ASSOCIATIONS (Week 4)

mode, manner, way; aunt, grandmother, sister; uniform, standardized, regular; Berlin, Frankfurt, Munich; imitate, mimic, ape; quantity, amount, portion; lofty, majestic, noble; building, edifice, skyscraper. From scratch.

SUDOKU (Week 4)

4	3	1	2	5	6	9	8	7
9	2	6	7	3	8	4	5	1
5	8	7	9	1	4	2	6	3
7	5	3	6	2	1	8	9	4
8	6	2	3	4	9	1	7	5
1	9	4	5	8	7	6	3	2
3	4	8	1	6	5	7	2	9
6	7	5	4	9	2	3	1	8
2	1	9	8	7	3	5	4	6

MISSING DOMINOES (Week 4)

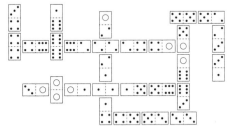

SQUARE LINKS (Week 4)

raindrop, cassette, turnpike, splashed, thorough.

RINGERS (Week 4)

1. swear, forum, bulge, adept; 2. groan, tepid, liner, stomp.

STAR WORDS (Week 4)

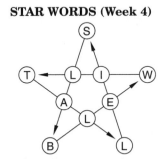

Your sequence of words may begin in any outer circle.

CIRCLE MATH (Week 4)

A = 2, B = 8, C = 3, D = 1, E = 5, F = 7, G = 9, H = 4, and I = 6.

BULL'S-EYE LETTER (Week 4)

The Bull's-Eye Letter is P: park, upon, copy, dump, sped, pave.

ALPHABET SOUP (Week 4)

Idaho.

GOING IN CIRCLES (Week 4)

1. operator; 2. treasure.

U.S. H'S (Week 4)

1. Hawaii; 2. Utah; 3. Massachusetts; 4. Ohio; 5. Rhode Island; 6. New Hampshire.

OVERLAY (Week 5)

Diagram A.

COMPOUND IT (Week 5)

1. oat; 2. meal; 3. time; 4. out; 5. post; 6. card; 7. board; 8. walk; 9. way; 10. farer (oatmeal, mealtime, timeout, outpost, postcard, cardboard, boardwalk, walkway, wayfarer).

IN THE MONEY (Week 5)

1. $4.80; 2. $4.67; 3. $4.85; 4. $4.75. Bag #3 has the most money.

CROSS PATHS (Week 5)

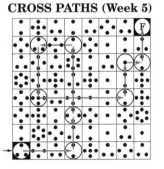

POP! (Week 5)

speared, spared, pared, pare, par, pa, a.

TRIANGULAR SQUARE (Week 5)

IN THE MONEY (Week 5)
1. $29.10; 2. $26.25; 3. $22.30; 4. $29.23.
Bag #4 has the most money.

HOLE IN ONE (Week 5)
The golf ball in the hole is 7395.

POP! (Week 5)
bridges, bridge, ridge, ride, rid, id, I.

CROSS PATHS (Week 5)

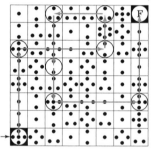

VISION QUEST (Week 5)
Row 4.

**ALTERNATING PRESIDENTS
(Week 5)**
1. George Washington; 2. Woodrow Wilson; 3. Thomas Jefferson; 4. Abraham Lincoln; 5. Martin Van Buren: 6. Andrew Jackson; 7. Calvin Coolidge; 8. John Quincy Adams.

SLIDE RULE (Week 5)
dare, darn, dart, dose, dude, dust, earl, earn, ease, east, nail, node, nose, nude, sail, skin, skit, soil, sore, sort, suit, sure.

DOUBLE DUTY (Week 5)
vacation time.

WORD CHARADE (Week 6)

H	Y	P	E	N	C	J	O
Z	Ⓤ	B	W	G	E	Q	X
N	W	Z	Ⓤ	K	D	S	A
T	I	A	R	T	R	Ⓞ	P
O	C	D	Y	Ⓤ	V	Ⓛ	Q
F	P	Ⓥ	Ⓔ	Q	H	X	F
A	R	K	X	S	Ⓤ	A	J
N	Ⓤ	L	G	B	I	P	S

volume

EASY PICKINGS (Week 6)
"History is the biography of great men."

CARD SENSE (Week 6)
The bottom card isn't the nine (clue 2) or the three, six, or king (clue 3), so it is the ace. The top card isn't the three or six (clue 1) or the nine (clue 4); it is the king. Since the six is somewhere above the nine (clue 4) and the nine is somewhere above the three (clue 2), the six is second from the top, the nine is third, and the three is fourth. In summary, from top to bottom: king of diamonds, six of hearts, nine of spades, three of hearts, and ace of clubs.

QUICK FILL (Week 6)
excavation.

WORD WHEEL (Week 6)
mail, mailbox, ail, box, boxcar, car, cart, cartwheel, art, whee, wheel, heel, eel, elf, fat, father, the, there, her, here, repair, pair, air, airy, you, your, our, urn.

KEEP ON MOVING (Week 6)
Move one square up, three squares left, two squares up, four squares right, and one square down to the asterisk.

WORD EQUATIONS (Week 6)
1. for + tune = fortune; 2. car + pet = carpet; 3. war + den = warden; 4. ox + Ford = oxford; 5. pun + gent = pungent.

SQUARE LINKS (Week 6)
magician, sergeant, colonist, boosting, stranger.

ELIMINATION (Week 6)
1. hydrogen, cobalt, iodine; 2. two, heads, are, better, than, one (two heads are better than one); 3. "Network," "Shaft," "Giant," "Jaws," "Vertigo"; 4. agitate, granola (Atlanta, Georgia); 5. sponge; 6. sole; 7. house, guest (houseguest, guesthouse). Penny and penny will soon become many.

BLOCK PARTY (Week 6)

WORD HUNT (Week 6)
bath, both, math, moth, myth, oath, path, pith, that, thaw, them, then, they, thin, this, thud, thug, with.

ROUND TRIP (Week 6)

ONLINE NETWORK (Week 7)
Opportunity not welcomed will not come again.

ANAGRAM MAZE (Week 7)

1	2	3			6
7		9	10		12
13	14		16	17	18
	20	21			
		27			
31	32	33			

The path through the maze, with only one anagram given for each, is 6. fats; 12. stab; 18. glue; 17. shoe; 16. real; 10. team; 9. owns; 3. diet; 2. pals; 1. none; 7. lime; 13. trio; 14. atom; 20. went; 21. male; 27. thaw; 33. wand; 32. ripe; 31. lean.

SKILLS TEST (Week 7)
feign, felon, flown, frown, futon.

SUDOKU (Week 7)

1	8	9	3	5	7	4	2	6
2	5	3	6	9	4	8	1	7
7	6	4	8	2	1	3	9	5
6	3	1	9	4	2	7	5	8
8	4	2	5	7	3	1	6	9
9	7	5	1	8	6	2	4	3
3	9	8	2	1	5	6	7	4
4	1	6	7	3	9	5	8	2
5	2	7	4	6	8	9	3	1

LICENSE PLATES (Week 7)
1. Caracas, Venezuela; 2. Bogotá, Colombia; 3. Quito, Ecuador; 4. Lima, Peru; 5. Montevideo, Uruguay; 6. Santiago, Chile.

MAGIC NUMBER SQUARES (Week 7)

1.

9	24	30	31
29	32	16	17
30	21	25	18
26	17	23	28

2.

18	8	7	21
13	15	16	10
17	11	12	14
6	20	19	9

THE LINEUP (Week 7)

1. J; 2. daffodil; 3. L; 4. guzzle; 5. keep, milk, mare.

MAGNIFIND (Week 7)

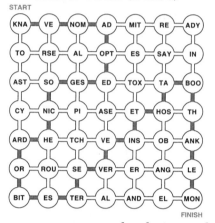

ANTONYMS QUIZ (Week 7)

1. b; 2. a; 3. c; 4. a; 5. b; 6. a; 7. c; 8. c.

TIPS OF THE ICEBERG (Week 7)

1. Inez ($11.30); 2. Hank ($8.00); 3. Laura and Noel ($9.05)

RINGERS (Week 7)

1. whirl, globe, vapor, mound; 2. havoc, plead, chimp, audit.

CODE WORD (Week 7)

Code Word: upholstering. Swans have an air of being proud, stupid, and mischievous; qualities that go well together.

TRI, TRI AGAIN (Week 8)

FUN WITH FACTS AND FIGURES (Week 8)

1. $2 \times 5 = 10$; 2. $10 + 88 = 98$; 3. $98 \div 2 = 49$; 4. $49 - 7$ (New York) $= 42$; 5. $42 \div 6 = 7$.

GRAND TOUR (Week 8)

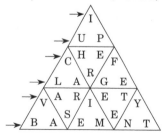

knave, venom, nomad, adopt, opted, edges, gesso, sonic, niche, heard, ardor, orbit, bites, ester, terse, sever, verve, veins, inset, ethos, hosta, taboo, booth, thank, ankle, lemon.

DOVETAILED WORDS (Week 8)

1. clock, watch; 2. frosty, humid; 3. sugar, flour; 4. moral, lesson; 5. laugh, giggle.

MARCHING ORDERS (Week 8)

SKILLS TEST (Week 8)

The revolution of the moon around the earth is irregular because of its elliptical orbit.

COUNTDOWN (Week 8)

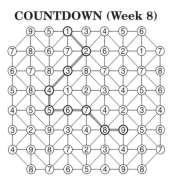

WAYWORDS (Week 8)

Live life as a sheep and forever fear the wolf.

STAR WORDS (Week 8)

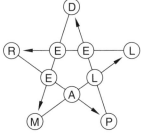

Your sequence of words may begin in any outer circle.

ASSOCIATIONS (Week 8)

surpass, exceed, eclipse; reduce, decrease, lessen; mix, blend, mingle; involved, complicated, complex; Packers, Giants, Eagles; twine, string, cord; Beethoven, Mozart, Brahms; league, association, partnership. Scream doors.

RING LOGIC (Week 8)

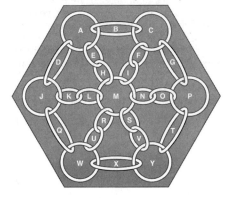

ALL IN A ROW (Week 8)

Row C. Row A contains four groups: 972, 1566, 9621, and 621234. Row B contains five groups: 21555, 5517, 51732, 17325, and 594. Row C contains six groups: 5553, 369, 333333, 3339, 99, and 981.

LETTER, PLEASE (Week 8)

A fool must now and then be right by chance.

F COUNT (Week 8)

There are 43 F's.

IN THE ABSTRACT (Week 9)

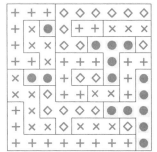

CROSS-UPS (Week 9)

1. bookmark; 2. headache; 3. sailboat; 4. backbone.

FILLING STATION (Week 9)

1. Pittsburgh; 2. refrigerator; 3. "West Side Story"; 4. glazed doughnut; 5. grizzly bear.

SKILLS TEST (Week 9)

Bob sold 1,100 nails on Monday, 1,300 on Tuesday, 900 on Wednesday, 1,400 on Thursday, and 800 on Friday.

LOOSE TILE (Week 9)

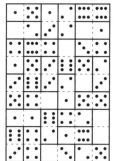

The 4-5 is the loose tile.

MISSING DOMINOES (Week 9)

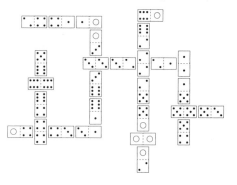

CIRCLE SEARCH (Week 9)

ball, ballad, bare, bask, deer, dell, den, mall, man, mask, read, reader.

CHANGELINGS (Week 9)

1. FIND, fine, five, live, LOVE. 2. FILE, fill, fall, fail, NAIL; 3. SWAP, swat, seat, seal, DEAL.

VISION QUEST (Week 9)

Column E.

SEVEN WORD ZINGER (Week 9)

ash, dye, eon, gum, map, pin, shy.

SUDOKU (Week 9)

9	2	3	5	4	1	8	7	6
7	5	6	2	3	8	9	4	1
1	8	4	9	7	6	2	5	3
8	7	9	3	1	2	4	6	5
6	4	2	7	9	5	1	3	8
3	1	5	8	6	4	7	2	9
4	6	8	1	2	3	5	9	7
5	3	7	4	8	9	6	1	2
2	9	1	6	5	7	3	8	4

ALPHABET SOUP (Week 9)

"M*A*S*H."

CARD SENSE (Week 10)

The bottom card isn't the two or seven (clue 2), ace (clue 3), or five (clue 4), so it is the four. Also by clue 4, the five is second from the bottom. The ace is second from the top (clue 1). By clue 3, the two is third from the top. By elimination, the seven is on top. In summary, from top to bottom: seven of diamonds, ace of spades, two of hearts, five of clubs, four of diamonds.

DEDUCTION PROBLEM (Week 9)

Dark-haired Clea wore a pink gown and a pink camellia. She wasn't Jack's date who wore yellow roses, Tim's who wore white, or Mark's who is a blonde, so she was Lou's date. Since Bea is a junior and both Tim's and Mark's dates are seniors, Bea was Jack's date. Tim's date wasn't Amy; she was Donna. By elimination, Mark's date was Amy. In summary: Jack and Bea, Lou and Clea, Mark and Amy, and Tim and Donna.

U.S. R's (Week 10)

1. California; 2. New York; 3. Vermont; 4. Oregon; 5. Colorado; 6. Arizona.

WORD HUNT (Week 10)

sad, said, sailed, salad, salted, sand, scold, seed, seeded, send, sewed, skewed, skied, skid, sled, slid, slinked, slowed, sold, solid, sordid, sound, sounded, sowed, sped, speed, spend, steed, steeped, sword.

CIRCLE MATH (Week 10)

A = 1, B = 2, C = 8, D = 7, E = 4, F = 5, G = 3, H = 9, and I = 6.

GOING IN CIRCLES (Week 10)

1. aviation; 2. ruthless.

RELATIONSHIPS QUIZ (Week 10)

1. c; 2. a; 3. c; 4. d; 5. b.

HEXAGON HUNT (Week 10)

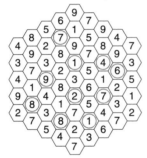

LETTER, PLEASE (Week 10)

A man convinced against his will is not convinced.

COMPOUND IT (Week 10)

1. cat; 2. fish; 3. tail; 4. pipe; 5. line; 6. up; 7. wind; 8. fall; 9. back; 10. ground (catfish, fishtail, tailpipe, pipeline, lineup, upwind, windfall, fallback, background).

WORD WHEEL (Week 10)

was, wash, washer, ash, she, sherbet, her, herb, bet, etch, chill, hill, ill, illegal, leg, legal, gal, gall, gallop, all, lop, opal, pal, pale, palette, ale, let, letter, terrace, err, race, ace.

BULL'S EYE LETTER (Week 10)

The Bull's-Eye Letter is T: taxi, stir, city, zest, quit, tree.

WHAT'S YOUR NUMBER? (Week 10)

77. In each row, column, and diagonal, the black box separates a number and that number minus six.

ANIMAL CHARADES (Week 10)

crocodile.

COUNT ON IT! (Week 11)

Practice makes perfect.

WORD CHARADE (Week 11)

export

G COUNT (Week 11)

There are 37 G's.

ELIMINATION (Week 11)

1. balustrade, laboratory, albatross; 2. Wolverines, Hurricanes, Volunteers; 3. all, my, loving ("All My Loving"); 4. coffee, Chianti, lemonade, ale; 5. defrost; 6. empire, state, building (Empire State Building); 7. cent (percent), form (perform), oxide (peroxide), severe (persevere). The punishment for vanity is flattery.

QUICK FILL (Week 11)

pinpointed.

TARGET SHOOT (Week 11)

1. OU: amount, blouse, enough; 2. ME: camera, cement, homely.

373

TRI, TRI AGAIN (Week 11)

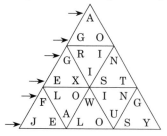

ARROW MAZE (Week 11)

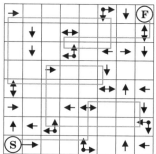

SUDOKU (Week 11)

4	8	3	6	9	1	7	2	5
5	9	2	4	3	7	1	8	6
7	6	1	8	2	5	9	4	3
9	4	7	1	8	3	6	5	2
6	2	5	7	4	9	3	1	8
3	1	8	5	6	2	4	7	9
1	3	9	2	7	8	5	6	4
8	7	4	3	5	6	2	9	1
2	5	6	9	1	4	8	3	7

WAYWORDS (Week 11)
Seven days on a crash diet can make one weak.

ALL IN A ROW (Week 11)
Row A. Row A contains six groups: 16437, 64371, 437133, 33294, 948, and 158124. Row B contains five groups: 948, 15951, 9516, 2595, and 33384. Row C contains five groups: 72381, 3819, 1965, 5961, and 9714.

FUN WITH FACTS AND FIGURES (Week 12)
1. $2 + 2 = 4$; 2. $4 \times 23 = 92$; 3. $92 - 60 = 32$; 4. $32 + 3$ (March, May, June) $= 35$; 5. $35 \div 7 = 5$.

ANIMAL CHARADES (Week 11)
tortoise.

STACKED UP (Week 12)
Boxes 3, 5, and 6.

KEEP ON MOVING (Week 11)
Move three squares up, two squares right, three squares down, two squares right, and one square down to the asterisk.

SKILLS TEST (Week 12)
Diplomacy is to do and say / The nastiest thing in the nicest way.

COUNT TO TEN (Week 11)
1. the fifth row; 2. the first row; 3. the tenth row.

SLIDE RULE (Week 12)
chug, chum, clam, club, coax, crab, crag, cram, crux, dorm, drab, drag, dram, drub, drug, drum, flab, flag, flax, flex, flub, flux, foam, form, shag, sham, slab, slag, slam, slug, slum.

WORD EQUATIONS (Week 12)

1. Mel + low = mellow; 2. ante + lope = antelope; 3. bum + pier = bumpier; 4. con + science = conscience; 5. chart + reuse = chartreuse.

RHYMING REPLACEMENTS (Week 12)

1. song & dance; 2. tried & true; 3. said & done; 4. rant & rave; 5. meek & mild; 6. cat & mouse; 7. wax & wane; 8. bill & coo; 9. thick & thin; 10. Stars & Stripes; 11. rock & roll; 12. sights & sounds.

HEXAGON HUNT (Week 12)

OVERLAY (Week 12)
Diagram C.

ANAGRAM MAZE (Week 12)

1	2	3	4	5	
				11	
		15	16	17	
	20	21			
	26		28	29	30
	32	33	34		36

The path through the maze, with only one anagram given for each, is 1. peek; 2. tans; 3. dose; 4. fate; 5. chin; 11. leap; 17. dust; 16. arid; 15. mash; 21. knee; 20. toga; 26. blow; 32. beak; 33. rare; 34. café; 28. mare; 29. dome; 30. ever; 36. earn.

EASY PICKINGS (Week 12)

"Hope is independent of the apparatus of logic."

IN THE ABSTRACT (Week 12)

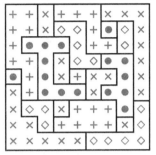

WHAT'S YOUR NUMBER? (Week 12)

20. On each spoke, the number in the circle plus the square of the number in the square equals 120, the number in the diamond.

SUDOKU (Week 12)

2	1	3	5	4	7	9	8	6
6	8	9	2	1	3	7	5	4
4	7	5	6	9	8	3	2	1
1	9	7	3	5	2	6	4	8
5	4	2	8	6	9	1	3	7
3	6	8	1	7	4	2	9	5
8	2	4	7	3	1	5	6	9
9	5	1	4	2	6	8	7	3
7	3	6	9	8	5	4	1	2

FILLING STATION (Week 12)

1. shuffleboard; 2. Humphrey Bogart; 3. "Murder, She Wrote"; 4. contact lenses; 5. Hansel and Gretel.

ARROW MAZE (Week 13)

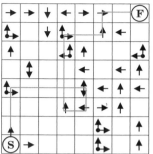

QUICK FILL (Week 13)
proverbial

COUNT TO TEN (Week 13)
1. row 9; 2. row 8; 3. row 6.

EASY PICKINGS (Week 13)
Enemies are made, not born.

THE LINEUP (Week 13)
1. V; 2. correct; 3. M; 4. sponge; 5. three words (taxi, slim, bump).

SUDOKU (Week 13)

3	5	2	1	7	8	9	6	4
9	8	7	4	2	6	3	1	5
1	6	4	5	3	9	7	8	2
6	4	3	7	9	2	1	5	8
7	9	1	8	4	5	6	2	3
5	2	8	3	6	1	4	7	9
4	3	5	2	1	7	8	9	6
2	7	6	9	8	3	5	4	1
8	1	9	6	5	4	2	3	7

IN THE ABSTRACT (Week 13)

B COUNT (Week 13)
There are 38 B's.

HEXAGON HUNT (Week 13)

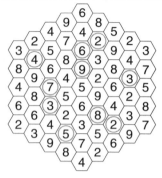

COMPOUND IT (Week 13)
1. clean; 2. up; 3. wind; 4. burn; 5. out; 6. run; 7. down; 8. turn; 9. over; 10. come (cleanup, upwind, windburn, burnout, outrun, rundown, downturn, turnover, overcome).

ONLINE NETWORK (Week 13)
channel, ditch, trench; molar, bicuspid, tooth.

COUNT THE TRIANGLES (Week 13)
There are 27 triangles: ABC, ABD, ABF, ACD, ADG, AFG, AFJ, AGI, AIJ, BDE, BDF, BDG, BEG, BFG, BFJ, DEF, DFG, DGI, EFG, FGH, FGI, FGJ, FHI, FIJ, GHJ, GIJ, and HIJ.

LICENSE PLATES (Week 13)
1. Tony Danza; 2. Wayne Brady; 3. Bert Parks; 4. Regis Philbin; 5. Donny Osmond; 6. Mario Lopez.

LOOSE TILE (Week 14)

The 3-4 is the Loose Tile.

ALL IN A ROW (Week 14)

Row A. Row A contains six groups: 361, 532, 28, 2611, 6112, and 11242. Row B contains three groups: 415, 11233, and 64. Row C contains four groups: 217, 21421, 46, and 451.

TIPS OF THE ICEBERG (Week 14)

1. Flora ($13.55); 2. Al ($6.10); 3. Dena and Ed ($12.75).

COUNTDOWN (Week 14)

SYMBOL-ISM (Week 14)

When you can't control the wind direction, you must adjust your sails.

MAGNIFIND (Week 14)

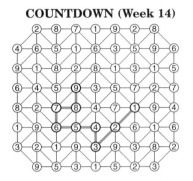

ANTONYMS QUIZ (Week 14)

1. b; 2. a; 3. a; 4. c; 5. a; 6. b; 7. c; 8. a.

ANIMAL CHARADES (Week 14)

canary

CODE WORD (Week 14)

Code Word: regulations. No one is ever too old to learn, which is why some people keep putting it off.

ELIMINATION (Week 14)

1. best, vest, test, rest; 2. Angel, Royal, Twin, Ranger; 3. remedy, cure, heal; 4. grand, rapids (Grand Rapids); 5. intestines; 6. regulation; 7. porter, stout. There is always someone ready to say you can't.

GOING IN CIRCLES (Week 14)

1. envelope; 2. dynamite.

ANAGRAM MAZE (Week 14)

1		3	4	5	6
7	8	9			12
			16	17	18
	20	21	22		
	26				
	32	33	34	35	36

The path through the maze, with just one anagram given for each, is 1. cask; 7. hums; 8. deaf; 9. dads; 3. oils; 4. hewn; 5. hare; 6. hate; 12. cola; 18. lain; 17. grin; 16. peas; 22. owes; 21. awry; 20. lamp; 26. earl; 32. dust; 33. saps; 34. bean; 35. turn; 36. care.

WHAT'S YOUR NUMBER? (Week 14)

50 (starting with the 5 in the center of the diagram, the numbers increase by five in a spiral pattern).

STAR WORDS (Week 15)

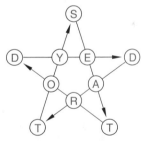

Your sequence of words may begin in any outer circle.

ASSOCIATIONS (Week 15)

promise, vow, oath; area, region, locale; join, connect, link; Orlando, Tampa, Miami; guide, steer, direct; Clinton, Bush, Obama; strict, severe, harsh; prohibit, ban, forbid. In dew time.

BULL'S-EYE LETTER (Week 15)

The Bull's-Eye Letter is V: oval, envy, five, vain, even, very.

SLIDE RULE (Week 15)
can, cat, cee, con, coo, cot, coy, cue, cut, jay, jet, jot, joy, jut, man, mat, may, men, met, moo, sat, say, see, set, she, shy, son, soy, sue, sun, tan, tat, tee, ten, the, toe, ton, too, tot, toy, tut.

OVERLAY (Week 15)
Diagram B.

CIRCLE SEARCH (Week 15)
babe, ban, barn, beet, earn, eat, home, horn, hornet, hot, meet, neat, tea, thorn.

WORD VISIBLITY (Week 15)
1. erode; 2. apple; 3. moose; 4. truth; 5. orbit; 6. mimic.

CARD SENSE (Week 15)
The bottom card is not the six or seven of spades (clue 1), three of clubs (clue 2), or jack of hearts (clue 3); it is the four of diamonds. The top card is not the jack of hearts (clue 1), six of spades (clue 2), or three of clubs (clue 4), so it is the seven of spades. Since the jack of hearts is below the six of spades (clue 1) and the six of spades is below the three of clubs (clue 2), the three of clubs is second from the top, the six of spades is third, and the jack of hearts is fourth. In summary, from top to bottom: seven of spades, three of clubs, six of spades, jacks of hearts, four of diamonds.

VISION QUEST (Week 15)
Row 4.

DEDUCTION PROBLEM (Week 15)
By clue 1, Leslie is 10, the girl wearing blue is 12, and Diane is 14. The girl wearing yellow is 11 and the girl wearing green is 13 (clue 2). By clue 3, Abigail is 12 and Janice is 11. By elimination, Nancy is 13. Diane is wearing pink (clue 4). By elimination, Leslie's dress is red. In summary: Abigail, 12, blue; Diane, 14, pink; Leslie, 10, red; Nancy, 13, green; Janice, 11, yellow.

RELATIONSHIPS QUIZ (Week 15)
1. d; 2. c; 3. a; 4. a; 5. b.

WAYWORDS (Week 15)
One thing we never run out of is surprise.

SUDOKU (Week 16)

7	8	5	9	4	2	6	3	1
6	2	3	1	8	5	9	4	7
9	4	1	7	6	3	8	5	2
3	9	2	6	1	7	4	8	5
4	1	6	2	5	8	7	9	3
8	5	7	4	3	9	2	1	6
1	3	4	8	7	6	5	2	9
5	6	9	3	2	4	1	7	8
2	7	8	5	9	1	3	6	4

FUN WITH FACTS AND FIGURES (Week 16)
1. $31 + 9 = 40$; 2. $40 \div 20 = 2$; 3. $2 \times 5 = 10$; 4. $10 + 60 (15 \times 4) = 70$; 5. $70 \div 10 = 7$.

LETTER, PLEASE (Week 16)
The road to success is dotted with many tempting parking spaces.

SEVEN WORD ZINGER (Week 16)
cry, ewe, gym, ink, joy, nor, she.

GRAND TOUR (Week 16)

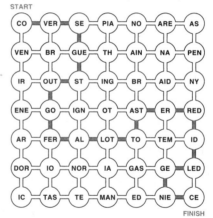

cover, verse, segue, guest, stout, outgo, gofer, feral, allot, lotto, toast, aster, erred, redid, idled, ledge, genie, niece.

SKILLS TEST (Week 16)
1. rough and gruff; 2. could & good; 3. limb & hymn; 4. choir & tire; 5. broad & fraud; 6. half & laugh.

COUNT ON IT! (Week 16)
Man can't live by bread alone.

FILLING STATION (Week 16)
1. "Raiders of the Lost Ark"; 2. penguin; 3. Venezuela; 4. Harry Potter; 5. Grand Canyon.

TARGET SHOOT (Week 16)
1. WE: fewest, unwell, towels; 2. AC: teacup, placid, beacon.

U.S. O'S (Week 16)
1. Connecticut; 2. New York; 3. Iowa; 4. Idaho; 5. Ohio; 6. Oregon.

KEEP ON MOVING (Week 16)
Move 3 squares down, 3 squares left, 2 squares down, 4 squares right, and 3 squares up to the asterisk.

DOVETAILED WORDS (Week 16)
1. verb, noun; 2. honey, sugar; 3. skunk, mole; 4. snake, venom; 5. conch, shell.

WORD HUNT (Week 16)
aunt, bent, bunt, cant, dent, dint, font, hint, hunt, lint, mint, pant, pent, punt, rant, rent, runt, tent, tint, want, wont.

MARCHING ORDERS (Week 16)

1. FINISH

17	21	19	39	41	44
16	22	15	36	34	31
12	11	14	16	19	29
9	10	8	19	17	26
6	5	12	14	21	24
4	7	9	10	15	19

START

2. FINISH

27	30	32	27	37	38
22	28	35	33	22	21
14	19	27	23	16	18
11	9	10	15	13	17
6	4	8	12	25	21
3	7	9	13	15	19

START

MISSING DOMINOES (Week 17)

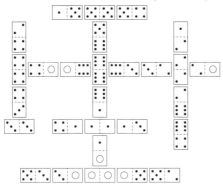

CROSS PATHS (Week 17)

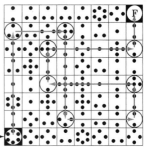

IN THE BALANCE (Week 17)
Eight diamonds. One triangle equals two circles (scale 1), and one circle equals two squares (scale 2), so one triangle equals four squares. Since one square equals two diamonds (scale 3), one triangle equals eight diamonds and would balance scale 4.

HOLE IN ONE (Week 17)
The golf ball in the hole is 3268.

POP! (Week 17)
stowing, towing, owing, wing, win, in, I.

TRIANGULAR SQUARE (Week 17)

CROSS PATHS (Week 17)

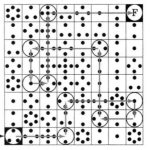

HOLE IN ONE (Week 17)
The golf ball in the hole is 7954.

IN THE BALANCE (Week 17)

Two triangles. One triangle equals two circles (scale 1), and one circle equals three squares (scale 2), so two circles equal six squares. One triangle, then, equals six squares. By scale 3, six squares equal three diamonds, so one triangle equals three diamonds. Two triangles, then, equal six diamonds, and would balance scale 4.

NEXT TO NOTHING (Week 17)
Marcus

WORD WHEEL (Week 17)

spa, spar, spare, par, pare, are, area, read, readmit, admit, itch, char, charm, harm, arm, armor, more, moreover, ore, over, overboard, verb, boa, boar, board, oar, dim, dimply, imp, imply, ply.

ONLINE NETWORK (Week 17)

cheetah, jaguar, leopard; diamond, emerald, garnet.

ELIMINATION (Week 18)

1. raven, cardinal, vulture; 2. ever, glades (Everglades); 3. operation, accumulate, permissible; 4. good, vibrations ("Good Vibrations"); 5. canoe, trivia, fatigue, ennui; 6. base, dimension, world (third base, third dimension, Third World); 7. reed (reputed). Better to dare great things than dare nothing.

BLOCK PARTY (Week 18)

IN THE ABSTRACT (Week 18)

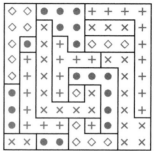

TRI, TRI AGAIN (Week 18)

WORD CHARADE (Week 18)

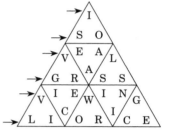

warden

EASY PICKINGS (Week 18)

There are more idle brains than idle hands.

ALPHABET SOUP (Week 18)

Texas

SKILLS TEST (Week 18)

Figure 5. When all the arrows are pointing up, the only arrow coming from the left side of the oval shape is that in figure 5.

ARROW MAZE (Week 18)

CONDENSED PRESIDENTS (Week 18)

1. Abraham Lincoln; 2. Barack Obama; 3. John Quincy Adams; 4. Ronald Reagan; 5. Ulysses Grant; 6. Martin Van Buren; 7. Theodore Roosevelt; 8. Harry Truman; 9. Richard Nixon; 10. Lyndon Johnson.

CHANGELINGS (Week 18)

1. NAME, same, sane, sang, SONG.
2. PEEP, beep, beet, best, NEST.
3. DEER, peer, peek, perk, PARK.
(Using the same number of changes, other answers may be possible for each Changeling.)

RING LOGIC (Week 18)

HEXAGON HUNT (Week 18)

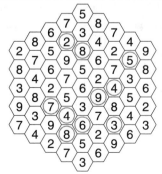

RINGERS (Week 18)

1. claim, proud, lurch, value; 2. steak, lodge, braid, glory.

CARD SENSE (Week 19)

The bottom card is not the ace of clubs or queen of clubs (clue 1), five of hearts (clue 2), or king of diamonds (clue 4); it is the queen of spades. The king of diamonds is somewhere above the five of hearts (clue 4), which is somewhere above the queen of clubs (clue 2). By clue 3, there's a black card between the king of diamonds and the five of hearts, so the king of diamonds is on top, the ace of clubs is second from the top, the five of hearts is third, and the queen of clubs is fourth. In summary, from top to bottom: king of diamonds, ace of clubs, five of hearts, queen of clubs, queen of spades.

WAYWORDS (Week 19)

The guilty think that all talk is of them.

ROUND TRIP (Week 19)

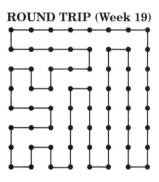

C COUNT (Week 19)

There are 27 C's.

SUDOKU (Week 19)

1	6	2	8	5	4	9	7	3
8	3	7	9	2	6	5	4	1
4	9	5	1	3	7	6	8	2
2	8	9	3	4	1	7	5	6
5	4	3	7	6	8	1	2	9
7	1	6	5	9	2	4	3	8
9	5	4	6	8	3	2	1	7
3	2	1	4	7	9	8	6	5
6	7	8	2	1	5	3	9	4

FILLING STATION (Week 19)

1. Minneapolis; 2. Pulitzer Prize; 3. Sandra Bullock; 4. "The Office"; 5. Christmas.

ON THE LINE (Week 19)

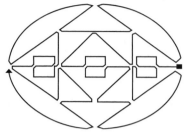

SLIDE RULE (Week 19)

fiat, firm, fist, flat, flaw, flay, flow, foam, foot, form, fort, frat, fray, from, list, loam, loom, loot, lost, plat, play, plot, plow, ploy, port, post, posy, pram, pray, prom, prow, riot, roam, room, root, rosy.

RELATIONSHIPS QUIZ (Week 19)

1. d; 2. b; 3. c; 4. a; 5. d.

MAGIC NUMBER SQUARES (Week 19)

1.

3	31	29	9
25	13	15	19
17	21	23	11
27	7	5	33

2.

10	38	36	16
32	20	22	26
24	28	30	18
34	14	12	40

ANAGRAM MAZE (Week 19)

1	2	3	4	5	
7					
13	14		16	17	18
	20	21	22		24
				29	30
	32	33	34	35	

The path through the maze, with just one anagram given for each, is 5. bowl; 4. cone; 3. done; 2. lake; 1. arch; 7. ever; 13. taco; 14. lies; 20. lilt; 21. abut; 22. file; 16. veto; 17. mare; 18. does; 24. felt; 30. ride; 29. gels; 35. tend; 34. lacy; 33. slat; 32. rove.

ALL IN A ROW (Week 19)

Row B. Row A contains five groups: 572, 3164, 1643, 33332, and 25412. Row B contains six group: 149, 491, 7421, 51332, 13325, and 59. Row C contains four groups: 37211, 11165, 842, and 353111.

STACKED UP (Week 19)

Boxes 2, 4, and 5.

SQUARE LINKS (Week 19)

marinate, fatigued, sidekick, vertical, treasure.

LICENSE PLATES (Week 20)

1. Brussels, Belgium; 2. Bangkok, Thailand; 3. Beijing, China; 4. Baghdad, Iraq; 5. Berlin, Germany; 6. Budapest, Hungary.

THE LINEUP (Week 20)

1. D; 2. scratch; 3. H; 4. excess; 5. three words (husk, time, hare).

U.S. E'S (Week 20)

1. Nevada; 2. Texas; 3. Tennessee; 4. Maine; 5. New Jersey; 6. Delaware.

SENTENCE TEASER (Week 20)

1. no, only women enjoy surfing (D); 2. yes, she is a singer who likes milk and is therefore a good driver (B), so could like to surf (D), but nothing in D states that she must like to surf; 3. yes, he is an athlete, so likes milk (A), and therefore likes sailing (C); 4. yes, singers who do like milk are good drivers (B), but nothing in B states that those who do not like milk cannot be good drivers. Similarly, men who like milk like sailing (C), but nothing in C states that those are the only people who enjoy sailing.

MAGNIFIND (Week 20)

STAR WORDS (Week 20)

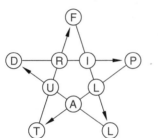

Your sequence of words may begin in any outer circle.

ALPHABET CIRCLE MAZE (Week 20)

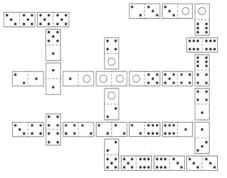

WHAT'S YOUR NUMBER? (Week 20)

16 (the number in each square is one-third of the sum of the numbers in the circles surrounding it).

OVERLAY (Week 20)

Diagram C.

ASSOCIATIONS (Week 20)

finish, complete, end; sleep, doze, nap; active, lively, animated; work, toil, labor; Rome, Milan, Naples; collapse, crash, breakdown; victory, triumph, conquest; thyme, marjoram, oregano. A wise quacker.

VISION QUEST (Week 20)

Column C.

COMPOUND IT (Week 20)

1. barn; 2. yard; 3. stick; 4. ball; 5. park; 6. way; 7. lay; 8. man; 9. power; 10. house (barnyard, yardstick, stickball, ballpark, parkway, waylay, layman, manpower, powerhouse).

CIRCLE MATH (Week 20)

A = 7, B = 8, C = 4, D = 1, E = 2, F = 6, G = 5, H = 9, and I = 3.

SYMBOL-ISM (Week 20)

People don't build their reputations on things they are always intending to do.

MISSING DOMINOES (Week 21)

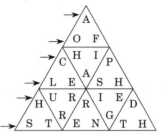

TRI, TRI AGAIN (Week 21)

A
O F
C H I P
L E A S H
H U R R I E D
S T R E N G T H

CODE WORD (Week 21)

Code Word: cabinetworks. Love is not soft like water; it is hard like rock, on which the waves of hatred beat in vain.

SUDOKU (Week 21)

8	4	1	3	9	6	2	5	7
2	9	5	8	1	7	3	4	6
7	3	6	2	5	4	8	9	1
9	7	8	6	3	1	5	2	4
5	1	3	9	4	2	7	6	8
4	6	2	7	8	5	1	3	9
6	2	9	1	7	3	4	8	5
3	5	7	4	6	8	9	1	2
1	8	4	5	2	9	6	7	3

ANTONYMS QUIZ (Week 21)
1. c; 2. b; 3. b; 4. a; 5. c; 6. c; 7. b; 8. b.

TIPS OF THE ICEBERG (Week 21)
1. Jack ($8.70); 2. Marty ($5.70); 3. Inez and Noel ($5.75).

WORD CHARADE (Week 21)

mystic

ALPHABET SOUP (Week 21)
radish

KEEP ON MOVING (Week 21)
Move 4 squares right, 2 squares up, 3 squares left, 4 squares down, 2 squares right, and 3 squares up to the asterisk.

COUNT ON IT! (Week 21)
Let's face the music and dance!

TARGET SHOOT (Week 21)
1. QU: acquit, sequel, liquid; 2. MB: fumble, bamboo, combat.

WORD HUNT (Week 21)
(Spiro) Agnew, (Joe) Biden, (George H.W.) Bush, (Dick) Cheney, (Gerald) Ford, (Albert) Gore, (Lyndon) Johnson, (Walter) Mondale, (Richard) Nixon, (Dan) Quayle, (Harry) Truman.

COUNT TO TEN (Week 22)
1. row 6; 2. row 4; 3. row 10.

WHAT'S YOUR NUMBER?
(Week 22)
1. 49 (7 x 2 = 14, 14 − 1 = 13, 13 x 2 = 26, 26 − 1 = 25, 25 x 2 = 50, 50 − 1 = 49); 2. 282 (2 x 3 + 3 = 9, 9 x 3 + 3 = 30, 30 x 3 + 3 = 93, 93 x 3 + 3 = 282).

GOING IN CIRCLES (Week 22)
1. question; 2. favorite.

RING LOGIC (Week 22)

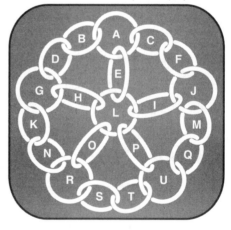

SEVEN WORD ZINGER (Week 22)
arm, dew, keg, spa, tab, wit, you.

STACKED UP (Week 22)
Boxes 1, 3, and 4.

GRAND TOUR (Week 22)

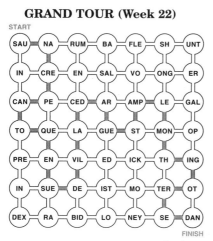

sauna, nacre, crepe, pecan, canto, toque, queen, ensue, suede, devil, villa, laced, cedar, argue, guest, stamp, ample, lemon, month, thing, ingot, otter, terse, sedan.

EASY PICKINGS (Week 22)
People with horse sense know when to say "nay."

ROUND TRIP (Week 22)

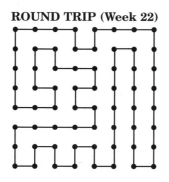

LETTER, PLEASE (Week 22)
Look before you leap.

SUDOKU (Week 22)

6	3	7	9	8	2	1	5	4
2	8	4	5	3	1	7	6	9
5	1	9	7	4	6	2	8	3
8	6	2	3	1	5	9	4	7
9	5	3	4	7	8	6	1	2
4	7	1	6	2	9	8	3	5
7	2	5	1	6	4	3	9	8
1	4	8	2	9	3	5	7	6
3	9	6	8	5	7	4	2	1

ARROW MAZE (Week 22)

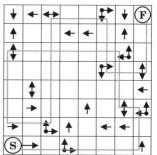

ALL IN A ROW (Week 22)
Row A. Row A contains six groups: 92536, 367162, 71629, 62953, 534562, and 213595. Row B contains four groups: 94516, 516238, 238273, and 273661. Row C contains five groups: 34576, 576223, 6223291, 2232916, and 835135.

HEXAGON HUNT (Week 22)

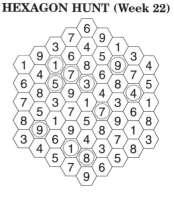

CIRCLE SEARCH (Week 23)
ape, apricot, apt, cot, leap, leapt, pie, piece, pile, pole, pot, rice, tap, tape.

SWITCHEROO (Week 23)
1. d; 2. a; 3. c; 4. a; 5. c; 6. b.

MARCHING ORDERS (Week 23)

1.
FINISH

7	10	6	16	24	29
9	8	13	21	26	21
3	4	9	14	19	23
5	1	7	12	10	18
0	3	6	8	17	20
2	4	5	10	12	15

START

2.
FINISH

6	11	12	14	11	15
9	10	8	9	10	13
5	8	7	10	8	9
3	7	4	11	12	11
6	2	5	6	10	8
4	1	3	7	5	9

START

DEDUCTION PROBLEM (Week 23)

If Melinda lied and came in last, then Jerri would also be a liar. If Jerri lied, then Melinda came in last and Melinda would be a liar too. Eileen, then, was the liar and came in last. Melinda and Jerri told the truth, so Melinda came in first and Jerri came in second. In summary, from first to last: Melinda, Jerri, Eileen.

SKILLS TEST (Week 23)

compact, company, compare, compass.

SLIDE RULE (Week 23)

back, balk, ball, bask, beak, beat, bell, belt, best, boat, boll, bolt, buck, bulk, bull, bust, deal, deck, dell, desk, dock, doll, dolt, dual, duck, duct, dull, dusk, dust, rack, rasp, real, reap, rest, rock, roll, rust, yell, yelp, yolk.

LOOSE TILE (Week 23)

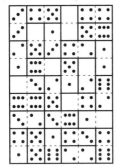

The 3-5 is the Loose Tile.

QUICK FILL (Week 23)
invalidate

COUNTDOWN (Week 23)

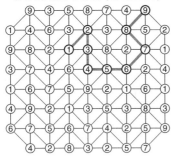

BLOCK PARTY (Week 23)

P

ANIMAL CHARADES (Week 23)
gorilla

WORD WHEEL (Week 23)

fir, fire, firearm, ire, rear, rearm, ear, arm, armor, moral, oral, aloft, loft, often, ten, tent, entwine, twin, twine, win, wine, inexact, inexactly, exact, exactly, act, lye, yell, yellow, ell, low.

ASSOCIATIONS (Week 23)

baron, viscount, duke; astound, surprise, amaze; mustard, ketchup, relish; flaunt, parade, exhibit; biology, physics, chemistry; petticoat, pinafore, sarong; refuge, sanctuary, asylum; support, back, uphold. A drill pickle.

WAYWORDS (Week 23)

Why is it that people won't listen when history repeats itself?

DOVETAILED WORDS (Week 24)

1. oven, kiln; 2. orange, green; 3. crochet, knit; 4. canoe, yacht; 5. spinach, lettuce.

ELIMINATION (Week 24)

1. church, ill (Churchill); 2. tails, aura (Australia); 3. shouldn't, throw, stones (shouldn't throw stones); 4. costume, indefinite; 5. snake, nasty, sanitary; 6. fiber, wine, hour (fiberglass, wineglass, hourglass); 7. birds, of, a, feather, flock, together (birds of a feather flock together). Demand excellence and be willing to pay for it.

ANAGRAM MAZE (Week 24)

		3	4	5	6
					12
13	14	15			18
19		21	22	23	24
25					
31	32	33	34		

The path through the maze, with just one anagram given for each, is 3. flit; 4. hoes; 5. acne; 6. team; 12. chin; 18. pace; 24. step; 23. pier; 22. hams; 21. furs; 15. leap; 14. slip; 13. live; 19. stub; 25. nude; 31. neon; 32. wake; 33. rock; 34. prod.

CROSS-UPS (Week 24)
1. clothesline; 2. clockwork.

RINGERS (Week 24)
1. antic, prove, mulch, gloat; 2. worth, radio, blunt, derby.

FUN WITH FACTS AND FIGURES (Week 24)
1. $3 \times 5 = 15$; 2. $15 + 3 = 18$; 3. $18 - 2 = 16$; 4. 16×5 (Egypt) $= 80$; 5. $80 - 4 = 76$.

IN THE ABSTRACT (Week 24)

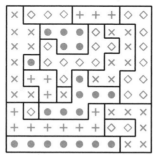

BULL'S-EYE LETTER (Week 24)
The Bull's-Eye Letter is S: jars, shin, fish, eggs, size, bask.

SQUARE LINKS (Week 24)
platform, yielding, digested, whatever, baseball.

CARD SENSE (Week 24)
The three red cards are the eight of hearts, the king of hearts, and the eight of diamonds. Since the king of hearts is somewhere between the eight of hearts and the eight of diamonds (clue 1), the eight of diamonds and the king of hearts are adjacent (clue 3), and at least one other card is between the eight of hearts and king of hearts. The jack of clubs is not adjacent to the king of hearts (clue 4), so the four of spades is. By clue 2, the four of spades is above both the king of hearts and the jack of clubs. In summary, from top to bottom: eight of hearts, four of spades, king of hearts, eight of diamonds, jack of clubs.

ON THE LINE (Week 24)

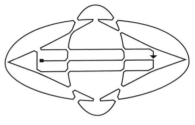

CIRCLE MATH (Week 24)
$A = 5$, $B = 4$, $C = 7$, $D = 9$, $E = 6$, $F = 2$, $G = 8$, $H = 1$, and $I = 3$.

HOLE IN ONE (Week 25)
The golf ball in the hole is 6134.

POP! (Week 25)
craters, crater, crate, rate, rat, at, a.

CROSS PATHS (Week 25)

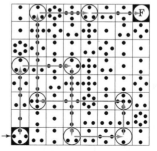

IN THE BALANCE (Week 25)
Two triangles. Scale 1 shows that two triangles equal three circles. Since scale 2 shows that one circle equals two squares, three circles equal six squares. Two triangles, then, equal six squares and one triangle equals three squares. Scale 3 shows that three squares equal two diamonds, so one triangle equals two diamonds. Two triangles, then, equal four diamonds, and would balance scale 4.

387

IN THE ABSTRACT (Week 25)

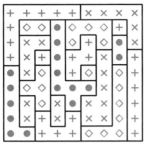

EASY PICKINGS (Week 25)

"I've been rich and I've been poor; rich is better."

COUNTDOWN (Week 25)

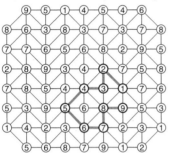

CODE WORD (Week 25)

Code Word: Speculation. We feel much worse by the contempt of fools than by the lukewarm approval of men of intelligence.

SUDOKU (Week 25)

9	2	7	8	1	4	5	3	6
5	1	4	7	3	6	9	8	2
3	8	6	5	9	2	4	7	1
2	9	5	4	6	3	8	1	7
7	4	8	1	2	5	3	6	9
1	6	3	9	8	7	2	5	4
4	7	1	2	5	8	6	9	3
8	3	9	6	4	1	7	2	5
6	5	2	3	7	9	1	4	8

GOING IN CIRCLES (Week 25)

1. somebody; 2. humidity.

TRI, TRI AGAIN (Week 25)

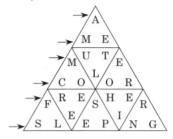

ANIMAL CHARADES (Week 25)

walrus

MAGNIFIND (Week 25)

ALL IN A ROW (Week 25)

Row B. Row A contains five groups: 1246, 463, 1561, 193, and 2722. Row B contains six groups: 3334, 49, 1174, 742, 382, and 517. Row C contains four groups: 4171, 85, 346, and 373.

THE LINEUP (Week 26)

1. Q; 2. garment; 3. G; 4. crying; 5. foxy, slit, muse.

QUICK FILL (Week 26)

productive

ELIMINATION (Week 26)

1. con, cord (Concord); 2. few (curfew), rent (current), tail (curtail); 3. turban, bowler, fedora; 4. basket; 5. vied (visited); 6. it, happened, one, night ("It Happened One Night"); 7. great, Dane (Great Dane). Dig your well before you are thirsty.

LICENSE PLATES (Week 26)
1. Michael Caine; 2. Ewan McGregor; 3. Anthony Hopkins; 4. Colin Firth; 5. Ralph Fiennes; 6. Hugh Grant.

CARD SENSE (Week 26)
There are three black cards and two red cards, and the second and fourth cards in the pile are red (clue 1). By clue 3, then, the second card from the top is the seven of diamonds and the fourth card is the ace of hearts. The two of spades is the top card and the seven of spades is third (clue 2). By elimination, the queen of clubs is the bottom card. In summary from top to bottom: two of spades, seven of diamonds, seven of spades, ace of hearts, and queen of clubs.

WORD HUNT (Week 26)
avow, blow, brow, chow, crow, flow, glow, grow, know, meow, plow, prow, scow, show, slow, snow, stow.

ONLINE NETWORK (Week 26)
operate, work, manage; smooth, even, uniform.

ROUND TRIP (Week 26)

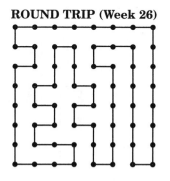

DOVETAILED WORDS (Week 26)
1. conceal, hide; 2. filling, cavity; 3. shell, beach; 4. book, novel; 5. prize, reward.

ASSOCIATIONS (Week 26)
dune, hill, ridge; verdict, decision, finding; Vermont, Connecticut, Massachusetts; error, mistake, blunder; doubt, question, dispute; intuition, feeling, sense; diamond, ruby, sapphire; ship, rowboat, catamaran. Answer: A plastic sturgeon.

BULL'S-EYE LETTER (Week 26)
The Bull's-Eye Letter is N: into, pony, next, yawn, zinc, navy.

MISSING DOMINOES (Week 26)

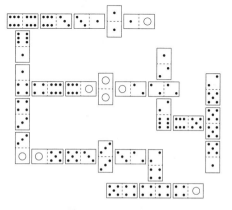

SLIDE RULE (Week 27)
ail, air, are, art, awe, awl, bit, boy, but, buy, die, doe, dot, dry, due, lie, lit, lot, oil, ore, our, out, owe, owl.

OVERLAY (Week 27)
Diagram B.

ARROW MAZE (Week 27)

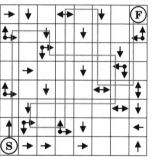

BLOCK PARTY (Week 27)

WORD CHARADE (Week 27)

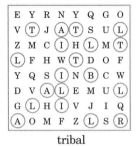

tribal

WHAT'S YOUR NUMBER?
(Week 27)

12. In each square, the upper-left number times the lower-right number equals the upper-right number times the lower-left number.

SQUARE LINKS (Week 27)

whatever, sailboat, limerick, engineer, daybreak.

WORD EQUATIONS (Week 27)

1. dead + line = deadline; 2. can + did = candid; 3. off + ice = office; 4. page + ant = pageant; 5. ref + use = refuse.

TIPS OF THE ICEBERG (Week 27)

1. Brenda ($15.85); 2. Greta ($10.70); 3. Ed and Flora ($14.65).

VISION QUEST (Week 27)

Column D.

SKILLS TEST (Week 27)

Answer b. Since two bicyclists cover 15 miles in two hours, a motorcyclist covers 30 miles in two hours, and 15 miles in one hour.

D COUNT (Week 27)

There are 29 D's.

TARGET SHOOT (Week 27)

1. IG: bright, enigma, frigid; 2. OP: eloped, floppy, people.

ALPHABET SOUP (Week 28)

Maine

FUN WITH FACTS AND FIGURES
(Week 28)

1. $25 \div 5 = 5$; 2. $5 \times 240 = 1,200$; 3. $1,200 - 1,000 = 200$; 4. $200 + 400 = 600$; 5. $600 \div 2 = 300$.

ANAGRAM MAZE (Week 28)

1			4	5	6
7		9	10		12
13	14	15			18
			22	23	24
			28		
			34	35	36

The path through the maze, with just one anagram given for each, is 1. file; 7. trio; 13. rage; 14. rock; 15. step; 9. ruby; 10. bane; 4. beak; 5. real; 6. none; 12. beat; 18. ride; 24. loaf; 23. ream; 22. moat; 28. refs; 34. bare; 35. tugs; 36. pans.

COUNT ON IT! (Week 28)

Out of sight, out of mind.

LOOSE TILE (Week 28)

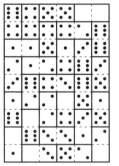

The 0-5 tile is the loose tile.

COMPOUND IT (Week 28)

1. fort; 2. night; 3. stand; 4. off; 5. shore; 6. bird; 7. bath; 8. house; 9. hold; 10. over (fortnight, nightstand, standoff, offshore, shorebird, birdbath, bathhouse, household, holdover).

GRAND TOUR (Week 28)

tutor, torte, tenor, north, thank, ankle, leash, ashen, endow, dowel, elope, opera, raced, cedar, arrow, rowdy.

WORD VISIBLITY (Week 28)

1. pulse; 2. later; 3. snoop; 4. icing; 5. young; 6. marsh.

COUNT THE SQUARES (Week 28)

The 18 squares are: ABMJ, ACYW, BCPM, DEMK, DFVT, EFOM, GHML, GISQ, HINM, JBPX, JMXW, KEOU, KMUT, LHNR, LMRQ, MNSR, MOVU, and MPYX.

RINGERS (Week 28)

1. touch, juicy, pupil, rivet; 2. wharf, liken, voice, credo.

WAYWORDS (Week 28)

The closed mouth will gather no feet.

ANTONYMS QUIZ (Week 28)

1. c; 2. a; 3. a; 4. b; 5. c; 6. a; 7. b; 8. b.

SEVEN WORD ZINGER (Week 28)

got, ink, nun, oil, rid, sew, wet.

CIRCLE MATH (Week 28)

A = 6, B = 2, C = 3, D = 8, E = 7, F = 4, G = 9, H = 1, and I = 5.

STACKED UP (Week 29)

Boxes 2, 3, and 5

SUDOKU (Week 29)

1	6	4	7	5	2	3	8	9
2	3	5	9	8	4	7	6	1
7	9	8	6	3	1	4	2	5
6	2	9	4	7	5	1	3	8
5	7	3	1	2	8	9	4	6
8	4	1	3	9	6	2	5	7
3	5	6	2	1	9	8	7	4
9	8	7	5	4	3	6	1	2
4	1	2	8	6	7	5	9	3

RING LOGIC (Week 29)

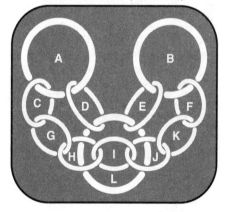

CIRCLE SEARCH (Week 29)

bag, bail, bare, draw, drawing, fad, fail, fare, gin, rare, raw, rein, win, wing.

IN THE MONEY (Week 29)
1. $5.50; 2. $4.50; 3. $5.83; 4. $6.05. Bag #4 has the most money.

NEXT TO NOTHING (Week 29)
Janice.

CROSS PATHS (Week 29

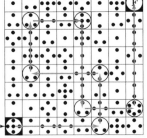

COUNT TO TEN (Week 29)
1. the fourth row; 2. the seventh row; 3. the second row.

U.S. T'S (Week 29)
1. Connecticut; 2. West Virginia; 3. Montana; 4. Texas; 5. Utah; 6. Vermont.

HOLE IN ONE (Week 29)
The golf ball in the hole is 8976.

IN THE BALANCE (Week 29)
Three triangles. Scale 1 shows that one triangle equals two circles, so three triangles equal six circles. Since scale 2 shows that three circles equal four squares, six circles equal eight squares. Three triangles, then, equal eight squares. Scale 3 shows that two squares equal one diamond, so eight squares equal four diamonds. Three triangles, then, equal four diamonds, and would balance scale 4.

KEEP ON MOVING (Week 29)
Move three squares up, two squares left, four squares down, three squares right, and one square down to the asterisk.

HEXAGON HUNT (Week 29)

STAR WORDS (Week 29)

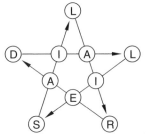

Your sequence of words may begin in any outer circle.

STACKED UP (Week 30)
Boxes 3, 4, and 6.

SUDOKU (Week 30)

8	6	9	7	5	4	2	1	3
3	1	7	8	2	6	5	9	4
2	5	4	1	9	3	7	6	8
4	3	1	9	7	8	6	2	5
9	7	6	5	3	2	8	4	1
5	8	2	6	4	1	9	3	7
1	9	8	3	6	7	4	5	2
7	2	5	4	1	9	3	8	6
6	4	3	2	8	5	1	7	9

FILLING STATION (Week 30)
1. Philadelphia; 2. microwave oven; 3. "The English Patient"; 4. spaghetti; 5. rhinoceros.

MAGIC NUMBER SQUARES (Week 30)

1.

18	8	7	21
13	15	16	10
17	11	12	14
6	20	19	9

2.

10	21	17	22
24	15	19	12
23	16	20	11
13	18	14	25

WORD WHEEL (Week 30)
mess, message, ess, sag, sage, age, gem, map, phone, hone, honey, one, eye, yea, year, ear, arrange, ran, rang, range, angel, gel, eleven, eve, even, event, vent, entry, try, rye.

CHANGELINGS (Week 30)
1. SOUP, sour, soar, star, STIR; 2. VINE, vane, sane, sang, HANG; 3. LONG, lone, line, like, HIKE.

CODE WORD (Week 30)
Code Word: Tragicomedy. Great deeds are done by women who are smart enough to know they can, or too ignorant to think they cannot.

IN THE ABSTRACT (Week 30)

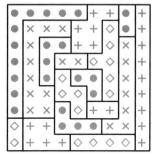

LETTER, PLEASE (Week 30)
A friend in need is a friend indeed.

PROGRESSION (Week 30)
Figures 2, 4, and 5.

COUNTDOWN (Week 30)

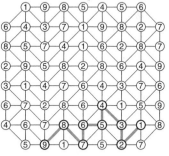

SYMBOL-ISM (Week 30)
Only those who are faithful to duty in small matters will fulfill it in great ones.

ONLINE NETWORK (Week 30)
high, elevated, towering; mature, adult, developed.

393

MARCHING ORDERS (Week 31)

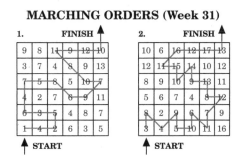

QUICK FILL (Week 31)
fragmented

GOING IN CIRCLES (Week 31)
1. artifact; 2. chemical.

WORD CHARADE (Week 31)

modern

WHAT'S YOUR NUMBER?
(Week 31)

32. In each circle, the number at the top equals the difference between the numbers in the squares times the number in the triangle.

RELATIONSHIPS QUIZ (Week 31)
1. a; 2. d; 3. c; 4. d; 5. a.

ELIMINATION (Week 31)
1. golden, gate, bridge (Golden Gate Bridge); 2. Pierce (Franklin), Grant (Ulysses); 3. peruse (Peru); 4. pride (lions), pack (wolves), flock (sheep); 5. fiddle, nature, banana; 6. if, the, shoe, fits, wear, it (If the shoe fits, wear it); 7. book, case (bookcase, casebook). Always give credit where credit is due.

EASY PICKINGS (Week 31)
"Government after all is a very simple thing."

ALPHABET SOUP (Week 31)
Egypt

DOVETAILED WORDS (Week 31)
1. cactus, desert; 2. velvet, linen; 3. zebra, horse; 4. beret, fedora; 5. peanut, cashew.

MISSING DOMINOES (Week 31)

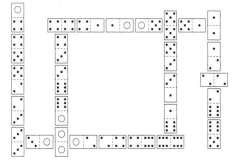

VISION QUEST (Week 32)
Row 5.

ANIMAL CHARADES (Week 32)
swordfish

TRI, TRI AGAIN (Week 32)

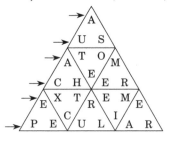

WAYWORDS (Week 32)
Try to make a point without making an enemy.

394

OVERLAY (Week 32)
Diagram A

CIRCLE SEARCH (Week 32)
beat, been, den, end, lane, lap, late, neat, pat, pen, pend, plane, plate, spat, spend.

ROUND TRIP (Week 32)

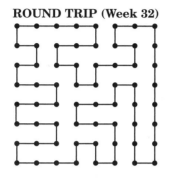

TARGET SHOOT (Week 32)
1. CT: cactus, doctor, hectic; 2. NG: danger, bungle, fungus.

SUDOKU (Week 32)

7	5	2	8	3	1	6	9	4
1	9	4	6	7	2	3	8	5
6	3	8	9	4	5	2	7	1
9	4	6	2	5	7	1	3	8
3	7	1	4	8	9	5	6	2
2	8	5	3	1	6	9	4	7
5	2	9	7	6	8	4	1	3
8	1	3	5	9	4	7	2	6
4	6	7	1	2	3	8	5	9

MAGNIFIND (Week 32)

LOOSE TILE (Week 32)

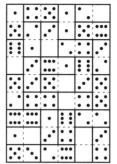

The 1-4 tile is the Loose Tile.

ASSOCIATIONS (Week 32)
cold, nippy, brisk; June, July, August; initiate, start, begin; riddle, pun, joke; taco, burrito, enchilada; unusual, odd, irregular; calculus, geometry, algebra; lion, tiger, jaguar. Answer: People who reed.

ANAGRAM MAZE (Week 32)

1	2	3	4		
7					
13		15	16	17	18
19	20	21			24
				29	30
		33	34	35	

The path through the maze, with just one anagram given for each, is 4. slow; 3. clay; 2. bowl; 1. jets; 7. hubs; 13. vest; 19. calm; 20. deli; 21. lilt; 15. coin; 16. cars; 17. page; 18. ante; 24. face; 30. shut; 29. cure; 35. cats; 34. poem; 33. sent.

E COUNT (Week 32)
There are 36 E's.

SLIDE RULE (Week 33)

jail, jest, jury, just, mail, main, mart, mast, meal, mean, meat, mist, must, rail, rain, real, rein, rest, ruin, rust, vain, vary, vast, veal, veil, vein, very, vest, vial.

THE LINEUP (Week 33)

1. Y; 2. magnet; 3. A; 4. knuckle; 5. jack, exit, made.

BULL'S-EYE LETTER (Week 33)

The Bull's-Eye Letter is R: rind, zero, mark, true, jeer, your.

SQUARE LINKS (Week 33)

external, railroad, stairway, opposite, recovery.

RING LOGIC (Week 33)

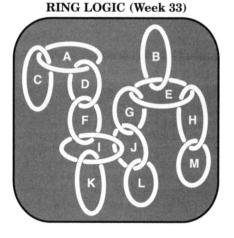

ALL IN A ROW (Week 33)

Row C. Row A contains three groups: 68, 1157, and 482. Row B contains five groups: 51215, 59, 36212, 2129, and 77. Row C contains six groups: 72212, 2129, 293, 9311, 419, and 257.

WHIRLIGIG (Week 33)

1. upsweep; 2. upscale; 3. upfront; 4. upstart; 5. upsurge; 6. upraise; 7. upstage; 8. upriver; 9. upright; 10. upgrade; 11. upswing; 12. updated.

COMPOUND IT (Week 33)

1. cross; 2. road; 3. work; 4. horse; 5. fly; 6. paper; 7. back; 8. fire; 9. trap; 10. door (crossroad, roadwork, workhorse, horsefly, flypaper, paperback, backfire, firetrap, trapdoor).

FUN WITH FACTS AND FIGURES (Week 33)

1. 2 x 4 = 8; 2. 8 + 40 = 48; 3. 48 − 5 (Alaska, California, Hawaii, Oregon, Washington) = 43; 4. 43 x 5 (Japan) = 215; 5. 215 − 15 = 200.

HEXAGON HUNT (Week 33)

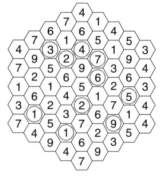

WORD EQUATIONS (Week 33)

1. ramp + age = rampage; 2. had + dock = haddock; 3. bell + hop = bellhop; 4. ran + sack = ransack; 5. sat + ire = satire.

CARD SENSE (Week 33)

The bottom card is not a heart or diamond (clue 1) or the three of clubs (clue 2), so it is the seven of spades. Since the top card is not the three of clubs (clue 2) or four of diamonds (clue 4), it is a heart. By clue 2, then, the second card from the top is the three of clubs and the third card is a heart. By elimination, the fourth card is the four of diamonds. The third card is the queen of hearts (clue 3). By elimination, the top card is the two of hearts. In summary from top to bottom: two of hearts, three of clubs, queen of hearts, four of diamonds, seven of spades.

CIRCLE MATH (Week 33)

A = 2, B = 8, C = 7, D = 6, E = 9, F = 3, G = 1, H = 5, and I = 4.

ANTONYMS QUIZ (Week 33)

1. a; 2. b; 3. a; 4. c; 5. b; 6. a; 7. c; 8. b.

CROSS-UPS (Week 34)

1. headline; 2. downpour; 3. backhand; 4. lifelong.

U.S. I'S (Week 34)

1. Illinois; 2. Iowa; 3. Wisconsin; 4. Missouri; 5. Hawaii; 6. Ohio.

SUDOKU (Week 34)

4	2	1	8	7	9	5	3	6
3	7	5	6	2	4	1	9	8
6	8	9	3	1	5	7	4	2
9	6	8	4	5	2	3	1	7
1	4	3	7	9	8	6	2	5
7	5	2	1	6	3	4	8	9
5	3	4	9	8	7	2	6	1
2	9	6	5	3	1	8	7	4
8	1	7	2	4	6	9	5	3

WORD HUNT (Week 34)

quack, quail, quake, qualm, quart, query, quest, quick, quiet, quilt, quirk, quite, quota, quote.

KEEP ON MOVING (Week 34)

Move one square right, two squares down, three squares left, four squares up, and four squares right to the asterisk.

ARROW MAZE (Week 34)

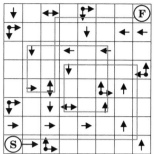

LICENSE PLATES (Week 34)

1. Washington Redskins; 2. Detroit Lions; 3. Chicago Bears; 4. Dallas Cowboys; 5. Atlanta Falcons; 6. Seattle Seahawks.

RINGERS (Week 34)

1. gnash, occur, above, tweet; 2. blend, sable, flaky, hover.

COUNT TO TEN (Week 34)

1. the first row; 2. the third row; 3. the fifth row.

BLOCK PARTY (Week 34)

TIPS OF THE ICEBERG (Week 34)

1. Jack ($11.80); 2. Inez ($5.10); 3. Hank and Noel ($6.75).

TRI, TRI AGAIN (Week 34)

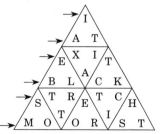

LETTER, PLEASE (Week 34)

Great minds think alike.

STAR WORDS (Week 35)

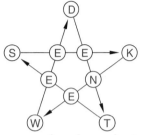

Your sequence of words may begin in any outer circle.

WORD VISIBILITY (Week 35)

1. bribe; 2. draft; 3. witty; 4. straw; 5. roost; 6. hedge.

WORD WHEEL (Week 35)

reap, reappear, appear, pea, pear, ear, earmuff, arm, muff, muffle, muffled, fled, led, ledge, edge, edgewise, wise, sea, seat, seating, eat, eating, tin, ting, ingrate, grate, rat, rate, ate, tee, teem.

SYMBOL-ISM (Week 35)

Some of the most far-reaching and exciting events of our lives arise from unexpected encounters.

COUNT ON IT! (Week 35)

A man's home is his castle.

RELATIONSHIPS QUIZ (Week 35)

1. b; 2. a; 3. d; 4. c; 5. b.

FILLING STATION (Week 35)

1. badminton; 2. Marlon Brando; 3. "Desperate Housewives"; 4. laptop computer; 5. Oliver Twist.

MARCHING ORDERS (Week 35)

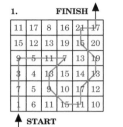

COUNT THE TRIANGLES (Week 35)

The 23 triangles are: ABK, ACK, ADF, ADH, ADK, AFH, AHK, BDE, BDK, CGH, CHK, DEK, DFK, DGK, DHK, DIK, EFK, EGK, EHK, FGK, FHK, GHK, and HJK.

SHIFTING GEARS (Week 35)

Cogs B, D, and F will turn counterclockwise.

ELIMINATION (Week 35)

1. his, money, are, soon, parted (his money are soon parted); 2. soybean, methane, subpoena; 3. schnapps, sprightly, growths; 4. piano, violin, saxophone; 5. soldier, field (Soldier Field); 6. rain, reign, rein; 7. cheese, garnet (Athens, Greece). Use tasteful words in case you have to eat them.

PROGRESSION (Week 35)

Figures 1 and 3.

WHAT'S YOUR NUMBER? (Week 35)

42. On each spoke, the number in the square plus the product of the numbers in the circles equal the number in the diamond.

SKILLS TEST (Week 35)

Answer a. Sam has 52 CDs and Tom has 29, 23 fewer than Sam.

IN THE ABSTRACT (Week 36)

ARROW MAZE (Week 36)

PRESIDENTIAL LIMITS (Week 36)

1. Barack Obama; 2. Ronald Reagan; 3. George Washington; 4. Franklin Roosevelt; 5. Harry Truman; 6. Gerald Ford; 7. Herbert Hoover; 8. John Kennedy; 9. Dwight Eisenhower; 10. Ulysses Grant.

WAYWORDS (Week 36)

Some people are a few trees short of a forest.

SEVEN WORD ZINGER (Week 36)

arc, cab, din, eye, jar, yam, woe.

EASY PICKINGS (Week 36)

"Even weak men when united are powerful."

SUDOKU (Week 36)

SWITCHEROO (Week 36)

1. a; 2. c; 3. b; 4. a; 5. d; 6. d.

ASSOCIATIONS (Week 36)

Atlanta, Montgomery, Nashville; suave, debonair, urbane; thin, slender, slim; happy, merry, joyful; Harvard, Princeton, Yale; senior, junior, sophomore; original, novel, unique; year, decade, century. Beacon and eggs.

SLIDE RULE (Week 36)

hail, hair, head, heal, hear, heed, heel, heir, hoed, hoer, hood, said, sail, seal, sear, seed, seen, seer, shad, shed, shin, shod, soar, soil, soon, tail, teal, tear, teed, teen, than, then, thin, toad, toed, toil, tool, wail, wean, wear, weed, when, whir, wood, wool.

ANAGRAM MAZE (Week 36)

The path through the maze, with just one anagram given for each, is 6. acme; 12. what; 11. cape; 10. raps; 4. diet; 3. does; 2. feet; 1. list; 7. news; 13. knee; 14. coal; 15. rely; 21. much; 22. drop; 23. arid; 29. hear; 35. ripe; 34. vane; 33. fast; 32. nuts; 31. newt.

ALL IN A ROW (Week 36)

Row A. Row A contains eleven groups: 32154, 21543, 438, 825, 384, 843, 4371, 627, 7215, 2157, and 762. Row B contains nine groups: 636, 825, 2517, 78, 321234, 12345, 5541, 54132, and 276. Row C contains ten groups: 1923, 9231, 31191, 1914, 1464, 6423, 2382, 825, 52233, and 69.

COUNTDOWN (Week 37)

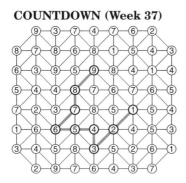

QUICK FILL (Week 37)
deplorable

SUDOKU (Week 37)

6	9	5	7	1	3	2	4	8
8	4	7	2	9	6	5	1	3
3	1	2	4	8	5	7	6	9
5	8	3	1	7	2	4	9	6
2	6	9	8	3	4	1	5	7
4	7	1	6	5	9	8	3	2
9	3	8	5	4	7	6	2	1
7	2	4	3	6	1	9	8	5
1	5	6	9	2	8	3	7	4

A COUNT (Week 37)
There are 32 A's.

HEXAGON HUNT (Week 37)

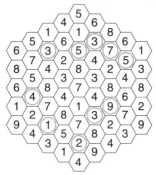

CODE WORD (Week 37)
Code Word: atmospheric. The closest to perfection a person comes is when he or she fills out an employment application.

EASY PICKINGS (Week 37)
Modesty is for those who have no talent.

ANAGRAM MAZE (Week 37)

		3	4	5	
				11	12
13	14	15			18
19		21	22	23	24
25					
31	32	33	34		

The path through the maze, with just one anagram given for each, is: 3. felt; 4. dire; 5. beak; 11. step; 12. lacy; 18. pier; 24. sham; 23. furs; 22. idle; 21. leap; 15. list; 14. slip; 13. live; 19. stub; 25. pace; 31. heat; 32. neon; 33. skid; 34. rove.

WORD CHARADE (Week 37)

E	A	D	N	L	Q	H	M
G	G	U	V	K	W	Z	P
B	I	L	G	H	A	S	J
Z	(M)	Q	H	M	T	C	U
A	H	Z	(L)	J	F	Q	K
C	O	X	A	E	C	(E)	U
T	N	E	I	D	E	(B)	O
(U)	V	Y	O	I	N	Z	J

lumber

ALL IN A ROW (Week 37)
Row A. Row A contains six groups: 4131, 711, 11412, 621, 1314, and 45. Row B contains three groups: 225, 3312, and 12141. Row C contains four groups: 22122, 81, 153, and 36.

TARGET SHOOT (Week 37)
1. UN: plunge, county, brunch; 2. FT: gifted, soften, deftly.

IN THE ABSTRACT (Week 37)

LICENSE PLATES (Week 37)

1. Charles Barkley; 2. Isiah Thomas; 3. Bill Russell; 4. Larry Bird; 5. Michael Jordan; 6. Wilt Chamberlain.

COUNT TO TEN (Week 37)

1. row 9; 2. row 3; 3. row 8.

BULL'S-EYE LETTER (Week 38)

The Bull's-Eye Letter is I: idol, sigh, into, prim, jail, size.

WAYWORDS (Week 38)

A foolish leader will make others foolish.

CIRCLE SEARCH (Week 38)

badge, base, bath, chat, each, ease, edge, plea, please, pledge, seat, see, that, thatch.

RING LOGIC (Week 38)

ARROW MAZE (Week 38)

DOVETAILED WORDS (Week 38)

1. film, photo; 2. bride, groom; 3. tardy, punctual; 4. baton, stick; 5. scarf, sarong.

ONLINE NETWORK (Week 38)

faithful loyal, true; danger, peril, hazard.

LOOSE TILE (Week 38)

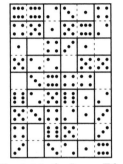

The 1-4 is the Loose Tile.

GOING IN CIRCLES (Week 38)

1. complete; 2. original.

FUN WITH FACTS AND FIGURES (Week 38)

1. $31 - 13 = 18$; 2. $18 + 50 = 68$; 3. $68 \div 34 = 2$; 4. 2×7 (Germany) $= 14$; 5. $14 - 9 = 5$.

COMPOUND IT (Week 38)

1. air; 2. brush; 3. work; 4. horse; 5. back; 6. fire; 7. power; 8. house; 9. hold; 10. over. (airbrush, brushwork, workhorse, horseback, backfire, firepower, powerhouse, household, holdover).

DEDUCTION PROBLEM (Week 38)

By clue 2, Jessica had bacon. Malcolm didn't have sausage (clue 1), so he had pepperoni. Penelope, then, had sausage. Since the one who ordered peppers isn't Jessica (clue 2) or Malcolm (clue 3), Penelope had peppers. By clue 1, Malcolm didn't order onions, so Jessica did. By elimination, Malcolm got mushrooms. In summary:

Jessica: bacon and onions
Malcolm: pepperoni and mushrooms
Penelope: sausage and peppers

SEVEN WORD ZINGER (Week 38)
elk, hum, jab, mow, pun, vie, zoo.

TRI, TRI AGAIN (Week 39)

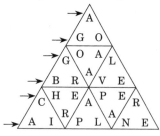

STACKED UP (Week 39)
Boxes 1, 3, and 6.

ANIMAL CHARADES (Week 39)
panther

KEEP ON MOVING (Week 39)
Move two squares left, three squares up, two squares left, four squares down, and two squares right to the asterisk.

CARD SENSE (Week 39)
The two of spades is adjacent to the two of diamonds (clue 2), so by clue 1, the king of hearts is fourth from the top and the eight of clubs is on the bottom. By clue 2, the top card is the eight of diamonds. The two of diamonds isn't second from the top (clue 3); it's third and the two of spades is second. In summary, from top to bottom: eight of diamonds, two of spades, two of diamonds, king of hearts, eight of clubs.

SLIDE RULE (Week 39)
lab, lap, lay, let, lip, lit, lob, lop, lot, map, mat, may, met, mob, moo, mop, pat, pay, pep, pet, pip, pit, pop, pot, pro, pry, rap, rat, ray, rep, rib, rip, rob, rot, zap, zip, zoo.

TIPS OF THE ICEBERG (Week 39)
1. Dena ($15.80); 2. Al ($7.05); 3. Brenda and Flora ($12.55).

WORD HUNT (Week 39)
also alto, auto, halo, hero, into, judo, logo, memo, onto, peso, polo, silo, solo, taro, trio, typo, undo, zero.

SUDOKU (Week 39)

6	3	7	8	2	5	4	1	9
1	9	4	7	6	3	2	8	5
2	5	8	9	4	1	3	7	6
5	8	1	2	9	4	7	6	3
4	2	6	3	1	7	5	9	8
9	7	3	6	5	8	1	2	4
3	1	2	4	8	6	9	5	7
7	6	5	1	3	9	8	4	2
8	4	9	5	7	2	6	3	1

MISSING DOMINOES (Week 39)

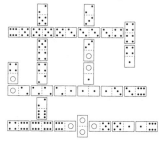

GETTING IN SHAPE (Week 39)
Boxes 3 and 4 have the same shapes.

RELATIONSHIPS QUIZ (Week 39)
1. b; 2. d; 3. c; 4. a; 5. c.

GRAND TOUR (Week 40)

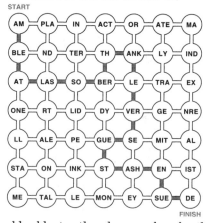

amble, bleat, atlas, lasso, sober, berth, thank, ankle, lever, verse, segue, guest, stash, ashen, ensue, suede.

SYMBOL-ISM (Week 40)

We will not get far without enthusiasm, nor will we go far if that is all we have.

ASSOCIATIONS (Week 40)

Montreal, Calgary, Toronto; prey, victim, quarry; abandon, relinquish, surrender; shield, protect, guard; spur, goad, prod; helicopter, airplane, dirigible; seduce, lure, entice; pick, choose, select. Hailing taxis.

WORD VISIBLITY (Week 40)

1. murky; 2. chase; 3. spore; 4. maxim; 5. cobra; 6. aroma.

COUNT THE RECTANGLES (Week 40)

There are 38 rectangles: ABFE, ABMK, ABTR, ABYX, ACHE, BCHF, DERQ, DFTQ, DIVQ, DJWQ, EFMK, EFTR, EFYX, EGNK, EIPK, EJWR, EJZX, FGNM, FIPM, FIVT, FJWT, FJZY, GIPN, IJWV, KLSR, KMTR, KMYX, KOUR, KPVR, LMTS, LOUS, LPVS, MOUT, MPVT, OPVU, RTYX, RWZX, and TWZY.

THE LINEUP (Week 40)

1. B; 2. suggest; 3. U; 4. sludge; 5. jest, thud, exam.

STAR WORDS (Week 40)

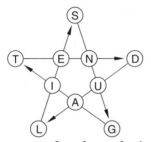

Your sequence of words may begin in any circle.

MAGNIFIND (Week 40)

ALPHABET SOUP (Week 40)

plum

ELIMINATION (Week 40)

1. dough, bread, cabbage; 2. chickens, before, they, are, hatched; 3. support, torso, rusty, pronoun; 4. able-bodied, short-lived, quick-witted; 5. church, temple, mosque; 6. break (breakdown, breakfast, breakneck, breakthrough); 7. bridge, hearts. He who hesitates is often the wisest.

ANTONYMS QUIZ (Week 40)

1. a; 2. b; 3. b; 4. a; 5. c; 6. a; 7. c; 8. b.

WHAT'S YOUR NUMBER? (Week 40)

34. In each rectangle, the bottom two numbers add up to one more than the top number.

MARCHING ORDERS (Week 40)

1.		FINISH			
24	25	29	31	34	36
18	13	26	21	19	35
9	12	24	18	22	16
8	3	7	11	14	19
5	6	9	12	14	17
4	7	8	10	11	16

START

2.		FINISH			
14	17	18	21	28	34
12	13	16	22	23	33
8	7	20	11	25	30
6	9	12	24	26	29
5	3	8	9	20	18
2	4	7	10	14	16

START

RINGERS (Week 40)

1. imply, niche, patio, deign; 2. munch, count, prime, wharf.

CROSS PATHS (Week 41)

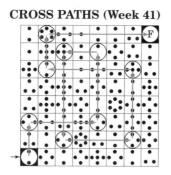

POP! (Week 41)
planets, plants, plant, pant, pan, an, a.

IN THE BALANCE (Week 41)
One triangle. Scale 1 shows that one triangle equals two circles, so two triangles equal four circles. Scale 2 shows that four circles equal three squares, so two triangles equal three squares. Since scale 3 shows that one square equals four diamonds, three squares equal twelve diamonds. Two triangles, then, equal twelve diamonds; one triangle equals six diamonds, and would balance scale 4.

HOLE IN ONE (Week 41)
The golf ball in the hole is 8537.

TRIANGULAR SQUARE (Week 41)

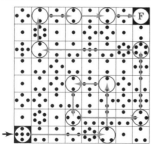

CROSS PATHS (Week 41)

HOLE IN ONE (Week 41)
The golf ball in the hole is 2938.

POP! (Week 41)
cheated, heated, hated, hate, hat, at, a.

BLOCK PARTY (Week 41)

OVERLAY (Week 41)
Diagram B.

MAGIC NUMBER SQUARE (Week 41)

3	16	9	22	15
20	8	21	14	2
7	25	13	1	19
24	12	5	18	6
11	4	17	10	23

QUICK FILL (Week 41)
electronic

CALL TO ORDER (Week 42)
7, 3, 1, 5, 2, 4, 8, 6.

ROUND TRIP (Week 42)

ALL IN A ROW (Week 42)

Row C. Row A contains seven groups: 712, 1261, 19, 22222, 253, 5311, and 181. Row B contains eight groups: 1117, 172, 253, 3331, 82, 28, 334, and 4411. Row C contains nine groups: 19, 91, 181, 6211, 2116, 2224, 2413, 46, and 55.

COUNT THE TRIANGLES (Week 42)

There are 50 triangles: AEF, ALN, AY2, BGH, BNP, BTW, BZ4, CIJ, CPR, C25, DEL, DGZ, ELM, EFM, EGT, EY1, FMN, FGN, FI2, GNO, GTV, GZ3, GIV, HIP, HK4, IPQ, IVX, IKX, JKR, LYZ, LNZ, MNT, NTU, NZ2, NOU, NP2, OUV, OPV, PVW, P24, PR4, QRX, R45, STZ, TZ1, UV2, V23, VW3, W34, WX4.

EASY PICKINGS (Week 42)

Home is the sweetest type of heaven.

ELIMINATION (Week 42)

1. masterpiece, toothbrush, bookshelf; 2. coat, jacket, parka; 3. curiosity, killed, the, cat (curiosity killed the cat); 4. princess, earl, baron; 5. susceptable (susceptible), manue-ver (maneuver), innoculation (inoculation); 6. apartment, dormitory, house; 7. duck, soup, horse, feathers ("Duck Soup," "Horse Feathers"). As we chase joy we may run past happiness.

STACKED UP (Week 42)

Boxes 3, 5, and 6.

WORD WHEEL (Week 42)

par, part, participate, art, tic, pat, pate, patent, ate, ten, tent, entire, tire, ire, return, returnable, turn, urn, nab, able, blend, lend, end, endless, less, lesson, ess, son.

ONLINE NETWORK (Week 42)

forgive, pardon, excuse; respect, admire, esteem.

ASSOCIATIONS (Week 42)

lime, lemon, orange; radical, extreme, ultra; impair, damage, injure; thumb, forefinger, pinkie; Sydney, Perth, Canberra; sleepy, drowsy, tired; defeat, vanquish, conquer; collapse, crash, fall. By hareplane.

DEDUCTION PROBLEM (Week 42)

The collie does not wear a red collar (clue 3) or green collar (clue 4), so the collie has a brown collar. By clue 5, Lisa owns the beagle. Sarah owns the terrier and the beagle wears a red collar (clue 3). By elimination, Andrew has the collie and the terrier wears a green collar. The beagle likes to chew on a piece of rope (clue 1). By clue 2, the terrier likes to play with an old shoe. By elimination, the collie chews on a doll. In summary:
beagle, Lisa, rope, red
collie, Andrew, doll, brown
terrier, Sarah, shoe, green

CODE WORD (Week 42)

Code Word: keyboardist. A remarkable memory doesn't make for a creative mind any more than an unabridged dictionary is a great book of literature.

FUN WITH FACTS AND FIGURES (Week 42)

1. $4 \div 2 = 2$; 2. $2 \times 8 = 16$; 3. $16 + 21 = 37$; 4. $37 - 20$ ($3 \times 2 + 2 \times 3 + 2 \times 4$) $= 17$; 5. $17 + 35 = 52$.

ARROW MAZE (Week 43)

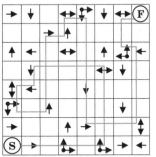

DOVETAILED WORDS (Week 43)

1. center, middle; 2. trout, salmon; 3. afghan, shawl; 4. deputy, sheriff; 5. ladle, tureen.

CIRCLE MATH (Week 43)

A = 8, B = 9, C = 5, D = 7, E = 6, F = 4, G = 3, H = 1, and I = 2.

WHAT'S YOUR NUMBER?
(Week 43)
8. In each square, the bottom number indicates the number of letters in each word above it.

ANAGRAM MAZE (Week 43)

1	2				
7			10	11	12
13	14		16		18
	20	21	22		24
				29	30
			35		

The path through the maze, with just one anagram given for each, is: 2. sore; 1. bane; 7. sobs; 13. sued; 14. coal; 20. chin; 21. shoe; 22. peas; 16. sent; 10. sack; 11. tied; 12. lope; 18. fear; 24. hums; 30. team; 29. rock; 35. hubs.

WORD VISIBLITY (Week 43)
1. debit; 2. hoard; 3. penny; 4. bugle; 5. verve; 6. rotor.

VISION QUEST (Week 43)
Column A.

SEVEN WORD ZINGER (Week 43)
ant, fig, our, pea, sew, ski, you.

WAYWORDS (Week 43)
Say what you must and not what you should.

WORD CHARADE (Week 43)

comply

FIGURE FUN (Week 43)
The diamond equals 4, the triangle equals 1, the square equals 3, and the circle equals 2.

SLIDE RULE (Week 43)
cake, clad, coat, code, coke, cote, crab, gate, glad, goad, goat, grab, grad, jade, joke, made, make, mate, moat, mode, mote.

ALPHABET CIRCLE MAZE
(Week 43)

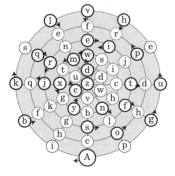

COMPOUND IT (Week 43)
1. grand; 2. father; 3. land; 4. mark; 5. down; 6. wind; 7. fall; 8. out; 9. board; 10. room (grandfather, fatherland, landmark, markdown, downwind, windfall, fallout, outboard, boardroom).

SUDOKU (Week 44)

9	3	2	4	5	6	8	7	1
1	5	6	7	9	8	4	3	2
7	8	4	2	1	3	9	6	5
6	7	5	8	2	9	3	1	4
2	4	3	1	6	7	5	9	8
8	9	1	3	4	5	7	2	6
3	6	7	5	8	2	1	4	9
4	2	8	9	7	1	6	5	3
5	1	9	6	3	4	2	8	7

IN THE ABSTRACT (Week 44)

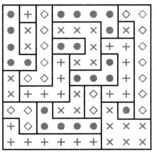

GOING IN CIRCLES (Week 44)
1. youthful; 2. broccoli.

HEXAGON HUNT (Week 44)

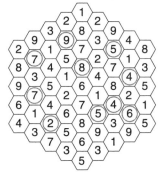

LETTER, PLEASE (Week 44)
As long as you can keep a secret, it is your servant. Once you reveal it, you make it your master.

CROSS EXAMINAITON (Week 44)
1. parenthesis; 2. electrician; 3. thermometer; 4. harpsichord; 5. catastrophe; 6. agriculture; 7. metropolitan; 8. investigate.

RELATIONSHIPS QUIZ (Week 44)
1. b; 2. c; 3. d; 4. a; 5. d.

STAR WORDS (Week 44)

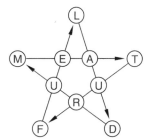

Your sequence of words may begin in any circle.

ANIMAL CHARADES (Week 44)
alligator

CHANGELINGS (Week 44)
1. GOLD, good, food, fool, FOIL.
2. HARD, herd, head, heat, SEAT.
3. PULL, hull, hall, hail, HAIR.
(Using the same number of changes, other answers may be possible for each Changeling.)

TARGET SHOOT (Week 44)
1. LL: collie, ballet, yellow; 2. AI: praise, brainy, quaint.

SYMBOL-ISM (Week 44)
Junk is stuff you will hoard for years then throw away just two weeks before you need it badly.

CIRCLE SEARCH (Week 44)
are, area, asea, cup, cure, exam, excuse, exit, pad, padre, pit, read, sea, seam, secure.

SWITCHEROO (Week 44)
1. c; 2. d; 3. a; 4. d; 5. b; 6. c; 7. a; 8. d.

TIPS OF THE ICEBERG (Week 45)
1. Laura ($11.10); 2. Jack ($8.80); 3. Hank and Marty ($9.85).

ZANY ZONES (Week 45)
1. Austin, Texas; 2. Topeka, Kansas; 3. Augusta, Maine; 4. Albany, New York; 5. Helena, Montana; 6. Madison, Wisconsin; 7. Salt Lake City, Utah; 8. Boston, Massachusetts.

THE LINEUP (Week 45)

1. F; 2. clarinet; 3. T; 4. should; 5. tuck, view, math.

TRI, TRI AGAIN (Week 45)

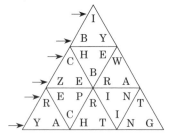

WORD HUNT (Week 45)

vain, vane, vary, vase, vast, vats, veal, veer, veil, vein, vend, vent, verb, very, vest, veto, vets, vied, view, vine, viol, void, volt, vote.

RINGERS (Week 45)

1. expel, prawn, ditch, valid; 2. spunk, labor, realm, drift.

ROUND TRIP (Week 45)

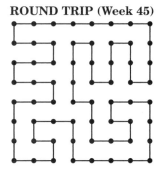

ALPHABET SOUP (Week 45)

Italy

SLIDE RULE (Week 45)

arid, away, awed, head, heap, heed, hoed, hood, hook, hoop, seed, seek, seep, soak, soap, swap, sway, teak, teed, toad, toed, took, trap, tray, trek, trey, trip, trod.

COUNT TO TEN (Week 45)

1. row 5; 2. row 7; 3. row 10.

RING LOGIC (Week 45)

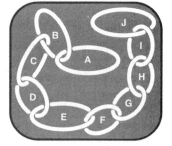

WORD CHARADE (Week 45)

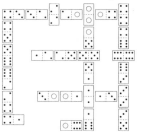

icebox

WORD VISIBLITY (Week 45)

1. finch; 2. curio; 3. idiom; 4. saint; 5. awful; 6. lofty.

MISSING DOMINOES (Week 46)

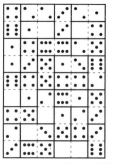

LOOSE TILE (Week 46)

The 0-5 is the Loose Tile.

LICENSE PLATES (Week 46)

1. Gordon Ramsay; 2. Emeril Lagasse; 3. Rachael Ray; 4. Bobby Flay; 5. Mario Batali; 6. Wolfgang Puck.

CARD SENSE (Week 46)

By clue 1, the ace of spades, four of clubs, and jack of spades are first, second, and third in some order and the four of diamonds and nine of hearts are fourth and fifth in some order. The four of clubs, then, is third and the four of diamonds is fourth (clue 2). By elimination, the nine of hearts is on the bottom. Since the ace of spades isn't on top (clue 3), it's second from the top and the jack of spades is on top. In summary, from top to bottom: jack of spades, ace of spades, four of clubs, four of diamonds, nine of hearts.

WHAT'S YOUR NUMBER? (Week 46)

630. In each group, the number in the square is one half the product of the four numbers in the circles.

ANAGRAM MAZE (Week 46)

1	2	3	4	5	
				11	
		15	16	17	
	20	21			
	26		28	29	30
	32	33	34		36

The path through the maze, with just one anagram given for each is: 1. stud; 2. cone; 3. done; 4. lake; 5. arch; 11. awry; 17. ever; 16. taco; 15. lies; 21. lilt; 20. file; 26. veto; 32. does; 33. bore; 34. gels; 28. thaw; 29. neat; 30. last; 36. blow.

WAYWORDS (Week 46)

Every problem is a chance for us to do our best.

BULL'S-EYE LETTER (Week 46)

The Bull's-Eye Letter is M: milk, hump, term, omen, smog, exam.

VISION QUEST (Week 46)

Row 5.

GETTING IN SHAPE (Week 46)

Boxes 1 and 6 have the same shapes.

SEVEN WORD ZINGER (Week 46)

bed, cab, cry, gym, jog, nor, was.

ANTONYMS QUIZ (Week 47)

1. c; 2. a; 3. a; 4. b; 5. a; 6. c; 7. c; 8. a.

BLOCK PARTY (Week 47)

MAGNIFIND (Week 47)

QUICK FILL (Week 47)

vegetarian

Z COUNT (Week 47)

There are 28 Z's.

LETTER, PLEASE (Week 47)

A man who wants to have his family tree traced should just go into politics and have his opponents do it for him.

ONLINE NETWORK (Week 47)

guard, shelter, protect; thrive, flourish, bloom.

OVERLAY (Week 47)

Diagram A.

MAGIC NUMBER SQUARE (Week 47)

6	10	25	22	2
11	18	3	14	19
17	21	13	5	9
7	12	23	8	15
24	4	1	16	20

ALL IN A ROW (Week 47)

Row B. Row A contains four groups: 7121, 191, 1361, and 6212. Row B contains seven groups: 65, 3413, 137, 74, 128, 281, and 353. Row C contains five groups: 263, 254, 5411, 1424, and 245.

COUNTDOWN (Week 47)

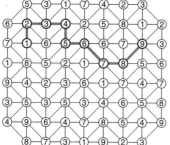

HEXAGON HUNT (Week 47)

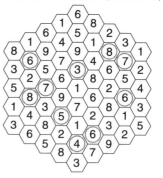

KEEP ON MOVING (Week 47)

Move four squares left, three squares up, two squares right, one square down, and three squares left to the asterisk.

EASY PICKINGS (Week 48)

Regardless of the past, you may have a spotless future.

GRAND TOUR (Week 48)

uncle, clean, angle, gleam, ample, plead, adult, ultra, radio, diode, debut, butte, testy, style, least, astir.

410

ASSOCIATIONS (Week 48)

skillful, expert, proficient; avoid, shun, evade; cafe, restaurant, diner; Laos, Thailand, Cambodia; terrible, dreadful, awful; king, emperor, czar; emphasize, stress, accentuate; rubbish, trash, garbage. A good night's sleep.

IN THE ABSTRACT (Week 48)

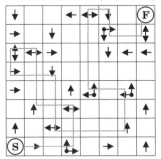

QUOTATION MARKS (Week 48)

It's amazing that the amount of news that happens in the world every day always . . . exactly fits the newspaper.

ARROW MAZE (Week 48)

CODE WORD (Week 48)

Code Word: tenaciously. Humility is a virtue that many may preach and few will practice; however, it's something that everyone is happy to hear that others possess.

CROSS-UPS (Week 48)

1. stepladder; 2. shutterbug; 3. overpower; 4. postmaster.

DOVETAILED WORDS (Week 48)

1. quote, proverb; 2. drama, comedy; 3. popular, trendy; 4. zipper, button; 5. orchid, tulip.

COMPOUND IT (Week 48

1. flood; 2. water; 3. color; 4. blind; 5. side; 6. step; 7. child; 8. like; 9. wise; 10. crack (floodwater, watercolor, colorblind, blindside, sidestep, stepchild, childlike, likewise, wisecrack).

ELIMINATION (Week 48)

1. apple, day, doctor, away; 2. depot, tenor, ponder, rodent; 3. euro, peso, yen, pound; 4. potato, salad, fried, chicken, cold, cuts (potato salad, fried chicken, cold cuts); 5. north, by, northwest ("North by Northwest"); 6. light (stoplight, flashlight, daylight, limelight); 7. make, hay, while, the, sun, shines (Make hay while the sun shines). Grudges and anger only grow with constant care.

CIRCLE MATH (Week 48)

A = 4, B = 1, C = 6, D = 7, E = 9, F = 2, G = 5, H = 8, and I = 3.

SUDOKU (Week 48)

8	4	6	3	7	2	5	9	1
1	9	3	4	6	5	8	7	2
7	2	5	1	8	9	3	4	6
4	7	9	6	3	8	1	2	5
3	5	1	2	9	7	4	6	8
6	8	2	5	4	1	9	3	7
5	1	7	9	2	3	6	8	4
2	3	4	8	5	6	7	1	9
9	6	8	7	1	4	2	5	3

VISION QUEST (Week 49)
Row 5.

QUICK FILL (Week 49)
motorcycle

ONLINE NETWORK (Week 49)
leave, separate, part; pepper, nutmeg, thyme.

COUNT TO TEN (Week 49)
1. row 2; 2. row 6; 3. row 9.

EASY PICKINGS (Week 49)
The capital of New York is Albany.

SUDOKU (Week 49)

5	7	6	1	8	4	3	2	9
9	1	4	7	2	3	5	8	6
8	3	2	5	9	6	1	4	7
3	2	1	8	7	9	6	5	4
6	8	7	4	5	1	2	9	3
4	9	5	6	3	2	7	1	8
1	6	9	3	4	5	8	7	2
2	5	8	9	6	7	4	3	1
7	4	3	2	1	8	9	6	5

LICENSE PLATES (Week 49)
1. Peter O'Toole; 2. Liam Neeson; 3. Pierce Brosnan; 4. Colin Farrell; 5. Richard Harris; Gabriel Byrne.

MAGNIFIND (Week 49)

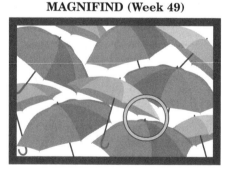

WAYWORDS (Week 49)
The greatest error in life is giving up.

HEXAGON HUNT (Week 49)

ALPHABET SOUP (Week 49)
lime

FUN WITH FACTS AND FIGURES (Week 49)
1. $2 + 300 = 302$; 2. $302 - 200 = 102$; 3. $102 \div 2 = 51$; 4. $51 \times 5 = 255$; 5. $255 + 111 = 366$.

TRI, TRI AGAIN (Week 49)

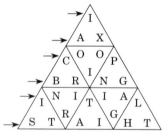

IN THE ABSTRACT (Week 50)

CODE WORD (Week 50)
Code Word: pathfinders. Some people will get credit for having nice personalities when they are merely proud of their teeth.

GRAND TOUR (Week 50)

cabin, bingo, goner, nerve, veins, inset, ether, heron, onion, ionic, icing, ingot.

SYMBOL-ISM (Week 50)

The dearest friends began their relationship first of all as strangers.

TIPS OF THE ICEBERG (Week 50)

1. Hank ($7.40); 2. Laura ($5.40); 3. Inez and Marty ($7.00).

LOOSE TILE (Week 50)

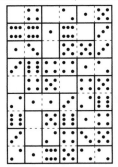

The 3-4 is the Loose Tile

R COUNT (Week 50)

There are 26 R's in the sentence.

SEVEN WORD ZINGER (Week 50)

ark, lip, now, oat, spa, wry, you.

WHAT'S YOUR NUMBER? (Week 50)

108. The number in the square divided by the sum of the numbers in the circles equals the number in the diamond.

THE LINEUP (Week 50)

1. B; 2. connected; 3. I; 4. fitting; 5. three words (axle, lime, jump).

SKILLS TEST (Week 50)

1. Romania; 2. Bulgaria; 3. Belgium; 4. Albania; 5. Croatia.

U.S. A'S (Week 50)

1. Nevada; 2. Iowa; 3. Maryland; 4. Oklahoma; 5. Maine; 6. Idaho.

ASSOCIATIONS (Week 50)

help, aid, assist; price, cost, expense; receive, get, acquire; suitable, proper, fitting; Berlin, Munich, Frankfurt; college, university, school; kitchen, bathroom, basement; flaw, defect, blemish. A spelling bee.

ARROW MAZE (Week 51)

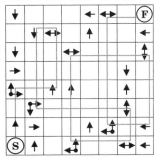

WORD VISIBLITY (Week 51)

1. razor; 2. frown; 3. adopt; 4. jelly; 5. slope; 6. quote.

STACKED UP (Week 51)

Boxes 1, 2, and 4.

DOVETAILED WORDS (Week 51)

1. raise, boost; 2. frost, snow; 3. jungle, forest; 4. petite, slight; 5. panda, bamboo.

COUNTDOWN (Week 51)

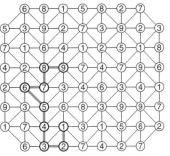

CHANGELINGS (Week 51)

1. PICK, pink, pins, pens, PEAS; 2. NAVY, wavy, wary, ward, YARD; 3. WISE, wide, wade, wads, DADS.
(Using the same number of changes, other answers may be possible.)

SQUARE LINKS (Week 51)

umbrella, virtuous, eventful, offering, beanpole.

WORD WHEEL (Week 51)

boa, boar, oar, arc, arch, archer, cherub, her, rub, bat, bath, bathe, the, them, hem, emigrate, migrate, grate, rat, rate, ate, tea, tear, ear, earmuff, arm, muff, muffin, fin, final, finale, ale.

ELIMINATION (Week 51)

1. poem, novel, essay; 2. strangers, in, the, night ("Strangers in the Night"); 3. permanent, manicure, facial; 4. chic, ago (Chicago); 5. try (tray), stem (steam), chin (chain); 6. dormant, rodeo, ordinary; 7. animal, farm ("Animal Farm"). None are so empty as those full of themselves.

COMPOUND IT (Week 51)

1. hat; 2. check; 3. up; 4. hold; 5. over; 6. kill; 7. joy; 8. stick; 9. ball; 10. park (hatcheck, checkup, uphold, holdover, overkill, killjoy, joystick, stickball, ballpark).

ANAGRAM MAZE (Week 51)

	2	3	4		
			10	11	12
13	14	15			18
19		21	22	23	24
25					
31	32	33	34	35	

The path through the maze, with just one anagram given for each, is 2. bear; 3. left; 4. hoes; 10. kale; 11. pays; 12. lied; 18. taps; 24. save; 23. ring; 22. care; 21. mugs; 15. apes; 14. soil; 13. vote; 19. clay; 25. lilt; 31. hear; 32. dent; 33. rock; 34. luge; 35. rams.

ALL IN A ROW (Week 51)

Row B. Row A contains four groups: 5131, 3142, 14221, and 73. Row B contains six groups: 712, 28, 1324, 244, 3232, and 172. Row C contains five groups: 514, 244, 181, 23113, and 811.

TARGET SHOOT (Week 52)

1. UT: pouted, clutch, brutal; 2. RG: forget, jargon, gargle.

DEDUCTION PROBLEM (Week 52)

By clue 1, three hens in order from heaviest to lightest were C, D, and E. Hen A weighed less than E (clue 2). By clue 3, Hen B weighed the most, so the order from heaviest to lightest was: B, C, D, E, and A.

BULL'S-EYE LETTER (Week 52)

The Bull's-Eye Letter is O: oath, cozy, plop, also, hoax, obey.

FILLING STATION (Week 52)

1. seersucker; 2. praying mantis; 3. Sri Lanka; 4. "American Idol"; 5. table tennis.

MISSING LINKS (Week 52)

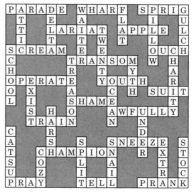

CARD SENSE (Week 52)

The black cards are adjacent (clue 1), so the three of spades is directly above the seven of clubs (clue 2). Also by clue 2, the seven of clubs is somewhere above the queen of hearts. Since neither heart is on the bottom (clue 3), the ten of diamonds is. By clue 4, the three of spades isn't the top card; the ace of hearts is. In summary, from top to bottom: ace of hearts, three of spades, seven of clubs, queen of hearts, and ten of diamonds.

DOVETAILED WORDS (Week 52)

1. earth, soil; 2. science, history; 3. porch, patio; 4. sport, game; 5. canoe, dinghy.

COUNT THE DIAMONDS (Week 52)

The figure contains 34 diamonds: ACEB, BEHD, CFIE, FJNI, EIMH, DHLG, GLQK, HMRL, INSM, JOTN, OUAAT, NTZS, MSYR, LRXQ, KQWP, PWCCV, QXDDW, RYEEX, SZFFY, TAAGGZ, UBBHHAA, AFMD, CJSH, BIRG, DMXK, ENYL, FOZM, AJYG, BNEEK, COFFL, JUGGS, ITFFR, HSEEQ, and GRDDP.

STAR WORDS (Week 52)

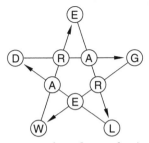

Your sequence of words may begin in any circle.

CIRCLE MATH (Week 52)

A = 7, B = 5, C = 1, D = 2, E = 3, F = 6, G = 4, H = 8, and I = 9.

SUDOKU (Week 52)

2	1	5	4	3	6	9	8	7
4	3	8	7	9	5	2	6	1
6	7	9	8	1	2	5	3	4
9	2	4	1	5	8	6	7	3
3	5	7	9	6	4	8	1	2
1	8	6	2	7	3	4	5	9
8	9	3	6	2	1	7	4	5
7	6	1	5	4	9	3	2	8
5	4	2	3	8	7	1	9	6

MISSING DOMINOES (Week 52)

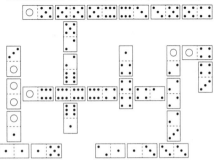

415